COLD WAR AND McCARTHY ERA

Selected Titles in ABC-CLIO's Perspectives in American Social History Series

African Americans in the Nineteenth Century: People and Perspectives

American Revolution: People and Perspectives

Baby Boom: People and Perspectives

British Colonial America: People and Perspectives

Civil Rights Movement: People and Perspectives

Civil War: People and Perspectives

Cold War and McCarthy Era: People and Perspectives

Early Republic: People and Perspectives

Great Depression: People and Perspectives

Industrial Revolution: People and Perspectives

Jacksonian and Antebellum Age: People and Perspectives

Jazz Age: People and Perspectives

Making of the American West: People and Perspectives

Reconstruction: People and Perspectives

Vietnam War Era: People and Perspectives

Women's Rights: People and Perspectives

PERSPECTIVES IN
AMERICAN SOCIAL HISTORY

Cold War and McCarthy Era

People and Perspectives

Caroline S. Emmons, Editor
Peter C. Mancall, Series Editor

 ABC-CLIO

Santa Barbara, California • Denver, Colorado • Oxford, England

Library of Congress Cataloging-in-Publication Data

Cold War and McCarthy era : people and perspectives / Caroline S. Emmons, editor.
    p. cm. — (Perspectives in American social history)
  Includes bibliographical references and index.
   ISBN 978-1-59884-103-9 (hard copy : alk. paper) — ISBN 978-1-59884-104-6 (e-book) 1. Cold War—Social aspects—United States. 2. Anti-communist movements—United States—History—20th century. 3. United States—History—1945-1953. 4. United States—Social conditions—1945-1953. United States—Social life and customs—1945-1970. 6. United States—Politics and government—1945-1953. I. Emmons, Caroline S.
  E169.Z8C649 2010
   973.918—dc22   2010007778

ISBN: 978-1-59884-103-9
EISBN: 978-1-59884-104-6

14 13 12 11 10   1 2 3 4 5

This book is also available on the World Wide Web as an eBook.
Visit www.abc-clio.com for details.

ABC-CLIO, LLC
130 Cremona Drive, P.O. Box 1911
Santa Barbara, California 93116-1911

This book is printed on acid-free paper ∞
Manufactured in the United States of America

My husband Tommy and daughter Zoe were not only tolerant of the time and energy I spent on this project, but were unfailingly cheerful and encouraging about it too. With all my love and thanks, I dedicate this work to them.

Contents

Acknowledgments, ix
Series Introduction, xi
Introduction, xv
About the Editor and Contributors, xxvii
Chronology, xxix

1 Catalyst of Empire: Joseph McCarthy, Anti-Communism, and
Early Cold War Political Culture, 1

Jeffrey D. Bass

2 Federal Loyalty Oath Program, 15

Martin Manning

3 McCarthy's Forgotten Defenders: Political and Social Conservatism in
1950s Pop Culture, 33

Bryan E. Vizzini

4 McCarthy and the Media: How the "Red Scare" Affected Radio,
TV, and Film, 49

Donna L. Halper

5 An Unlikely Team: The Social Aspects of the Ground Observer Corps, 63

David Mills

6 McCarthyism and the Cold War against Organized Labor in
the United States, 79

Saranna Thornton

7 "Racist Saints and Communist Devils": African Americans, McCarthyism,
and the Cold War, 95

S. Ani Mukherji

8 Sexuality and Gender in Cold War America: Social Experiences, Cultural
Authorities, and the Roots of Political Change, 111

Howard H. Chiang

9 Mothers, Spy Queens, and Subversives: Women in the McCarthy Era, 129

Michella M. Marino

10 Duck and Cover: Children's Cold War Experiences in 1950s America, 145

Margaret Peacock

Primary Documents, 163
Reference, 181
Bibliography, 197
Index, 215

Acknowledgments

I have incurred many debts while assembling this collection and am grateful for the encouragement and patience that have been extended to me. First of all, I'd like to thank the contributors for their hard work and for the important contributions they are making to the field. I'd also like to thank the series editor, Peter Mancall, for giving me the opportunity to try something new in editing an essay collection; John Grigg, who brought me into this project; and James Sherman and Kim Kennedy White at ABC-CLIO, for their assistance and encouragement. I also want to thank Hampden-Sydney College for all the support it has offered me over the years, particularly the librarians at the Bortz Library.

Series Introduction

Social history is, simply put, the study of past societies. More specifically, social historians attempt to describe societies in their totality and hence often eschew analysis of politics and ideas. Although many social historians argue that it is impossible to understand how societies functioned without some consideration of the ways that politics works on a daily basis or what ideas could be found circulating at any given time, they tend to pay little attention to the formal arenas of electoral politics or intellectual currents. In the United States, social historians have been engaged in describing components of the population that had earlier often escaped formal analysis, notably women, members of ethnic or cultural minorities, or those who had fewer economic opportunities than the elite.

Social history became a vibrant discipline in the United States after it had already gained enormous influence in Western Europe. In France, social history in its modern form emerged with the rising prominence of a group of scholars associated with the journal *Annales Économie, Société, Civilisation* (or *Annales ESC,* as it is known). In its pages and in a series of books from historians affiliated with the École des Hautes Études en Sciences Sociales in Paris, brilliant historians such as Marc Bloch, Jacques Le Goff, and Emanuel LeRoy Ladurie described seemingly every aspect of French society. Among the masterpieces of this historical reconstruction was Fernand Braudel's monumental study, *The Mediterranean and the Mediterranean World in the Age of Philip II,* published first in Paris in 1946 and in a revised edition in English in 1972. In this work, Braudel argued that the only way to understand a place in its totality was to describe its environment, its social and economic structures, and its political systems. In Britain, the emphasis of social historians has been less on questions of environment, per se, than on a description of human communities in all their complexities. For example, social historians there have taken advantage of that nation's remarkable local archives to reconstruct the history of the family and details of its rural past. Works such as Peter Laslett's *The World We Have Lost,* first printed in 1966, and the multi-authored *Agrarian History of England and Wales,* which began to appear in print in 1967, revealed that painstaking work could reveal the lives and habits of individuals who never previously attracted the interest of biographers, demographers, or most historians.

Social history in the United States gained a large following in the second half of the 20th century, especially during the 1960s and 1970s. Its development sprang from political, technical, and intellectual impulses deeply embedded in the culture of the modern university. The politics of civil rights and social reform fueled the passions of historians who strove to tell the stories of the underclass. They benefited from the adoption by historians of statistical analysis, which allowed scholars to trace where individuals lived, how often they moved, what kinds of jobs they took, and whether their economic status declined, stagnated, or improved over time. As history departments expanded, many who emerged from graduate schools focused their attention on groups that had previously been ignored or marginalized. Women's history became a central concern among U.S. historians, as did the history of African Americans, Native Americans, Latinos, and others. These historians pushed historical study in the United States farther away from the study of formal politics and intellectual trends. Although few Americanists could achieve the technical brilliance of some social historians in Europe, collectively they have been engaged in a vast act of description, with the goal of describing seemingly every facet of life from 1492 to the present.

The 16 volumes in this series together represent the continuing efforts of historians to describe U.S. society. Most of the volumes focus on chronological areas, from the broad sweep of the colonial era to the more narrowly defined collections of essays on the eras of the Cold War, the baby boom, and the United States in the age of the Vietnam War. The series also includes entire volumes on the epochs that defined the nation, the American Revolution and the Civil War, as well as volumes dedicated to the process of westward expansion, women's rights, and African American history.

This social history series derives its strength from the talented editors of individual volumes. Each editor is an expert in his or her own field, who selected and organized the contents of his or her volume. Editors solicited other experienced historians to write individual essays. Every volume contains first-rate analysis, complemented by lively anecdotes designed to reveal the complex contours of specific historical moments. The many illustrations to be found in these volumes testify as well to the recognition that any society can be understood not only by the texts that its participants produce but also by the images that they craft. Primary source documents in each volume allow interested readers to pursue some specific topics in greater depth, and each volume contains a chronology to provide guidance to the flow of events over time. These tools—anecdotes, images, texts, and timelines—allow readers to gauge the inner workings of the United States in particular periods and yet also to glimpse connections between eras.

The articles in these volumes testify to the abundant strengths of historical scholarship in the United States in the early years of the 21st century. Despite the occasional academic contest that flares into public notice, or the self-serving cant of politicians who want to manipulate the nation's past for partisan ends—for example, in debates over the Second Amendment to the U.S. Constitution and what it means about potential limits to the rights of gun ownership—the articles here all reveal the vast increase in knowledge of the American past that has taken place over the previous half century. Social historians do not dominate history faculties in U.S. colleges and universities, but no one could deny them a seat at the intellectual table. Without their efforts, intellectual, cultural, and political historians would be hard pressed to understand why certain ideas circulated when they did, why some religious movements prospered or foundered, how developments in fields such as medicine and engineering reflected larger concerns, and what shaped the world we inhabit.

Fernand Braudel and his colleagues envisioned entire laboratories of historians, in which scholars working together would be able to produce *histoire totale*: total history. Historians today seek more humble goals for our collective enterprise. But, as the richly textured essays in these volumes reveal, scholarly collaboration has in fact brought us much closer to that dream. These volumes do not and cannot include every aspect of U.S. history. However, every page reveals something interesting or valuable about how U.S. society functioned. Together, these books suggest the crucial necessity of stepping back to view the grand complexities of the past rather than pursuing narrower prospects and lesser goals.

Peter C. Mancall
Series Editor

Introduction

According to most popular understandings of wartime, wars usually have clearly defined beginnings and endings. Conventional definitions of war require clearly demarcated combatants, with each side typically able to articulate what it hopes to achieve. Most wars leave physical evidence of the struggle, either in the form of battlefields, widespread destruction, or other kinds of visible effects. Most wars are fought in order to attain or retain control of land or property or political hierarchies. For U.S. citizens, most wars have been fought by those "over there," where the fighting occurred, or "over here," on the home front.

The Cold War turned all of these assumptions upside down, and historians continue to debate the meanings and legacies of this complex historical era. When did the Cold War begin? When did it end (or has it ended)? Who were the most important combatants: military leaders, political leaders, or ordinary men, women and children? Where were the most important battlefields? Were they in Europe, China, Vietnam, Korea, U.S. communities, or even within the hearts and minds of individual citizens? What were the objectives of the combatants? Were the United States and the Soviet Union trying to destroy one another or simply to maintain their own spheres of influence?

These questions have resulted in significant and long-running debates over the timeline, interpretation, and consequences of the Cold War era. In this volume of essays, the Cold War is dated from roughly the end of World War II through the early 1960s. Although U.S. involvement in the Vietnam War was undoubtedly motivated by Cold War concerns, its role in the shaping of recent U.S. history is so significant that it is best treated in a separate volume. As with the other volumes in this series, this collection of essays focuses on social history. This refers to the study of ordinary men, women, and children, rather than on better known political and military figures; it is often referred to as history from the "ground up" rather than the "top down." The study of history, also referred to as historiography, traditionally focused on elites and so-called great men (and occasionally women). Beginning in the 1960s, this approach underwent criticism and reconsideration by a new generation of historians that had been shaped by the dramatic social turmoil of that decade. These new historians began to focus more on the experiences of men, women, and children who did not necessarily occupy powerful, wealthy, or influential roles in society. This new type of historical interpretation became known as social history; in the last several decades, it has enormously complicated and enriched our understanding of various historical epochs.

Social history must always take into account political, economic, and diplomatic developments, especially so in the case of this volume's theme. However, social history emphasizes the experiences of average Americans, rather than examining the experiences of political leaders and elites. Essays in this volume discuss women, children, gays and lesbians, African Americans, laborers, journalists, federal and civil defense workers, and popular culture, in addition to an essay looking at politicians who helped shape Cold War debates at the local and national level. Essays in this volume examine the ways in which Cold War anxieties and priorities helped shape U.S. attitudes about gender relations, child-rearing, sexual behavior, and other aspects of individual and community life; given that Cold War studies are usually military, political, or diplomatic in nature, these essays provide fresh ways of thinking about the effects and legacies of this period.

To understand the dramatic impact of the Cold War on U.S. life, it is important to consider the historical context. The Cold War resists easy or conventional bookends (i.e., years that define the beginning and ending of a particular era). The roots of the Cold War might, in some respects, be traced back to the publication of *The Communist Manifesto* in 1849. Although U.S. capitalism was by most measures still in its infancy at that time, many U.S. readers reacted with disapproval and strong rejection of the interpretation of history, economic relationships, and the future predictions put forward by Karl Marx and Fredrich Engels in that book. The public imagination was especially riveted and, for some, frightened by their prediction that capitalism would one day fail and be replaced with a state controlled by workers. But it would certainly be a stretch to say that the Cold War started in the 19th century.

Some have proposed that the Cold War started with the Russian Revolution of 1917, and indeed President Woodrow Wilson did authorize the deployment of U.S. Marines in an attempt to defeat the Bolsheviks. Although Soviet leaders were very critical of U.S. efforts to interfere with the revolution, the so-called invasion was short-lived and had limited effect. In the aftermath of World War 1, the United States had experienced its first "Red Scare," when Wilson's Attorney General, A. Mitchell Palmer, sought the arrest and/or deportation of hundreds of suspected political radicals, most of them accused of fomenting socialist revolution. For much of the past century, labor activism and socialism were seen by many as synonymous (and certainly some, but not all, labor activists were indeed socialists).

The Soviets resented the refusal of the United States to recognize the Soviet government until after the inauguration of Franklin D. Roosevelt in 1933; during the 1920s, this was another source of tension between the two nations. With the onset of the Great Depression in 1929, economic crisis brought renewed interest in critiques of capitalism, with a resurgence in union support and a proliferation of left-leaning political organizations. The Soviet Union sponsored the program known as the Popular Front, to encourage and support such movements, and to oppose the rise of fascism. Americans facing economic disaster were attracted to such groups in relatively large numbers, with membership in the Communist Party in the United States growing from 40,000 in 1936 to 82,000 by 1939; for many of these individuals, such associations would come back to haunt them in the postwar period. The Communist Party made a strong pitch for support, not only from labor groups and other traditional sources of recruitment but also African Americans. For some African American activists, even brief or tangential connections to the Communist Party would have long-term consequences in the postwar period.

World War II complicated the U.S.-Soviet relationship. Americans were outraged when Soviet Premier Joseph Stalin signed the Non-Aggression Pact with German Chancellor Adolf Hitler in 1939. In addition, by the late 1930s, rumors of the mass murders of suspected political opponents ordered by Stalin had also begun to circulate. The Popular Front collapsed in the wake of the Nazi-Soviet agreement, and Americans who had joined such organizations were left disorganized and on the defensive.

When Hitler ordered the invasion of the Soviet Union, Americans were forced to reconsider their anti-Soviet attitudes. Now, in the face of Hitler's onslaught against the European continent and the beginning of the war in the Pacific against Japan, the United States and Great Britain realized, reluctantly, that cooperation with Stalin was essential if the Allies were to win. The United States and Soviets formed an uneasy alliance during the war, with the United States providing millions of dollars in aid to the Russians through the Lend-Lease Act and other materiel support. In 1943, Roosevelt, British Prime Minister Churchill, and Stalin met at Yalta, where they agreed to work toward the creation of what became the United Nations. In addition, Stalin promised to hold open elections in Poland and other Soviet-occupied territories in East Europe. Roosevelt was later criticized for naiveté in accepting Stalin's word that he would permit elections to take place.

Although Americans were suspicious of the Soviet Union and its political system, the immediate threat presented by the Germans and Japanese sublimated those concerns. Indeed, the United States also cooperated with Chinese Communists in fighting the Japanese occupation of Manchuria and with Ho Chi Minh's struggle against the Japanese presence in Vietnam. In addition, many Americans recognized and admired the extraordinary sacrifices of the Soviet people in fighting Nazism, resulting in twenty million Russian deaths. As the war came to a conclusion in Europe in May 1945, this fragile accommodation began to fall apart. Roosevelt died in April 1945, and his successor, Harry Truman, inexperienced in foreign policy and only recently having joined Roosevelt's administration, was deeply suspicious of Stalin and his motives in Eastern Europe. At the Potsdam Conference in July 1945, Truman and Stalin took stock of one another and emerged with little reason to believe that the war time alliance would hold into peace time. It was at Potsdam that Truman learned that the team of scientists working on the Manhattan Project had successfully tested a nuclear bomb.

Truman wrote later that he knew this meant the end of the war with Japan; he also recognized that this new weapon could play a decisive role in securing U.S. supremacy over the Soviets.

The collapse of the World War II alliance between the United States and the Soviet Union presented a diplomatic dilemma, which quickly became a domestic controversy as well. Historians such as Ellen Schrecker have documented the network that was already in place, which was both prepared and committed to targeting and destroying allegedly subversive elements in U.S. society and politics. The passage of the Smith Act in 1940, which prohibited teaching or promoting the overthrow of the U.S. government, and the creation of the House Committee on Un-American Activities (HUAC) in 1938 provided critical tools for this network. From its inception, the FBI had initiated programs investigating alleged radicalism in U.S. society; in fact, this was a particular interest of the longtime FBI director, J. Edgar Hoover. This network included a number of prominent political leaders, as well as previously unknown individuals, who would find themselves in the spotlight as anxieties over Communism mounted. Indeed, evidence suggests that some of these individuals exaggerated alleged subversion as a way to promote their own career goals. In Jeffrey D. Bass's essay, included in this volume, he examines the careers of some of these Cold Warriors to assess their impact on local, state, and national politics.

Investigations into Communist infiltration in U.S. society began in Congress and in the executive branch. In 1947, HUAC began investigating claims that a group of Hollywood screenwriters, actors, and directors had unknowingly, or unwittingly, become agents for promoting Communist propaganda. The so-called Hollywood Ten was a group of writers who were ordered to testify before HUAC to answer questions about these claims. The men refused to cooperate, invoking Fifth Amendment rights, which protect accused citizens from having to give evidence against themselves. Although they insisted that this did not represent an admission of guilt, most of the Congressmen and many other Americans assumed that they must be guilty of the crimes with which they were charged. In fact, most of these men did have connections either to the Communist Party or to related organizations, although there is no evidence that they plotted revolution.

Others of those brought before the committee to testify were more cooperative, notably Ronald Reagan and Gary Cooper. Reagan, who at the time of his testimony was serving as president of the Screen Actor's Guild, an industry union, parlayed his appearance before the committee into a blossoming political career. Although Reagan's acting had received lukewarm reviews and showed no signs of leading to major stardom, he was a charismatic voice in warning of the dangers of Communism within Hollywood (and eventually much farther afield). This knack for politics encouraged Reagan to change careers.

Meanwhile, within the executive branch, President Truman sought to address allegations that he had not been tough enough on Communism within the federal government. Many young men and women had toyed with the idea of joining, or had actually joined, a variety of Popular Front, Communist, or radical labor organizations during the Great Depression;

some of these individuals later became federal employees. These earlier associations, many of them long-abandoned, were brought up as proof that Truman had permitted dangerous elements into the most important agencies of the federal government. To head off these charges, in 1947, Truman instituted the loyalty-security program through Executive Order 9835, which required federal employees to swear an oath of loyalty and a promise that the employee had never been a member of the Communist Party or had any "sympathetic" association with it. In 1950, the Department of Justice released a list of organizations, membership in which qualified as violating the oath. The list, called the Attorney General's List of Totalitarian, Fascist, Communist, Subversive, and Other Organizations (AGLOSO), mostly included fairly obscure and many obsolete organizations. Nevertheless, as Martin Manning documents in his essay on the effects of Cold War anxieties within the federal government, any individual who had, at any time, belonged to one of the named groups was potentially subject to being questioned and to losing his or her job.

Historians have debated why Truman was willing to impose such a sweeping and controversial program. With little foreign policy experience, surrounded by advisors who urged a hard line against Communism, Truman was persuaded that he could not afford to do any less. As China slipped farther under the control of Communists and in the wake of widely publicized cases of alleged (or proven) espionage, Truman was hammered by Republican political opponents for being weak on national security. Truman felt unable or unwilling to stand them down.

As Manning notes in his essay, the effects of the federal loyalty oath programs were real and, in many cases, devastating for individuals with long careers in public service. Among those who had experimented with membership in left-wing political and labor organizations was Alger Hiss, a State Department official, who had accompanied Roosevelt to the Yalta Conference held near the end of World War II; in 1948, a journalist and former Communist turned informant named Whittaker Chambers accused Hiss of also being a former Communist. Hiss strongly denied the allegation, and the case became the first of the high-profile McCarthy-era court cases. Hiss was never convicted of being a Soviet spy, but he was eventually forced to recant his testimony denying acquaintance with Chambers. Hiss was convicted of perjury and served several years in prison. (Recently released Soviet archives suggest that Hiss may, in fact, have been a Soviet operative. Hiss's possible guilt raises new questions about the McCarthy era and how to interpret the threat that Communist agents may have represented.)

Cold War anxieties seized the imagination of the U.S. public in 1949; it was a year when the fear of Communist infiltration moved from places such as Washington, D.C., and Hollywood, both of which were far from middle America, to every town and community in the country. During that year, China fell to the Communists, which many Americans viewed as a major foreign policy failure that had taken U.S. political leadership by surprise; far more ominously, it was also the year in which the Soviets detonated an atomic bomb. More than any other event, the Soviet acquisition of the bomb represented weakness and vulnerability for the United States. Even though the impact of political subversion and radical political ideologies might seem obscure, the potential effects of nuclear attack certainly did not.

In early 1950, Hiss was charged with perjury, for lying about his knowledge of Communists in Washington, and was sentenced to prison. Klaus Fuchs was arrested on suspicion of delivering atomic secrets to the Soviet Union. Several months later, David Rosenberg was the first arrest in the investigation that eventually led to the trial and execution of Julius and Ethel Rosenberg. The Korean War began in June; this was the first war of the Cold War era, in which U.S. forces (as part of a UN operation) sought to contain Communism in Asia. Coming on the heels of the Chinese Revolution, the cumulative impact of these events made it easy to understand why Americans were increasingly worried.

The best-known individual to seize on these anxieties and turn them to political advantage was Joseph McCarthy, elected to the Senate as a Republican from Wisconsin in 1946. McCarthy came to the issue of anti-Communism years after others, such as J. Edgar Hoover and Richard Nixon, Congressman from California and member of HUAC, had been warning of its dangers. Nevertheless, McCarthy's sensational speech, delivered on February 9, 1950, in front of a group of Republican women in Wheeling, West Virginia, in which he claimed that the State Department knowingly employed Communists, brought national attention to this little-known Wisconsin senator and proved to be the opening act in a political drama that dominated Washington for several years. McCarthyism is, in some ways, a misleading term because it tends to focus attention too narrowly on Joseph McCarthy himself, rather than conveying the true extent of political repression during this period, for which McCarthy himself was only partly responsible.

Changes in media coverage helped broadcast the warnings of McCarthy and others. HUAC had already successfully targeted Hollywood and the industry reeled under additional charges and countercharges. Some of the best known actors, directors and screenwriters found themselves blacklisted, unable to get work during a time when major studios still exercised strict control through contracts and other forms of reprisals. Those who were called in front of HUAC and other investigative bodies insisted that they had not belonged to any subversive organizations but they refused to provide information about colleagues and friends. They too suffered reprisals. The effects of these ideological struggles in Hollywood led to the production of a number of interesting media which sought directly or through metaphor and other narrative devices to challenge McCarthyism, as Bryan E. Vizzini discusses in his essay on film and other aspects of popular culture during this era.

Television was a new medium, appearing at approximately the same time that the Cold War began. Americans were able to watch HUAC hearings, news programs depicting the efforts of the military to contain Communism in Korea, and, most notoriously, the efforts of Joseph McCarthy and his associates to use Senate hearings as a way to investigate and expose alleged Communists. Television programming, like Hollywood films, also came under suspicion. In 1950, a publication entitled *Red Channels* provided listings of actors, directors, and others working in television who were accused of Communist or radical sympathies. As with the Hollywood Ten hearings, this document left many industry employees without work and unable to get any. Some of America's best-loved actors, such as Lucille Ball, came under attack through such publications. Journalists and other media figures had also long been accused of left-leaning sympathies. Donna L. Halper discusses in her essay not only the ways in which journalists were attacked by McCarthy and his allies but also the tools they used to fight back. Publications such as *Red Channels* were offset by the courageous efforts of Edward T. Murrow and others to use that same new medium, television, to broadcast evidence of McCarthy's slurs and unsupported allegations.

By the early 1950s, the effect of these programs and investigations had created an atmosphere of fear and distrust in many U.S. communities. Individuals such as McCarthy, Hoover, Nixon—and many more whose names are less familiar to us today—played a key role in shaping a political culture that left many Americans unsure whether they could trust neighbors, respected public officials, or beloved entertainment figures. Some of these individuals sincerely believed the Soviet rhetoric and were convinced that the United States was at imminent risk of a Communist takeover. Others, particularly McCarthy, seem to have used anti-Communism as a springboard for their own ambitions.

Beginning within a decade of the founding of the United States, Americans have struggled to reconcile protections of civil liberties with real or perceived threats to national security. Such demands are not unique to the era of the Cold War; they remain readily apparent in U.S. society today. But because Communism in the United States was often presented as operating clandestinely and because Communists were portrayed as "moles," living apparently normal lives while secretly working to promote Communist revolution, average Americans became increasingly alarmed about risks within their schools, businesses, and neighborhoods. In addition to such threats from within U.S. towns and cities, the potential for Soviet nuclear attacks added another layer of fear and anxiety.

In Dave Mills's essay, he looks at the development of civil defense societies in U.S. towns and communities. These organizations allowed average men and women to make a contribution to the Cold War effort by monitoring the skies for potential nuclear attacks. By mobilizing for this sort of surveillance, U.S. citizens experienced increased anxiety about the possibility of attack as well as a sense of reassurance by participating in events that would either prevent or limit the impact of an attack.

Some Americans supported monitoring not just the skies for Soviet bombers but also monitoring others' personal lives—to ferret out potential security weaknesses. In addition to those with questionable political associations, workers suspected of being homosexuals were also singled out, because it was argued that they would be more vulnerable to blackmail or extortion. Gays were disproportionately affected by the loyalty oath screenings, and their mistreatment by the federal government helped give rise to new civil rights protests. Federal employees working overseas in the U.S. Information Agency were also targeted by McCarthy aides, who challenged the inclusion of library materials (often materials that were common in many U.S. libraries) that allegedly promoted Communism.

In addition to federal employees, labor activists, long suspected in U.S. culture as being Communist sympathizers, faced renewed attacks. Labor experienced significant gains during World War II, as Roosevelt sought to extend labor protections as a way to promote efficient wartime production. Saranna Thornton, in her essay on McCarthyism and the labor movement, traces the long and contested road that unions have trod in U.S. history. With the advent of the Cold War, unions became an obvious target for McCarthy-style attacks. In an echo of earlier generations of labor unrest, accusations were made against union activists—on ethnic grounds as well as economic ones. Many labor activists represented groups whose arrival in the United States dated back perhaps only a few generations. Many of these individuals or their parents and grandparents came from eastern and southern Europe, areas traditionally viewed as especially "dangerous" for harboring political radicalism. Thus political and ethnic anxieties served to reinforce each other.

But McCarthyism touched others whose critiques of U.S. society were not based on Marxist analysis or even broader capitalist critiques. McCarthyism led to attacks on any political expression that sought to challenge the status quo, including challenges to white Protestant American norms. African Americans, for example, involved in the fast-emerging civil rights movement of the postwar period were also represented as radicals and political subversives. Attacks on civil rights activists demonstrate the ways in which McCarthyism used fears of Communism to try to protect a status quo under increasing pressure to change. Mainstream organizations such as the National Association for the Advancement of Colored People (NAACP) had to spend limited resources fending off charges of Communist infiltration and/or sympathy. As S. Ani Mukherji describes in his essay, blacks responded in a variety of ways to such charges. To be sure, some black Americans, disgusted by the hypocrisy of U.S. society, especially at a time when the United States increasingly defined itself as defender of the free world, turned to radical political solutions. W. E. B. Dubois and Paul Robeson perhaps best represent the bitter despair of some black leaders, who concluded that the United States would never live up to its promises of individual freedom and dignity. They were quickly targeted by federal agencies—with a variety of escalating punishments for their outspoken criticisms. Although most African American activists of the era adhered to the NAACP's staunchly anti-Communist rhetoric, white Southern legislators were able to use fears of Communism to constrain and challenge any efforts by blacks at securing more rights.

McCarthyism served to shore up other sorts of norms in U.S. society, in addition to those dealing with race and ethnicity. For the first time in mainstream America, sexual behavior became a subject of scientific inquiry and even dinner table conversation. Alfred Kinsey and his team of researchers produced two major studies of sexuality in the United States, one on men in 1948 and one on women in 1953. Although controversial, both at the time of publication and even today, these studies served to titillate but ultimately reinforce U.S. attitudes about sexuality and gender roles. The postwar period also ushered in the era of the baby boom, with Americans marrying younger and having more children. These demographic trends led to dramatic changes in U.S. society, seeming to demonstrate that, although homosexuality and other "deviant" behavior did exist in the United States, most Americans wanted to be part of a so-called nuclear family. (Nuclear refers to both the normative U.S. family structure of the era and the greatest perceived threat to that institution as well.) As Howard H. Chiang notes in his article on sexuality during this period, even individuals such as Christine Jorgensen, the first surgical transsexual, whose sexuality seemed far outside U.S. sexual norms, reaffirmed conventional expectations. Jorgensen sought to be transformed surgically into a woman, but her aspirations as a woman were strictly within traditional boundaries.

Michelle M. Marino notes in her essay on the women of this era that, as with African Americans, the effects of McCarthyism hindered the developing feminist movement but could not disrupt it entirely. Women, like homosexuals, were seen as particularly vulnerable to Communist recruitment and manipulation. Traditional views of women still attempted to maintain that women's weaker intellectual abilities left them susceptible to the diabolic schemes of Communist agents. One of the first individuals to make accusations against Communist agents in the United States was Elizabeth Bentley, who informed the FBI in late 1945 that a Communist cell had been in operation in Washington, D.C. Although some of her claims were eventually supported, she was, overall, not considered a credible witness, and her role in the early McCarthy period helped reinforce an image of women as politically vulnerable. But, as in other historical eras, women were able to use gender expectations to assert special responsibility to defend the home and used this responsibility to parlay for more political agency, such as the organization called Women Strike for Peace that eventually challenged McCarthyism.

Margaret Peacock's essay explores the impact of McCarthyism and Cold War fears on the children during this period of national anxiety. The baby boom led to a significant increase in the size of U.S. families, and media, advertising, and U.S. manufacturers responded to this growth with new products and services, aimed at the expanding middle class and its expanding families. But Communism represented a threat to this prosperity, both through the threat of nuclear attack and through insidious psychological attacks. Children were taught how to respond to nuclear attacks and how to guard themselves against the brainwashing techniques often attributed to Communist agents. In civil defense societies, as well as in organizations such as the Boy Scouts, children were considered an essential component in protecting U.S. ideals against Communist infiltration.

Eventually, as is often the case with political demagogues, McCarthy went too far. In 1954, he began holding a series of Senate hearings investigating whether, or the degree to which, the U.S. Army had been infiltrated by Communists. One of the attorneys smeared by McCarthy finally and passionately demanded whether McCarthy "had no decency." The medium of television broadcast the dramatic moment across the nation; as suddenly as the Wheeling speech had catapulted McCarthy to fame, the confrontation during the Army-McCarthy hearings brought about his collapse. Within a year, he had been censured by the U.S. Senate, and, in 1957, he died of liver failure. Although McCarthy's tenure as a major political force in Washington was relatively brief, it would be a mistake to assume that McCarthyism died along with its namesake.

For years to come, unfounded charges of Communism were directed at organizations and individuals who challenged the status quo in the United States. For example, the NAACP won its most important court victory in 1954, with the *Brown v. Board of Education* decision that prohibited segregated education. Southern legislatures immediately implemented a program of "Massive Resistance," the purpose of which was to delay or prevent the *Brown* ruling from being enforced. At the heart of many of these attacks on the NAACP and other civil rights groups were Southern legislators' claims that the civil rights movement was deeply influenced and even controlled by Communist agents. Indeed, virtually every reform organization of the 1950s and 1960s had to, at some point and to varying degrees, refute charges of Communist influence.

Several prominent Cold Warriors went on to expand their political influence by continuing to warn of Communist threats. Richard Nixon served two terms as vice president under Dwight Eisenhower and, in 1968, was elected president, running largely on promises to restore law and order to U.S. society and to show no leniency toward radicalism of any kind. Ronald Reagan served two terms as governor of California, making many of the same political appeals that Nixon had. He too eventually won election as president, promising to take a strong stand on radicalism at home and reenergizing Cold War debates abroad. J. Edgar Hoover, who, by the 1960s, was a formidable power broker within Washington and had files on virtually every major public figure in the capital, continued to serve as head of the FBI until his death in 1973. Like Southern legislators, Hoover was convinced that the civil rights movement harbored Communists within its ranks, and his attacks on the movement were a significant impediment to its work. By the 1960s, domestic debates over the Cold War and McCarthyism were incorporated into the broader social upheaval of the civil rights and Vietnam War era. The fears of political radicalism certainly did not go away, but the context in which they were expressed and deployed by political and media figures had changed.

The repressive climate that characterized the era of Joseph McCarthy and his associates had unexpected consequences. Although many forces germinating in the postwar period helped give rise to the explosion of social protest during the 1960s, McCarthyism played a key role. The more attacks that were made, particularly those based on unreliable or unfounded accusations, the more resistant were many individuals—not only those targeted by such attacks but by those who increasingly came to recognize (or remember) that the right of political dissent is profoundly American. Protests against McCarthy-style attacks were articulated through particular groups, such as those of women or African Americans or labor activists; some came from Hollywood, which began to satirize Cold War anxieties through films such as *Dr. Strangelove*; some came from the media, as a new generation of reporters sought to emulate the courageous example set by Edward R. Murrow. The cumulative effect of these protests was a backlash against McCarthyism. Although politicians like Nixon and Reagan, whose political careers began during the McCarthy era, went on to secure political power, they could not do so using the sort of heavy-handed investigative strategies of HUAC or McCarthy's Senate investigations.

The McCarthy and Cold War eras of the postwar period have left complex and often conflicting legacies. Americans were deeply unsettled by the new threats posed by the Cold War, in particular the threat of weapons of mass destruction and the threat of covert infiltration of U.S. communities and neighborhoods. The mood of the nation enabled McCarthy and his associates to manipulate those fears into a broad mandate to target and oftentimes harass those Americans who, because of their personal ideologies, class, race, gender or sexual orientation, seemed outside of U.S. norms and were thus suspect. This was not a new phenomenon in U.S. history and, in the post 9/11 world, we have seen this tendency continue to play out in some familiar ways. But when looking at the McCarthy era, it is equally striking to note the resiliency of U.S. civil liberties and rights, including the right to hold unpopular opinions and to attempt to reform U.S. society. The upheavals of the 1960s, resulting in a significant expansion of civil rights for all Americans, were inspired, at least in part, by a backlash against McCarthyism. In ways that Joseph McCarthy never envisioned, his influence over the long term may have helped create a more tolerant and diverse U.S. society.

Caroline S. Emmons
Hampden-Sydney College

References and Further Reading

Fried, Albert. *McCarthyism: The Great American Red Scare: A Documentary History*. New York: Oxford University Press, 1997.

Henriksen, Margot. *Dr. Strangelove's America: Society and Culture in the Atomic Age*. Berkeley: University of California Press, 1997.

Johnson, Haynes. *The Age of Anxiety: McCarthyism to Terrorism*. New York: Harvest Books, 2006.

Kuznick, Peter J., and James Gilbert, ed. *Rethinking Cold War Culture*. Washington, DC: Smithsonian Institution Press, 2001.

May, Elaine Tyler. *Homeward Bound: American Families in the Cold War Era*. New York: Basic Books, 1988.

Navasky, Victor S. *Naming Names*. New York: Penguin, 1980, 1991.

Oshinsky, David M. *A Conspiracy So Immense: The World of Joe McCarthy.* New York: Free Press, 1983.

Schrecker, Ellen. *The Age of McCarthyism: A Brief History with Documents.* Boston: Bedford/St. Martin's, 2002.

Schrecker, Ellen. *Many Are the Crimes: McCarthyism in America.* Boston: Little, Brown and Co., 1998.

Whitfield, Stephen. *The Culture of the Cold War.* Baltimore: Johns Hopkins University Press, 1991.

About the Editor and Contributors

Editor

Caroline S. Emmons is associate professor of history at Hampden-Sydney College in Hampden-Sydney, Virginia. She has published articles on the NAACP, civil rights leader Harry T. Moore, women in the civil rights movement in Virginia, and school desegregation battles in Florida. She was a Fulbright lecturer in Bratislava, Slovakia, an experience that piqued her interest in examining the legacies of the Cold War era in both Europe and the United States.

Contributors

Jeffrey D. Bass is adjunct history professor at Arizona State University, specializing in U.S. politics and foreign relations. He has a book on Congress and national security policy during the Cold War forthcoming in 2010 from McFarland & Company Publishing.

Howard H. Chiang is founding editor of *Critical Studies in History*, a journal devoted to the exploration of the intersections between critical theory and historiography. His research interests include the history and historical epistemology of biology, medicine, and the human sciences, the interdisciplinary study of gender and sexuality, and the history of modern China, East Asia, and the United States. He earned his graduate degrees from Columbia University and Princeton University.

Donna L. Halper is assistant professor of communications at Lesley University, Cambridge MA. She has also spent more than 35 years in broadcasting and print journalism and is the author of four books and many articles related to mass communication and popular culture. Ms. Halper's expertise is in media history, media stereotypes, and media ethics.

Martin Manning is a research librarian with the U.S. Department of State. He has degrees from Boston College and Catholic University. Manning has contributed to reference books and encyclopedias, and he is the author of the *Historical Dictionary of American Propaganda* (Greenwood, 2004) and is presently co-editing *Conflict and the Fourth Estate: Media and Propaganda in U.S. Military History* (expected to be published by ABC-CLIO, 2011).

Michella M. Marino is a PhD candidate at the University of Massachusetts-Amherst, where she concentrates on 20th-century U.S. social history, women's history, and the connections between women's sports and femininity.

David Mills is instructor of history at Minnesota West Community and Technical College. He has completed his PhD at North Dakota State University; his dissertation examines the Cold War on the northern plains. His research interests include the military and social aspects of the Cold War.

S. Ani Mukherji works at the intersections of U.S. foreign relations, political culture, and comparative ethnic studies. He is currently a doctoral candidate in the Department of American Civilization at Brown University, where he is finishing his dissertation, "The Anticolonial Imagination: Migrant Intellectuals and the Exilic Productions of American Radicalism in Interwar Moscow."

Margaret Peacock is assistant professor of Russian and Cold War history at the University of Alabama. Her research centers on visual culture during the Cold War. Her latest project examines how the Soviet and U.S. governments constructed particular visions of endangered and mobilized youth in order to legitimate their domestic and international Cold War policies from 1945 until 1968.

Saranna Thornton is professor of economics at Hampden-Sydney College. She is a member of the American Association of University Professors' National Council and chair of the AAUP's Committee on the Economic Status of the Profession. Her research interests include employment discrimination and labor law.

Bryan E. Vizzini is associate professor of history at West Texas A&M University. His recent publications include "Cold War Fears, Cold War Passions: Conservatives and Liberals Square off in 1950s Science Fiction," which appeared in 2009 in *Quarterly Review of Film and Video*, and "Hero and Holocaust: Graphic Novels in the Undergraduate History Classroom," a chapter in the forthcoming Modern Language Association volume *Approaches to Teaching the Graphic Novel*.

Chronology

This timeline covers the "Cold War and McCarthy era," which most historians date from about 1945 through approximately 1960. But the Cold War is an unusual war in that it does not have traditional beginning and ending points. Cold War tensions lasted long after 1960; indeed, some might say that the Cuban Missile Crisis in 1962 is the definitive Cold War moment in terms of U.S. foreign policy. Many historians argue that the Cold War did not "end" until 1989—when countries under Soviet domination began to reject Soviet power openly, most famously in the destruction of the Berlin Wall. Others argue that continued political instability in Russia and the former Soviet republics suggests that tension between Russia and the West amounts to an ongoing Cold War. However one wants to date these "bookends," the following timeline covers most of the major domestic and foreign policy issues during the height of the Cold War. It provides the reader with sufficient context in which to understand the accompanying essays. More detail can be found by exploring the items included in the bibliography.

1917

March Czar Nicholas II abdicates his throne in favor of his brother, who also subsequently abdicates.

April The United States declares war on Germany. The Committee on Public Information is created by President Woodrow Wilson to devise propaganda urging the U.S. public to support the war.

June With Wilson's support, the Espionage Act is passed, increasing penalties for those convicted of aiding the enemy (this act also singled out political subversives of the left).

November The Russian Revolution reaches its climax as the Bolshevik Party seizes power in Russia.

1918

March The Treaty of Brest-Litovsk is signed, and the Russians withdraw from World War I. President Wilson continues to refuse to recognize the Soviet government.

May The U.S. Congress passes the Sedition Act, increasing penalties for those found guilty of disloyal speech.

September U.S. troops land in the Soviet Union to try to prevent the consolidation of the Bolshevik Revolution. The Sisson Documents, forged documents purporting to show that Soviet leaders were actually German agents, are released by the Committee on Public Information.

October U.S. Congress passes the Alien Act, allowing for the deportation of alleged radicals from the United States.

November World War I ends with the signing of an armistice agreement.

1919

March The Third Congress of the Communist International (or Comintern, committing the Soviet Union to support Communist revolutions around the world) begins.

June Eugene Debs is arrested and eventually convicted under the Sedition Act.

August After the Socialist Party in the United States splits, the Communist Party of America and the Communist Labor Party are formed, with an estimated combined membership of 40,000 members in 1919 (Brune, 2005, 26).

November through January 1920 the Palmer Raids, including attacks on labor union offices, radical political organizations, left-wing newspaper and magazine offices, are carried out at the direction of U.S. Attorney General A. Mitchell Palmer.

1920

March The U.S. Senate votes to reject the Versailles Treaty and U.S. membership in the League of Nations.

April The final U.S. forces leave the Soviet Union.

July The United States resumes trade relations with the Soviets but does not extend formal recognition.

1921

July Nicola Sacco and Bartolommeo Vanzetti are found guilty of murder in a sensational Massachusetts trial that focused on the political radicalism (and foreign birth) of the defendants.

1922

April Stalin becomes Secretary-General of the Communist Party of the Soviet Union.

October Italian fascists seize control of Italy's government, under the leadership of Benito Mussolini.

December The Soviet Union officially adopts the name Union of Soviet Socialist Republics.

1924

January Vladimir Lenin dies.

1927

May U.S. Marines are dispatched to Nicaragua to prevent a takeover by leftist followers of Augusto Sandino (whose followers were called Sandinistas).

July The United States recognizes the Nationalist government of Chiang Kai-Shek in China.

August Sacco and Vanzetti are executed.

October Josef Stalin consolidates power over the Union of Soviet Socialist Republics.

1929

December Stalin begins forced collectivization of agriculture, leading to widespread starvation and displacement of rural populations.

1933

January Adolf Hitler and the Nazis take over control of Germany.

March Franklin D. Roosevelt is inaugurated as U.S. president.

November The United States officially recognizes the Union of Soviet Socialist Republics.

1934

The Union of Soviet Socialist Republics joins the League of Nations.

1935

July The United States and the Soviets sign a new trade agreement.

August The Soviet Union initiates the Popular Front, as a way to resist fascism and promote the Soviet Union internationally.
The Congress of Industrial Organizations (CIO) is formed.

1936

July The Spanish Civil War begins, and leftists in the United States defy U.S. laws prohibiting U.S. citizens from fighting in the war.

August Stalin's purge trials of Bolshevik leaders begin.

November The Anti-Cominterm pact is signed by Germany and Italy.

1938

August The House Committee on Un-American Activities is established to investigate anti-American (including fascist and Communist) ideologies in U.S. society.

September The Munich Conference is held, at which British Prime Minister Neville Chamberlain and other Allied leaders accepted Hitler's word that he will cease continued aggression if allowed to keep Sudetenland; this policy, known as "appeasement," was a powerful lesson to hardliners during the Cold War.

1939

August The Non-Aggression Pact is signed between the Soviet Union and Nazi Germany, bringing about the collapse of the Popular Front.

September World War II begins with Germany's attack on Poland. Whittaker Chambers informs the Assistant Secretary of State that there are Communist sympathizers within the federal government.

October Albert Einstein and other physicists warn Roosevelt that the Germans are seeking to develop an atomic bomb.

1940

June The Smith Act is passed, making it illegal to teach, advocate for, or join any group that teaches or advocates the overthrow of the U.S. government by force. The U.S. Supreme Court upholds Pennsylvania law allowing for the expulsion of schoolchildren refusing to salute the U.S. flag. The Selective Service and Training Act is passed, creating the first peacetime draft in U.S. history.

1941

January President Roosevelt delivers his Four Freedoms address, urging the Allies to fight for freedom of speech and worship and freedom from want and fear.

May The Federal Communications Commission (FCC) approves the broadcast of commercial television beginning in July.

June Germany attacks the Soviet Union, which subsequently joins the Allies. Roosevelt creates the Fair Employment Practices Committee to ensure that military contractors would not discriminate in hiring. The Office of Scientific Research and Development is created, which oversees development of nuclear weapons, radar, sonar, and other weapons innovations.

July Stalin begins asking the other Allied leaders to open a "second front" against Germany to relieve pressure on Soviets.

August Roosevelt and Churchill meet off the Canadian coast to draft the Atlantic Charter, a broad statement of support for self-determination and national sovereignty.

September The (Senate) Nye Committee investigates allegations of prowar propaganda produced by Hollywood.

November Roosevelt authorizes the extension of the Lend-Lease program to the Soviets.

December The United States comes into the war after the Japanese attack on Pearl Harbor.

1942

January The UN Declaration is signed in Washington, D.C., with 26 original signatories including the United States, the Union of Soviet Socialist Republics, Great Britain, and China.

February Roosevelt signs Executive Order 9066, allowing for the creation of detention camps for Japanese and Japanese Americans living in the United States.

June The Office of Strategic Services is set up to coordinate wartime intelligence activities; it is the forerunner of the Central Intelligence Agency.

November The Battle of Stalingrad begins between the Soviets and Germans; the hard-won Soviet victory is often described as the turning point of the war.

1943

January The Pentagon is completed in Washington, D.C., in order to house all branches of leadership of the U.S. Armed Forces.

May The Soviet Union agrees to dismantle the Comintern, at the request of the United States.

June The U.S. Supreme Court rules that schoolchildren cannot be expelled for refusing to salute the U.S. flag.

December The Teheran Conference is held; this is the first meeting between Roosevelt, Churchill, and Stalin.

1944

June The Normandy invasion by the Allies (better known as D-Day) begins.

September U.S. Ambassador to the Soviet Union Averell Harriman sends a telegram to Roosevelt warning of the worsening attitude of the Soviets toward the Americans.

1945

January The Soviet Army captures Warsaw, Poland, from the Germans.

February The Yalta Conference is held, at which Roosevelt, Churchill, and Stalin meet to discuss the postwar situation in Europe.

March A Communist government is formed in Romania.

April Roosevelt dies and is succeeded by Harry S Truman. The Soviet Union and Poland sign a twenty-year agreement of mutual assistance. Truman and Soviet Foreign Minister V. M. Molotov meet and exchange sharp words. The United Nations is created.

May Germany surrenders. Truman orders a reduction in the amount of Lend-Lease aid available to the Soviets.

June The trial in the *Amerasia* case begins, with a number of government employees accused of espionage.

July Earl Browder is expelled from the American Communist Party. The Potsdam Conference is held; this is Truman and Stalin's first meeting. The United States successfully tests a nuclear bomb in New Mexico.

August The United States drops a nuclear bomb on Hiroshima and Nagasaki, bringing World War II to a close. President Truman orders restoration of civilian production and collective bargaining. Allies divide Korea at the 38th parallel, with Soviet forces to the north and pro-Western to the south.

September Igor Gouzenko defects, heightening fears of Soviet spies in the United States. U.S. troops move into South Korea. Ho Chi Minh declares that Vietnam is independent from both Japan and France.

October Louis Budenz leaves the Communist Party.

November Elizabeth Bentley informs the FBI that she has information about a Communist spy ring within the United States. The Communist Party wins elections in Bulgaria. United Autoworkers begin a strike against General Motors in Detroit.

1946

January UN General Assembly holds its first meeting. It also creates the Atomic Energy Commission, for which the goal was to restrict atomic energy to peaceful purposes. Truman creates the Control Intelligence Group, another forerunner of the Central Intelligence Agency.

February Stalin gives a speech in which he declares that the Soviet Union cannot coexist with the West. George Kennan sends his "Long Telegram" to Truman, recommending that the United States take a hard line against the Soviets.

March Former British Prime Minister Winston Churchill gives his "Iron Curtain" address in Missouri. Truman signs Executive Order 9835, requiring background checks on all federal employment applicants.

June Bernard Baruch presents the "Baruch Plan," proposing international monitoring of nuclear materials.

September Secretary of Commerce (and former vice president) Henry Wallace resigns after criticizing Truman's hard-line policy toward the Soviet Union and warning against an arms race.

November Republicans win a Congressional majority in midterm elections; Truman creates the Temporary Commission on Employee Loyalty, which becomes the foundation for the loyalty-security program. Communist Party wins elections in Romania. France intensifies its effort to reassert control over Vietnam.

December Truman creates the Committee on Civil Rights, the first serious program by a U.S. president to investigate racial discrimination. The U.N. Security Council agrees to the implementation of the Baruch Plan, which in effect reinforced U.S. insistence on maintaining a monopoly on atomic weapons.

1947

January The Communist Party wins rigged elections in Poland.

March The Truman Doctrine is announced, promising U.S. aid to nations resisting "armed minorities or outside pressures"; Truman announces Executive Order 8802, requiring federal employees to sign a loyalty oath.

June Marshall Plan is announced; Taft-Hartley Act is passed, limiting unions' power and attacking Communist involvement in unions. Henry Wallace, former U.S. vice president, announces his plan to form a third party, following his break with Truman's Cold War policies.

July Kennan publishes the "Mister X" article in *Foreign Affairs,* urging the policy of containment of Soviet Communism. Soviets walk out of Marshall Plan talks in Paris; other East European nations follow suit. U.S. Congress passes National Security Act of 1947, creating the Department of Defense, including the Central Intelligence Agency (CIA) and National Security Council (NSC).

August Communist Party takes control of government in Hungary.

October Truman becomes the first U.S. president to make an address to the American people on television. Hollywood Ten hearings held before HUAC. Ronald Reagan appears before the Committee. Brig. Gen. Leslie Groves predicts that it will take twenty years for the Soviets to develop an atomic bomb. The Communist Information Agency (Cominform) is created by the Soviets and its allies for the purpose of centralizing Communist parties around the world.

November Attorney General's list of subversive organizations (AGLOSA) is released.

December Hollywood studios fire Hollywood Ten via Waldorf Statement. Screen Directors' Guild says Communists may not become members. Cominform is created in the Soviet Union. Henry Wallace begins third-party run for the presidency.

1948

February The Communists establish control in Czechoslovakia.

March The Brussels Treaty, a precursor to the North Atlantic Treaty Organization (NATO), is signed promising its signatories a plan for collective security. U.S. Supreme Court rules that religious training in public schools is unconstitutional.

June Yugoslavia is expelled from the Cominform. The United States and its allies make plans for the creation of a West German republic, and Stalin initiates the Berlin Blockade in response. Truman approves an airlift of supplies into Berlin.

July Eugene Dennis and other Communist leaders are arrested for violating the Smith Act. J. Strom Thurmond leads Southern Democrats in a walkout from the Democratic Party convention, forming the States Rights (or Dixiecrat) Party, which nominated Thurmond for president. The Progressive Party nominates Henry Wallace for president. Truman orders an end to segregation in the U.S. armed forces and federal civil service. Whittaker Chambers and Elizabeth Bentley testify to HUAC about the presence of Communists in the State Department in the 1930s.

August Whittaker Chambers accuses State Department employee Alger Hiss of having been a Communist; hearings begin before HUAC. Republic of South Korea is established. Peacetime draft registration in the United States begins.

October The Voice of America is created to broadcast anti-Communist programming in Eastern Europe.

November Truman is reelected over Republican Thomas Dewey, Progressive Party candidate Henry Wallace, and States Rights Party candidate J. Strom Thurmond.

December Chambers testifies about the "Pumpkin Papers," containing classified State Department documents that he says Hiss leaked to him. Hiss is indicted for perjury. Congressman Richard Nixon, a member of HUAC, accuses Truman of covering up evidence of Communist influence in the federal government.

1949

January Eugene Dennis is convicted of violating the Smith Act. Stalin agrees to negotiate with Truman over the situation in Berlin.
The University of Washington dismisses three professors accused of being Communists

February Richard Nixon and Karl Mundt introduce the Mundt-Nixon Bill to register Communists within the United States. The National Security Council (NSC) announces plans to investigate the extent of Communism within the United States.

March Judith Coplon arrested for espionage.

April The North Atlantic Treaty Organization (NATO) is formally established, with Belgium, Canada, Denmark, France, Great Britain, Iceland, Italy, Luxembourg, the Netherlands, Norway, Portugal, and the United States among the original members.

May Chiang Kai-Shek, leader of the Chinese Nationalists, is forced to retreat with his forces to the island of Formosa (Taiwan). China and North Korea sign a mutual defense treaty. The Federal Republic of Germany is established; the Berlin Blockade ends. The Hollywood Ten sue Hollywood producers after being blacklisted for refusing to testify before HUAC.

June University of California begins requiring faculty to take loyalty oath. Frank Sinatra, Lillian Hellman, and Charlie Chaplin are accused of being Communists. Mao Zedong declares that the Chinese Communist revolution had ended in victory.

July Hiss trial ends in hung jury. Soviets detonate a nuclear bomb. Senate ratifies the NATO treaty.

August Controversy erupts in Washington over whether or to what extent U.S. officials, especially members of Truman's administration, were responsible for the Chinese Communists' imminent victory.

September Mao declares the creation of the People's Republic of China.

October Eleven Communists found guilty of violating the Smith Act are sentenced to prison. The Soviet-allied German Democratic Republic is established.

November Congress of Industrial Organizations (CIO) throws left-leaning unions out. The Soviets and their allies challenge the seating of Nationalist Chinese on the Security Council.

December J. Parnell Thomas, chair of HUAC, is found guilty of payroll fraud and is sentenced to prison.

1950

January Hiss is convicted of perjury in his retrial and sentenced to prison. Truman announces plan to speed up development of the hydrogen bomb (or "super" bomb).

February Klaus Fuchs is arrested on suspicion of passing classified information to the Soviets. McCarthy delivers his famous Wheeling, West Virginia, address, in which he claimed to have the names of 205 Communists in the State Department. China and the Soviet Union sign a friendship agreement.

March The Chinese Nationalists in Taiwan declare the creation of the Republic of China.

April The National Security Council issues NSC-68, a policy paper recommending enormous increases in U.S. defense spending. The U.S. Supreme

Court upholds the conviction of Hollywood Ten screenwriters John Howard Lawson and Dalton Trumbo.

May The U.S. Supreme Court upholds sections of the Taft-Hartley Labor Act limiting access to the National Labor Relations Board if officers will not swear that they have no Communist affiliations.

June David Greenglass is arrested for passing classified information to Soviets, and he names Julius Rosenberg as a fellow conspirator. *Red Channels* is published, detailing the alleged connections between the television industry and Communism. The Korean War begins with an attack on South Korea by Communist forces of North Korea. Senator Margaret Chase Smith denounces McCarthy in a speech on the Senate floor.

July Julius Rosenberg is arrested for espionage; his wife Ethel is arrested a month later. A Senate subcommittee disputes the accuracy of charges made by Joseph McCarthy about the presence of Communists in the State Department, calling McCarthy's claims "a hoax and a fraud." Radio Free Europe begins its first broadcast to Czechoslovakia.

September McCarran Act forces Communist organizations to register with the federal government; Truman vetoes the bill and is overridden. Gen. Douglas MacArthur lands his forces at Inchon in South Korea and begins driving back the North Korean offensive. Truman approves NSC-68. Ralph Bunche becomes the first African American to win the Nobel Peace Prize for his work mediating conflict in the Middle East.

November The Chinese Communists enter the conflict in Korea in support of North Korea, forcing U.N. forces into retreat. Nixon defeats Helen Gehagen Douglas in California Senate race.

December Truman declares national state of emergency in response to the Korean War. Dwight D. Eisenhower is named supreme commander of NATO Allied Forces in Western Europe.

1951

February FBI begins program to investigate Communism in state government.

March Rosenberg Trial begins, and the defendants are quickly convicted.

April Judge Irving Kaufman sentences the Rosenbergs to death. Truman fires MacArthur for insubordination. Truman orders the Secretary of Commerce to take over the U.S. steel industry in order to avoid a strike. The first computer available for private purchase comes on the market, albeit with limited capabilities.

June More Smith Act prosecutions begin after arrests of party leaders throughout the country; conviction in *Dennis* case is upheld. CBS debuts the first one-hour color television program. Congress passes legislation lowering the draft age to 18 and extending the draft until 1955.

July Truce talks begin in Korea.

August McCarthy names 26 members of the State Department whom he accuses of subversive activity. Allen Dulles is appointed deputy director of the CIA.

September The United States, Australia, and New Zealand sign the ANZUS treaty, promising mutual protection. The United States also signs a mutual defense treaty with Japan.

October *I Love Lucy* debuts on CBS.

November Reagan is reelected president of the Screen Actors' Guild. Cease-fire declared in Korea. *See It Now*, hosted by Edward R. Murrow, debuts on CBS.

December John Service is fired by the State Department after the Civil Service Loyalty Review Board finds "reasonable doubt" about his loyalty. HUAC recommends the death penalty for anyone convicted of peacetime espionage in the United States. Americans for Democratic Action begin campaign to repeal the Smith Act.

1952

January *American Bandstand* and *Dragnet* both premiere on television.

February Churchill announces that Great Britain has developed an atomic bomb.

July Adlai Stevenson is selected as the Democratic nominee for president.

September Richard Nixon, Republican vice presidential nominee, delivers the Checkers Speech, in which he denied accepting illegal campaign gifts but insists that his family will keep the dog given to his children.

October Reports announce that the United States has detonated a hydrogen bomb. British announce successful nuclear bomb test. U.S. Supreme Court declines to review Rosenberg death penalty sentence.

November Dwight D. Eisenhower elected president over Democratic nominee Adlai Stevenson. *Bwana Devil*, the first 3-D movie, premieres.

December Owen Lattimore, accused of supporting the interests of Chinese Communists during the Chinese Revolution, is indicted for perjury. Eisenhower travels to Korea.

1953

January Allen Dulles becomes head of the CIA. His brother, John Foster Dulles, serves as Secretary of State.

March Stalin dies. Senator Robert Taft demands investigation into Voice of America radio station; Senate confirms Charles Bohlen as new ambassador to the Union of Soviet Socialist Republics despite McCarthy's protests

April Executive Order 10450 strengthens loyalty-security program. Joseph McCarthy's assistants, Roy Cohn and David Schine, return from touring U.S. Information Agency libraries in Europe and allege that these facilities are full of pro-Communist literature. Douglas MacArthur recommends that the United States attack China.

May U.S. Supreme Court declines again to review Rosenberg case.

June The Rosenbergs are executed.

August Soviets announce successful test of a hydrogen bomb. The CIA supports coup in Iran that overthrows left-leaning prime minister Mohammad Mossadegh; the Shah is returned to power with U.S. blessing.

September Nikita Khrushchev becomes Soviet leader, and the Soviets announce that they will provide Communist China with major economic assistance. Earl Warren appointed Chief Justice of the U.S. Supreme Court.

October United States and South Korea sign mutual protection treaty. George Marshall wins the Nobel Peace Prize.

December J. Robert Oppenheimer's security clearance is suspended pending an investigation.

1954

January The United States launches its first nuclear-powered submarine. The U.S. Army begins investigation of McCarthy aide David Schine.

February McCarthy charges Brig. Gen. Ralph Zwicker with tolerating Communists within the U.S. Army. Eisenhower declines further involvement in deteriorating French situation in Indochina. Trials of a polio vaccine developed by Jonas Salk begin.

March Battle of Dien Bien Phu between French and Viet Minh begins, ending a month later with a French defeat.

April–June The Army-McCarthy hearings are held; the Senate also investigates McCarthy for "alleged improprieties."

May The *Brown* decision is handed down by the U.S. Supreme Court.

June Nixon blames Truman for the loss of China. A CIA-sponsored coup overthrows leftist Guatemalan leader Jacobo Arbenz Guzman. Atomic Energy Commission agrees after investigation that J. Robert Oppenheimer is a potential security risk. Eisenhower signs bill adding the words "under God" to the Pledge of Allegiance.

July The Geneva Accords are signed between the French and Viet Minh, dividing Vietnam at the 17th parallel pending national elections. Elvis Presley releases his first single.

August U.S. Senate begins discussing possible censure of McCarthy. President Eisenhower signs legislation outlawing the Communist Party in the United States.

September The Southeast Asia Treaty Organization (SEATO) is signed. The first Miss America pageant is held.

October West Germany has military presence in NATO.

November Hiss is released from prison.

December The U.S. Senate votes 67–22 to censure Joseph McCarthy. United States signs mutual protection treaty with Republic of China.

1955

January President Eisenhower holds the first televised press conference.

February Great Britain announces plans to develop hydrogen bomb. The American Federation of Labor (AFL) and the Congress of Industrial Organizations (CIO) announce their merger.

March The Union of Soviet Socialist Republics threatens to establish regional security organization if West Germany is allowed to rearm.

April NATO admits West Germany. In Indonesia, the Non-Aligned Movement is established.

May The Warsaw Pact is signed by the Union of Soviet Socialist Republics, Albania, Bulgaria, Czechoslovakia, East Germany, Hungary, Poland, and Romania, promising mutual protection. *Brown II* is passed, requiring states to implement the *Brown* decision with "all deliberate speed." Ngo Dinh Diem consolidates his political control over the South Vietnamese government.

June Prosecution of Owen Lattimore is dropped by Justice Department. U.S. Court of Appeals rules that U.S. citizens may not have their passports revoked without due process.

July Disneyland in California opens, and *The Mickey Mouse Club* debuts on afternoon television.

September The Union of Soviet Socialist Republics and West Germany establish diplomatic relations. East Germany joins the Warsaw Pact. Actor James Dean is killed in a car accident. The accused killers of Emmett Till, a 14-year-old African American boy lynched in Mississippi, are acquitted by an all-white jury. President Eisenhower has a major heart attack, details of which are not released to the public.

October Allen Ginsberg gives first public reading of his poem *Howl*.

December Rosa Parks is arrested in Montgomery, Alabama, for refusing to give up her seat to a white man; the Montgomery Bus Boycott begins.

1956

February Khrushchev reveals extent of Stalin's brutality in speech to the 20th Congress of the Soviet Communist Party (the speech is published in the United States in June). Senator Harry Byrd (D-Virg.) urges "massive resistance" by Southern states to avoid implementation of the *Brown* decision.

April The U.S. Supreme Court overturns state sedition laws used to prosecute alleged Communists. The Union of Soviet Socialist Republics dissolves the Cominform.

June The Atomic Energy Commission allows the construction of the first privately run nuclear energy plant to begin in Illinois. The U.S. Supreme Court rules that only federal employees in sensitive jobs can be fired as security risks. U.S. Congress signs off on the Federal Aid Highway Act, providing funds for major expansion of the nation's highway system.

August The NAACP is prohibited from operation within Alabama after being investigated for alleged Communist ties; several other Southern state legislatures also investigate the NAACP for Communist infiltration.

The FBI begins its COINTELPRO program against the Communist Party.

September The first transatlantic phone cable goes into operation.

November The Soviets invade Hungary in order to put down an uprising against Communist rule. Khrushchev declares that the Soviet Union will "bury" the West. The U.S. Supreme Court rules in favor of Rosa Parks in the Montgomery bus segregation case; the bus boycott ends, but the civil rights movement continues to grow.

1957

March The Eisenhower Doctrine is released, promising U.S. aid to Middle Eastern countries that are resisting Communism.

May Joseph McCarthy dies. Great Britain detonates a hydrogen bomb.

June The U.S. Supreme Court exonerates John Service and limits HUAC's power by finding that Smith Act prosecutions must be based on more than allegations. The U.S. Senate approves the creation of the International Atomic Energy Commission.

August Congress passes the Civil Rights Act of 1957, which creates the Civil Rights Commission and is the first major civil rights bill since Reconstruction. The Soviets announce a successful test launch of an ICBM (intercontinental ballistic missile).

October The Union of Soviet Socialist Republics launches *Sputnik*, the first human-made satellite to orbit Earth successfully. *Leave It to Beaver* premieres.

September President Eisenhower orders the 101st Airborne to Little Rock, Arkansas, to protect African American students seeking to integrate Central High School.

November Secretary of State John Foster Dulles says the Soviets are winning the arms race.

December The United States successfully tests an ICBM.

1958

January The United States launches *Explorer*, its first satellite.

March Eisenhower indicates that he is willing to consider talks with the Soviet Union to end nuclear arms testing (the Union of Soviet Socialist Republics rejects his proposal in 1959). The Union of Soviet Socialist Republics announces a unilateral halt to nuclear arms tests. Elvis Presley enters the U.S. Army.

April Khrushchev refuses to sign onto Eisenhower's proposal to end nuclear testing.

June The U.S. Supreme Court rules that state orders requiring the NAACP to turn over membership lists is a First Amendment violation.

July U.S. Congress votes to create the National Aeronautic and Space Administration.

October The Union of Soviet Socialist Republics resumes nuclear testing.

1959

January Cuban leader Fulgencio Batista is forced to flee the country as Fidel Castro's forces enter Havana. Nikita Khrushchev announces details of his proposed "peaceful coexistence" with the West.

July The "Kitchen Debate" between Soviet Premier Khrushchev and U.S. Vice President Nixon occurs during Nixon's visit to Moscow.

September Nikita Khrushchev visits the United States, although his request to visit Disneyland in California is denied because of security concerns. He also meets with Eisenhower at Camp David.

1960

February France successfully tests an atomic bomb.

May Khrushchev announces that a U.S. spy plane had been shot down over Soviet airspace, and pilot Gary Francis Powers is held by the Soviets. Eisenhower refuses to apologize, and the upcoming summit between the two leaders is canceled.

June Soviet advisors are withdrawn from China, as the two nations disagree over Khrushchev's recommendation of "peaceful coexistence" with the West.

July In response to U.S. decline in orders for Cuban sugar, Castro nationalizes all U.S. property in Cuba. The United States successfully launches a Polaris missile from a submarine.

October The United States places an embargo on almost all Cuban products.

November John F. Kennedy defeats Richard Nixon in a very close U.S. presidential election.

1961

January The United States ends diplomatic relations with Cuba. Eisenhower delivers his Farewell Address, warning of the growing military-industrial complex that has the potential to secure broad influence in U.S. society and politics.

April The Soviets successfully launch the first human, Yuri Gagarin, into space. The U.S.-sponsored Bay of Pigs invasion by Cuban expatriates fails to overthrow the government of Fidel Castro.

May Kennedy announces that the United States will send a person to the moon by the end of the decade.

June Kennedy and Khrushchev meet in Vienna, where strong words are exchanged by both men.

August Construction on the Berlin Wall begins.

November Kennedy approves an increase in the number of U.S. military advisors stationed in South Vietnam.

1962

February Gary Francis Powers is released by the Soviets in exchange for U.S. release of Soviet spy Rudolf Abel.

October U.S. spy planes identify construction sites in Cuba that appear to be in preparation for Soviet ballistic missiles. The Cuban Missile Crisis develops over the next ten days, as Kennedy demands that Khrushchev stop construction on the missile sites. A compromise is eventually reached whereby the missile sites are dismantled in exchange for U.S. removal of missiles in Turkey and a promise not to attempt any future invasion of Cuba.

1963

May Protests against the rule of Ngo Dinh Diem in South Vietnam increase, including the self-immolation of a Buddhist monk.

June A split between Soviet and Chinese Communists becomes more pronounced. The United States and Soviets agree to a "hot line" to be used in order to avoid accidental nuclear war. Kennedy travels to Berlin and famously declares, "Ich bin ein Berliner!"

November Ngo Dinh Diem is assassinated during a coup in South Vietnam; three weeks later, Kennedy is assassinated in Dallas, Texas. Lyndon Johnson assumes the office of U.S. president.

1964

August Congress approves the Gulf of Tonkin resolution, which enables Johnson to escalate dramatically the U.S. military involvement in South Vietnam.

Catalyst of Empire: Joseph McCarthy, Anti-Communism, and Early Cold War Political Culture

Jeffrey D. Bass

The anti-Communist crusade launched by Senator Joseph McCarthy (R-Wisc.) in 1950 did not herald a new chapter in U.S. politics so much as it magnified preexisting trends in the social history of the U.S. republic. For groups marginalized by race, class, or sex, the loose association of their agendas with radicalism comprised an all-too-familiar occurrence. A long-standing sense of uniqueness and a noble destiny on the international stage (i.e., U.S. exceptionalism), further hindered the sort of self-scrutiny that breeds substantive and civil debate. As World War II created power vacuums left behind by fascist regimes and colonial empires, the environment proved ideal for a manipulator poised to prey upon popular fears, with a hoodwinked media for an accomplice. But McCarthy was merely the most outrageous of numerous opportunists willing to utilize a brand of scorched-earth politics in a quest for the spotlight. Even President Harry Truman unwittingly helped pave the way for these excesses by choosing the path of least resistance in mobilizing public opinion behind an aggressive national security posture.

Over the course of roughly four years, McCarthy reigned as the hottest political commodity in Washington, with two administrations generally unwilling to confront him directly. The stifling ideological climate fostered by him, and similar practitioners of the art of innuendo, impeded both social activism at home and the onset of détente with the Soviet Union and the People's Republic of China. In a reflection of the hysteria of the times, citizens censored themselves to an unparalleled degree. Although McCarthy proved to be his own undoing and plummeted into irrelevancy, apprehension over charges of "softness" toward Communism continued to haunt Americans across the political spectrum well into the 1960s. Whether at times by design or by the confluence of vast historical forces, this era of rampant anti-Communism forged a political consensus with dramatic implications for U.S. policy, both foreign and domestic. The apparent onslaught of international Communism, with its reputation for atheism, totalitarianism, and subversion, provided Americans with a reasonably common enemy, purpose, and sense of crisis. The resulting binary of good versus what Ronald Reagan subsequently dubbed the "evil empire" supplied a simplistic yet compelling template for shaping the trajectory of U.S. statecraft.

The uneasy U.S.-Soviet partnership during World War II provided fodder for politicians with the chutzpah to manipulate the issue of anti-Communism. Josef Stalin's assent to the Nazi-Soviet Non-Aggression Pact (1939) struck the U.S. public as the worst sort of perfidy. A mass grave in the Katyn Forest revealed the Soviet massacre of at least four thousand Polish officers while partitioning this land with Germany. In 1944, the Polish underground attacked its Nazi overlords, with the expectation that advancing Soviet armies would join the assault in a few days. But Stalin halted his forces in order to guarantee a mutual bloodletting. The resulting Warsaw Uprising doubly facilitated Soviet goals by weakening German defenses and the ability of the Poles to withstand postwar encroachments by the Kremlin. Such episodes encouraged a conflation of the extremes of the political left and right that scholars have termed "Red Fascism." This ideological transference conditioned Americans to mobilize against the Communist threat with an intensity worthy of the recent war effort. Soviet moves to dominate Eastern Europe, coupled with Marxist ideology of world revolution, appeared to be merely the opening salvoes in an unremitting campaign.

The Kremlin harbored mistrust as well. Anglo-American offensives that concentrated on the periphery of Axis power sustained suspicions that the Western Allies played their own version of killing two birds with one stone. The extraordinary carnage on the Eastern Front could fulfill the dual objectives of defeating Nazism and limiting Soviet power. When Truman hinted cryptically at the Potsdam Conference (1945) of the existence of a new weapon of unsurpassed destructiveness, Stalin (aware of the Manhattan Project through espionage) could question the degree of cooperation that remained between the two emerging superpowers. The Soviets grew to believe that the use of the atomic bomb against Japan was aimed, to some extent, at signaling Moscow to tread carefully in challenging U.S. postwar interests. A political marriage of convenience in the face of fascist aggression had lost its bloom, as both sides jockeyed for position amid the chaos of the birth of a new world order.

Although he never supported McCarthy, Truman fostered hypervigilance against Communism with a dubious government loyalty program in 1947, before the Wisconsin firebrand seized the political stage. Facing an incoming Congress with a Republican majority and numerous conservative Democrats, Truman hastily created the President's Temporary Commission on Employee Loyalty as a form of political cover. This fateful step led to investigations wherein tendencies in behavior, as well as actual crimes, constituted grounds for dismissal. Membership in organizations with varying reputations for Communist influence, such as unions, civil rights groups, and even cooperative bookstores, rendered one a target for scrutiny. In a style worthy of true Stalinism, accusers could anonymously level unsubstantiated charges, frequently taken at face value by prosecutors. A flamboyant lifestyle or a few offhand remarks functioned as a virtual indictment. At a time when the left wing of the Democratic Party aimed to market itself as the guarantor of civil liberties, Truman succumbed to political pressure in the name of expediency.

In fact, the president's acquiescence in the stirrings of a latter-day witch hunt fit into his grand vision for a revolutionary postwar foreign policy. The immediate aftermath of World War II left Truman in the unenviable position of selling a robust overseas military presence to a society that was weary from the twin burdens of the Great Depression and a global war on fascism. Unsure that he could measure up to the standards of his predecessor, Franklin Roosevelt, and inexperienced in diplomacy, Truman's insecurity likely contributed to the use of uninspiring tactics.

In order to enforce his containment doctrine, announced in 1947 as a remedy for Communist subversion, Truman needed to maintain a sizeable military, with new base construction and weapons research and development. An economically devastated Western Europe—with Britain unable to fulfill its traditional hegemonic role—was deemed vulnerable to Soviet machinations. A vanquished Germany and Japan hung in the balance; there was potential for both the cultivation of new allies and the sort of despondency that could turn to rage, as witnessed following World War I with the collapse of the Weimar Republic and the rise of Nazism. The perennial need for open markets further dictated to Truman that the United States could not shrink from the challenges of this uncertain era. Promoting stability more than democracy was regarded as the key to success. But the cost of manning these ramparts proved enormous at a time when both parties contained large blocs of fiscal conservatives. Particularly once he had received the NSC-68 report, with its alarmist assessment of Soviet capabilities and intentions, Truman needed an ace up the sleeve—found in riding the crest of anti-Communism.

Richard Nixon preceded and ultimately outlasted McCarthy in harnessing anti-Communist zeal for political gain. As a California House candidate fresh from naval service in the Pacific, Nixon triumphed in 1946 by inaccurately associating incumbent Democrat Jerry Voorhis with the left-leaning political action committee of the Congress of Industrial Organizations (CIO). The two squared off in a high school gym, where Nixon's knack for digging up political dirt produced one of his most effective ambushes. When Voorhis disavowed the CIO-PAC, Nixon confronted him, while brandishing an announcement that a local chapter of an associate organization, the National Citizens Political Action Committee (NC PAC), had cast its lot with the incumbent. Recognizing that the NC PAC was even more radical, Voorhis struggled to distinguish between the two groups. But in the raucous atmosphere of a bitterly fought campaign, he never regained momentum. Shortly before voters went to the polls, mysterious phone calls flooded this Congressional district with anonymous charges of Voorhis's Communism.

Angling for higher office, Nixon served with notoriety on the House Un-American Activities Committee (HUAC). He became a household name in helping convict former State Department official Alger Hiss of perjury for lying about ties with Communists in the 1930s. Hiss acted as a minor functionary at

Jerry Voorhis

Born in Kansas to the son of a salesman turned business executive, Voorhis graduated from Yale University with Phi Beta Kappa distinction in 1923. Rendered a pacifist and socialist by the spectacle of the World War I, he was enamored with Britain's Labour Party. He traveled to postwar Europe through Christian relief organizations to assist in recovery efforts.

Marrying into a staunch Republican family in 1924, Voorhis turned to teaching and a tamer brand of politics. He worked at several religious schools, as both an instructor and administrator, while completing his master's degree in 1928. His thesis entailed designing what would become the Voorhis School for Boys in San Dimas, California. Overseeing this institution while lecturing in history at Pomona College, Voorhis ran unsuccessfully for the state assembly in 1934 on the End Poverty in California (EPIC) ticket, headed by one-time muckraker Upton Sinclair.

In 1936, Voorhis triumphed as the Democratic candidate for California's 12th House District. As the EPIC movement faltered as a result of agitation by Communists and other radicals, Voorhis resigned from its board of directors. As a congressman, he served on HUAC and supported anti-Communist legislation, including the Voorhis Bill (1940), requiring the registration of all groups that advocated revolution against the U.S. government. In short, his anti-Communist credentials were more substantive than those of his 1946 opponent, Richard Nixon.

Exhausted and in poor health, the incumbent congressman proved no match for a no-holds-barred campaign style. Compounding the situation, Voorhis inexplicably offered the relatively unknown Nixon an opportunity to debate, which naturally elevated the stature of the challenger. Losing by a margin of 57–43 percent, Voorhis fell victim to a tendency in the early Cold War to portray the left wing of the political spectrum as little more than Communists and fellow travelers. His major legislative contributions were to the Fair Labor Standards Act (1938), the School Lunch Program, and a civilian-controlled Atomic Energy Commission. A reformer with strong principles, he spoke out against the wartime internment of Japanese Americans when white Californians overwhelmingly supported the measure.

the Yalta Conference (1945), over which suspicions were subsequently raised that a declining Franklin Roosevelt had been bamboozled by Stalin into accepting Soviet aggression. As the argument went, Hiss may have compromised the U.S. negotiating position. With an investigation that opened in 1948, HUAC relied heavily upon the testimony of former Communist Party member Whittaker Chambers. After a defiant Hiss seemed to refute Chambers's account, Nixon utilized a subcommittee to rehabilitate his witness and catch Hiss in some inconsistencies. Although a jury deadlocked in his first trial in 1949, Hiss was convicted the following year under less stringent rules of evidence.

Maintaining his innocence to the end of his life, Hiss evolved into a symbol for civil liberties on the political left. Material made available since the collapse of the Soviet Union in 1991 has supported the perjury charge. But the conduct of figures such as Nixon and McCarthy raised a broader question over the value of uncovering such bias or sympathy when weighed against the petty political atmosphere generated by these

Members of the House Committee on Un-American Activities visit the home of Chairman John Parnell Thomas in 1948; (l–r) Rep. Richard B. Vail, Rep. Thomas, Rep. John McDowell, Robert Stripling, chief counsel, and Rep. Richard M. Nixon. (Library of Congress)

investigations that ruined lives and reduced Washington life to little more than a three-ring circus.

The Hiss trials complemented Nixon's 1950 Senate campaign, which provided a study in political hyperbole. His opponent was liberal Helen Douglas, whom he dubbed the "Pink Lady." His thinly veiled male chauvinism seeped into numerous public statements over the rigors of a campaign for a woman and how she was "pink" right down to her undergarments. In response, Douglas created monikers such as, "Pipsqueak," "Peewee, and "Tricky Dicky," that dogged Nixon for the remainder of his career.

Nixon was soon tapped to join Dwight Eisenhower on the Republican ticket in 1952, although the master of negative campaigning found himself on the defensive over charges of an illegal "slush fund" amounting to at least $18,000. At a maudlin press conference, Nixon managed to deflect criticism by emphasizing the campaign contribution of a cocker spaniel, Checkers, to whom his daughters had grown attached. He also intimated that the entire affair amounted to no more than revenge for the Hiss case. As telegrams backing Nixon flooded the Eisenhower headquarters, the former general decided to retain the man whom he never completely trusted again.

By February 1950, the stage was set for the figure who came to embody an era of anxiety. The Soviets had recently tested their first atomic bomb while rumors proliferated over their success in penetrating the Manhattan Project. The Chinese Communists ousted the Nationalists from mainland Asia, which ignited the perennial Washington blood sport of finger pointing over the "loss" of China to U.S. influence. Joseph McCarthy immortalized himself with a speech in Wheeling, West Virginia, that became the stuff of legend. Undecided until the last moment as to whether the address would focus on housing or the Communist threat, he took the advice of his host and hastily prepared a tirade over traitors in the State Department. His claims of turncoats fluctuated dramatically in the following days and never panned out in most cases, but he kept his critics on the defensive and the press scrambling to keep pace with new charges. The outbreak of the Korean War in June heightened the sense of urgency necessary for large segments of the U.S. public to suspend rational judgment and fuel this crusade in little more than self-promotion.

McCarthy stumbled briefly in trying to capitalize on Truman's dismissal of General Douglas MacArthur as commander of U.N. forces in Korea for publicly criticizing the president's tactics in waging a limited war. Haranguing against an icon such as George Marshall (Secretary of State and former Army Chief of Staff) rang hollow with both political insiders and the public. Although he had seized upon the ideal issue of his time, McCarthy lacked the gravitas necessary to appear statesmanlike.

But the 1952 elections produced a Republican majority in Congress and the prospect of greater investigatory opportunities. Rightfully wary of his loyalty, the GOP leadership arranged for McCarthy to chair the innocuous Government Operations Committee. But this post gave him authority over the Permanent Subcommittee on Investigations, a body normally devoted to wasteful governmental practices. Soon the senator was back in the headlines, exasperating Democrats and Republicans alike with probes into subversive activities. Eisenhower fumed privately over his antics but refused to grant him the legitimacy of acknowledging the senator as a threat.

Among a variety of political offensives, McCarthy held up administration appointments and crippled the State Department's overseas libraries and the Voice of America broadcasting service. The ensuing fireworks made for great political theater, if nothing else. The McCarthy Select Committee experienced several resignations, however temporary, as a result of disputes over tactics. Democrats Stuart Symington (Mo.), Henry Jackson (Wash.), and John McClellan (Ark.) departed, while citing the hiring of a staff director who publicly labeled Protestant clergymen as a front for domestic Communists.

They subsequently returned, under the conditions of having minority counsel and a voice in personnel selections. McCarthy referred to Symington as "sanctimonious Stu," and, not to be undone, Symington later recommended that the chair seek psychiatric counseling (Fact Sheet, 1960). Symington grew so agitated with the proceedings that Jackson periodically grasped his knee under the table to encourage restraint. Ironically, Symington and Jackson were two of the most outspoken Senate hawks during their lengthy tenures in the upper house, owing in no small part to their support of what Eisenhower termed the "military-industrial complex."

Jackson was Nixon's first choice for Secretary of Defense following the 1968 presidential campaign, and Symington, running for the White House in 1960, was a proponent of the "missile gap" myth that exaggerated Soviet progress on strategic weapons. The Missouri senator changed his tune dramatically in the 1960s, as he assessed the economic impact of a protracted war effort in South Vietnam. But this clash revealed that McCarthy had gone too far, even for those whose public standing depended heavily upon railing against the Communist threat.

The McCarthy hearings produced plenty of theatrics away from the klieg lights. In June 1954, Robert Kennedy, then counsel for Senate Democrats, claimed that Roy Cohn, McCarthy's top lawyer, accosted him with the threat of exposing Henry Jackson for writings favorable to Communism. Bad blood between the two preceded this encounter, because Kennedy had been in the running for Cohn's position. Kennedy apparently retorted that Cohn's behavior was outrageous, to which the latter purportedly suggested fisticuffs. A tendency to resort to violence was not so uncommon in this supercharged political atmosphere. McCarthy had to be pulled off liberal columnist Drew Pearson by Nixon after the senator attacked the latter-day muckraker at a Washington, D.C., restaurant.

Flush from his skyrocketing political fortunes, McCarthy ventured into what was his greatest blunder. He began targeting the U.S. Army, an institution that was hardly noted for a shortage of patriotism. For more than a month in 1954, the public was treated to the spectacle of "Tail Gunner Joe" (a reference to his embellished war record) disrespecting distinguished veterans. McCarthy, reputedly drinking too much, appeared disheveled, rude, and megalomaniacal. The polls began to turn against him, and Senate Majority Leader Ralph Flanders (R-Vt.) moved to take disciplinary action.

But most senators were loathe to reconsider the assumptions that underpinned the entire anti-Communist crusade. Instead, several specific episodes of boorish behavior by McCarthy were chosen—namely, the handling of General Ralph Zwicker and the mistreatment of colleagues who had investigated charges against McCarthy in the previous Congress. Senate Republicans split over the censure vote; all Democrats present opted for the rebuke, in a final tally of 67–22. Citing poor health, John F. Kennedy (D-Mass.), whose father counted McCarthy as a friend, was notably absent from the proceedings.

John Stennis (D-Miss.) provided a good example of how McCarthy burned his bridges with many senators known themselves for anti-Communist zeal. Nicknamed the "conscience of the Senate" (despite his ardent segregationism), Stennis was the model of dignity and decorum over a career of more than forty years in the upper house. He could utter virulent statements on race and Communism without seeming vicious or partisan. Stennis made good use of the free association of Communism with reform movements (to include the NAACP) that threatened white Southern prerogatives.

But he was a real stickler when it came to how senators treated each other and managed their finances. Stennis, who later chaired the Select Committee on Standards and Conduct, was most alarmed by the fact that some of the money contributed to McCarthy to aid in his investigations wound up invested in commodities markets. As suspicions about McCarthy multiplied, the formerly quiescent press began to reassert itself. By late 1954, Eisenhower jokingly referred to "McCarthywasm," as whatever moral force once commanded by the senator had largely dissipated.

McCarthy did not fade away gracefully from the Washington arena. He endured as a pathetic hanger-on, virtually begging old friends for attention. The international climate shifted—against the same degree of hysteria that had so nurtured McCarthy just a few years before. The death of Stalin brought Nikita Khrushchev to power, a leader more willing to entertain a *modus vivendi* with the West. The armistice that halted fighting in Korea turned the attention of a weary nation inward.

During the 1956 campaign season, McCarthy grabbed a seat next to Vice President Nixon at a Milwaukee engagement. Shunted away by a staffer, McCarthy ended up sobbing nearby over his abandonment by a one-time friend. Nixon had often run political interference for McCarthy, to keep the White House in relatively good graces with the unstable senator. Now even a modicum of civility was unnecessary. A variety of illnesses took their toll on McCarthy, most seriously involving his liver, and he passed away in May of 1957.

Republicans did not hold a monopoly on opportunities to use the Communist threat. Senator George Smathers (D-Fla.) perfected the art of anti-Communist campaigning in building a career that political insiders initially believed might land him in the White House one day. Urged by Truman to "beat that son of a bitch Claude Pepper," Smathers launched a Senate bid in 1950 against the fellow Democrat and former mentor (Smathers, 1987). Pepper constituted an endangered political species in the early Cold War years, who argued that anti-Communist rhetoric lacked proportion and, in some cases, accuracy. His sympathy for expanding the New Deal into something resembling a European-style social democracy ruffled feathers as well.

Pepper hoped to transform the Democratic Party into a voice of unabashed liberalism, regardless of the consequences in a society noted more for its evolutionary than revolutionary political and social development. The vitriolic campaign, replete with references to Pepper's "pink" foreign policy views, vaulted Smathers into the limelight.

A close friend of both Nixon and Kennedy through their membership in the House "Class of '46," Smathers cultivated ties with several Latin American dictators, most notably Rafael Trujillo of the Dominican Republic. Dubbed the "senator from Latin America" by a colleague, Smathers typified the long-standing U.S. practice in foreign policy of embracing the extremes of the political right as a sort of inoculation against their counterparts on the left. His reluctance to differentiate Third World nationalism from Communism contributed to a myopia that limited U.S. gains during much of the Cold War. A member of Lyndon Johnson's inner circle, Smathers enjoyed a steady rise in influence until his financial connections to the convicted Senate Secretary for the Democrats, Bobby Baker, drove him to retire in 1969 at the conclusion of his third term.

Smathers joined fellow Senate Democrats Richard Russell (D-Ga.), John Stennis, Stuart Symington, and Henry Jackson, acting in concert to orient the United States against their perceptions of international Communism. Their militancy, coupled with substantial political clout, served as a counterweight to U.S. attempts at détente. Not known for a nuanced world view, Cold War axioms such as the domino theory, zero-sum game, monolithic Communism, and containment imbued their foreign policy stances with a constant sense of crisis.

Despite often knowing their arguments to be exaggerated, they stoked an already inflammatory political environment. At times, this coterie focused more on institutional rivalries than on ideological differences, particularly as the Vietnam War raised concerns over the constitutional separation of powers. These senators occupied a nebulous position, in that they were regarded as White House allies even as they embarrassed presidents with charges of timidity and missed opportunities. Rather than inspire constituents with a bold vision for the future, these hard-liners relied more on the tried and true path of fear-mongering.

The single-mindedness among U.S. leaders spawned by the early Cold War manifested itself on many occasions. One of the more revealing episodes transpired through a shouting match between Russell and President Kennedy during the Cuban Missile Crisis. On October 22, 1962, the president laid out his plans and sought Congressional endorsement for a naval quarantine of the embattled island where Soviet medium-range nuclear missile construction was in progress. An irate Russell believed that anything less than an immediate air strike would redound to the benefit of the Soviets by demonstrating a lack of resolve and placing U.S. bombers on lengthy alerts that degraded readiness. The senator insisted, "we've got to take a chance somewhere, sometime, if we're going to retain our position as a great world power" (May and Zelikow, 1997, 177). Russell's opposition helped explain why the president grew to feel trapped during the standoff by the persistently hard-line recommendations that he received and therefore could negotiate with Khrushchev (who faced a similar predicament).

Beyond the immediate exigencies of the Missile Crisis, Russell commented that "the time [is] going to come . . . when we're going to have to take this step [a military strike] in Berlin and Korea and Washington, D.C., and Winder, Georgia, for the nuclear war" (May and Zelikow, 1997, 172). The long-time chair of the Senate Armed Services Committee and de facto head of Appropriations seemed convinced of the inevitability of nuclear war and concluded that initiating the conflict sooner rather than later would produce better results. The extraordinary stress produced by this 13-day impasse may have led Russell to vent his frustrations without circumspection. But this sort of pessimistic ranting was common among those who milked anti-Communism for every bit of political value.

While elected officials manipulated the prevailing climate of anti-Communism on the hustings and in the corridors of power, bureaucrats joined in the act. FBI director J. Edgar Hoover had been raising the specter of revolution for decades before McCarthy emerged on the scene. The Bolshevik seizure of power in Russia during World War I helped spark the First Red Scare (1919–1920) within the United States. As the first head of the Radical Division of the Justice Department, Hoover provided much of the supposed justification for Attorney General A. Mitchell Palmer to conduct several thousand searches and seizures without probable cause.

During the 1940s to 1960s, Hoover sponsored numerous illegal wiretaps on a wide range of "radicals," including civil rights leader Martin Luther King, Jr. When agents discovered King's marital infidelity, they mailed portions of their recordings to his home. The agency utilized disinformation in an attempt to destabilize a variety of civil rights activists as well as foment discord between the Communist Party and the Mafia. Running the FBI from 1924 until his death in 1972, Hoover reputedly was untouchable because of accumulating files of questionable activities on numerous Washington power brokers. He was quick to conflate homosexuality with Communism despite a longtime relationship with a subordinate, Clyde Tolson, that sparked much speculation about his own sexual orientation.

Between Truman's effort to sell an internationalist foreign policy and the crass maneuvering of ambitious office seekers and bureaucrats building fiefdoms, a political realignment was born. Before long, Democrats and Republicans sought to outdo each other in claims of vigilance and foresight in stemming the tide of Soviet influence. The debate amounted far less to a question of tactics than one of commitment, judgment, and credibility, as epitomized in the 1960 presidential campaign between rising stars Kennedy and Nixon.

The Democrats, despite their bitter memories of McCarthyism, rallied behind a candidate who often sounded more hawkish on Communism than

J. Edgar Hoover, director of the FBI during the McCarthy era, was among the most active Cold Warriors of the time. (National Archives)

his opponent, who arguably was the dominant U.S. public figure of the 1950s, in no small part as a result of his anti-Communist stance. As the sitting vice president, Nixon was tied to Eisenhower's austerity program to reorient the U.S. military by drawing down conventional forces and relying more heavily on nuclear deterrence. Kennedy exploited this opportunity to argue that the U.S. strategic weapons advantage, dubbed the "missile gap," was rapidly closing and portended parity with the Soviets by the mid-1960s.

Once ensconced in the White House, Kennedy privately joked with military brass about irresponsible politicians who employed such tactics. But his administration soon felt the unremitting pressure of the anti-Communist imperative. As late as October 1963, shortly before the assassination in Dallas that stunned the world, Kennedy's National Security Council compiled a "check list" of global hotspots—where it served the mutual self-interest of the superpowers to posture against one another (Robert Komer to McGeorge Bundy). Each government feared constituencies and allies who potentially doubted their resolve against the other side. The locales where this joint saber rattling might produce political benefits included South Vietnam, Cuba, a divided Germany, and the territory disputed between Israel and its neighbors.

Although the U.S. two-party system has always tended to produce rather broad coalitions, the amount of common ground shared during the early Cold War years was striking. But the opportunity cost of winning conservative support plagued the Democratic Party for years afterward. Republicans and Southern Democrats demanded a loose definition of radicalism in this new political climate and utilized it for an assault upon labor unions, civil rights activists, New Dealers, and others deemed nonconformists.

Truman thus made what the liberal wing of his party might well have considered a Faustian bargain in selling its collective soul and limiting an agenda of social activism. The president desegregated the military by executive order in 1948, but he refrained from addressing a host of glaring racial inequities whose solutions required Congressional cooperation.

This bipartisan consensus on Cold War policy held reasonably firm until 1968, when the confluence of the shock of the Tet Offensive and a presidential campaign season led many Democrats to question the East-West prism through which the Vietnam War had been prosecuted. As the Democrats divided, most dramatically displayed at their nominating convention in Chicago, where protestors of various stripes clashed with law enforcement, their widespread uneasiness with the use of military force persists to this day.

The excesses committed in the name of anti-Communism should not convey the impression that the Soviet Union practiced a benign foreign policy or served as the exemplar of liberty to its own people. The gulags and suppressed uprisings behind the Iron Curtain offer considerable evidence to the contrary. The decryptions secured through the Anglo-American Venona project, primarily during World War II, attest to a vigorous program of Soviet espionage within U.S. borders. Although scholars continue to debate the reliability of these sources, clearly the Second Red Scare (a.k.a. McCarthyism) was not conjured up out of thin air or directed toward a blameless nation-state. But if Americans like to think that adversity brings out the best in their collective and individual characters, they must look askance at these critical years of Cold War crystallization.

Observations offered by Fidel Castro in 1959 captured the essence of how North Americans grappled with the question of Communism. The recently installed Cuban leader visited the United States amid a debate as to whether he was merely a leftist or a devotee of revolutionary socialism. During a private meeting with Nixon, Castro lauded the United States as a "great country—the richest, the greatest, the most powerful in the world." But the Cuban seemed perplexed over the lack of self-confidence, even self-esteem, that this success had engendered. "Your people, therefore, should be proud and confident and happy. But every place I go you seem to be afraid—afraid of Communism, afraid that if Cuba has land reform, it will grow a little rice and the market for your rice will be reduced—afraid that if Latin America becomes more industrialized American factories will not be able to sell as much abroad as they have previously . . . You in America should not be talking so much about your fear of what the Communists may do in Cuba or in some other country . . . you should be talking more about your own strength and the reasons why your system is superior to Communism or any other kind of dictatorship" (Richard Nixon to George Smathers, 1959).

Richard Nixon and Fidel Castro met in Washington in 1959, in a meeting described as "very friendly." (AP/Wide World Photos)

Although Castro's commitment to freedom remains dubious at best, he tapped into two key features of U.S. political culture during the early Cold War, namely a profound pessimism and a tendency to define the United States against a degraded "other" rather than on its own merits. The clarity with which this emerging adversary perceived the Cold War mind-set begs the question of why so many U.S. politicians languished in a self-pronounced misery (or at least found it useful to display such a persona). Although Nixon shared his account of Castro's remarks with fellow Cold Warrior George Smathers, he never appeared to have taken this critique to heart.

Examples for the early Cold War years that illustrate Castro's point included the CIA-sponsored coups in Iran (1953) and Guatemala (1954). In both cases, elected nationalist leaders, Mohammed Mossadeagh and Jacobo Arbenz Guzman, respectively, were toppled by "revolutions" with the thinnest veneer of popular support. Although of leftist orientation, both men were mischaracterized as Communists, or at least as pawns of the "Red menace."

Mossadeagh attempted to nationalize his nation's oil industry amid powerful Anglo-American influences in Iran. Arbenz intended merely to buy 400,000 unused acres from the United Fruit Company (with its formidable lobbying power in Washington) for redistribution to peasants, at a time when 2 percent of the population owned 70 percent of the land. Even if this plan had gone into effect, three-quarters of the countryside would have remained unaffected. In both cases, the result amounted to new regimes amenable to U.S. interests. Although he had already fled his homeland, U.S. authorities reinstalled Reza Pahlavi as the Shah of Iran. His subsequent brutality, buttressed by U.S. military hardware, sparked an uprising in 1979 that overthrew his government in favor of a militant theocracy and encouraged the taking of U.S. hostages for 444 days.

The writer F. Scott Fitzgerald once commented that the "mark of a first-rate intelligence is the ability to hold two opposed ideas in the mind at the same time and retain the ability to function." The U.S. society of the early Cold War years epitomized the struggle to achieve this ideal: the impact of Communism served as both a legitimate national security threat and one often misunderstood and manipulated to serve a variety of agendas.

Perhaps most tragically, the irrationality of anti-Communism helped ensure a lengthy engagement in Southeast Asian conflicts because numerous U.S. authorities hesitated to consider the region in any context other than as a subset of the Cold War. The nationalist aspirations of peoples, like the Vietnamese, who had only recently emerged from imperial rule, remained woefully underappreciated.

Although U.S. forces would not be deployed to South Vietnam in large numbers until the mid-1960s, the intensity and pervasiveness of Cold War assumptions took root in the 1950s, while the United States increasingly bankrolled a moribund French war effort and propped up a corrupt South Vietnamese regime.

The beauty of anti-Communism for its proponents lay in its elasticity. Regardless of the expenditure of resources or degree of vigilance, no one could ever do quite enough to meet the challenge. As a nation widely envisioned in the aftermath of World War II as a beacon of hope and progress, rather than turning to its own ideals for inspiration, the United States defined itself crudely in stark opposition to an insidious opponent.

References and Further Reading

Fact Sheet on Sen. Stuart Symington. *Congressional Quarterly,* June 10, 1960, 1002.

Fried, Richard. *Nightmare in Red: The McCarthy Era in Perspective.* New York: Oxford University Press, 1990.

Leffler, Melvyn. *The Specter of Communism: The United States and the Origins of the Cold War, 1917–1953.* New York: Hill and Wang, 1994.

Matthews, Christopher. *Kennedy and Nixon: The Rivalry That Shaped Postwar America.* New York: Simon and Schuster, 1996.

May, Ernest, and Philip Zelikow, eds. *The Kennedy Tapes: Inside the White House during the Cuban Missile Crisis.* Cambridge, MA: Norton, 1997.

Paterson, Thomas. *On Every Front: The Making and Unmaking of the Cold War.* New York: W. W. Norton, 1992.

Richard Nixon to George Smathers, April 24, 1959, Box 104, George Smathers Papers, George A. Smathers Libraries, University of Florida, Gainesville.

Robert Komer to McGeorge Bundy, October 16, 1963, National Security Files, Box 322, John F. Kennedy Library, Boston, MA.

Smathers, George, interview with University of Florida Oral History Program, February 26, 1987.

Federal Loyalty Oath Program

Martin Manning

2

Early investigations into subversive activity in the United States were made by the Fish and the McCormick-Dickstein committees in the 1930s and resulted from the change of policy in the world Communist movement from alienation to enticement, characteristics of the new partisans of the Left following this change, and their appearance in federal employment. However, this was just a prelude to the even darker period that followed, after World War II, as the Cold War tensions strengthened and the Communist menace became a looming presence to the way of life in the United States. One group that was particularly affected by these movements was federal employees, who were faced with the combined threats of a loyalty security program and of Senator Joseph McCarthy (R-Wisc.) and his Senate Subcommittee on Internal Security.

Background

Between 1940 and 1943, the federal government screened federal employees for loyalty using a secret AGLOSO (Attorney General's List of Subversive Organizations). The original legal basis for this list was the Hatch Act of August 1939, which banned from government employment any person who held membership in any political party or organization that advocated the overthrow of the constitutional form of government in the United States. Similar provisions were regularly included in Congressional appropriations acts. Pursuant to these Congressional mandates, Attorney General Francis Biddle created a temporary interdepartmental committee to investigate alleged subversion within the federal government. Biddle and the Dickinson Committee (named for special assistant to Attorney General Edwin Dickinson), which he created in early 1942, designated 47 organizations by May 1942 as falling within the Hatch Act criteria, membership in which raised a flag with regard to federal employees or applicants for federal jobs.

The federal employee loyalty program came after World War II, at the beginnings of the heightening Cold War tensions between the United States and the Soviet Union, as hundreds of employees were transferred to the U.S. Department of State and to other federal departments from wartime agencies, such as the Office of Strategic Services, Office of War Information, and Foreign Economic Administration, to carry on certain of the wartime functions. A screening committee was established to determine whether the loyalty of the particular individual was clearly to the United States and whether that person was eligible for federal employment.

At the end of World War II, a widespread belief that good relations with the Soviet Union would continue had briefly diminished the concern over alleged Communist and other subversive infiltration of the federal government that had led to the Hatch Act and the Biddle AGLOSO. In October 1945, the Gaston Committee (named for Assistant Secretary of the Treasury Herbert Gaston and created in early 1943 to replace the Dickinson Committee) recommended that it be abolished and its functions turned over to the U.S. Civil Service Commission. In December 1945, the new attorney general, Tom Clark, drafted a proposed executive order to implement this recommendation. However, the rapid development of Cold War tensions after 1945 and concerns about possible Communist infiltration of the government soon created a drastically changed political climate in the United States. President Truman, in late 1946, appointed yet another commission to study governmental employee loyalty.

Republicans made alleged Communist infiltration of the federal government a central theme of the 1946 Congressional elections. On November 25, 1946, two weeks after the election, President Truman announced the creation of the President's Temporary Commission on Employee Loyalty (TCEL) to make a sweeping study of federal loyalty programs. The TCEL's members, including representatives of six government departments, under the chairmanship of Special Assistant to the Attorney General A. Devitt Vanech, a Justice Department official who was close to FBI Director J. Edgar Hoover, was charged with determining federal loyalty standards and establishing procedures to remove or disqualify any disloyal or subversive person from federal service.

The TCEL heard testimony from Attorney General Clark, FBI Assistant Director D. Milton Ladd, and Gaston Committee chairman Herbert Gaston, but the most important testimony came from Clark, who told the TCEL that, although there were only two dozen Communists employed by the federal government, the seriousness of the problem needed to be considered not by the number of employees but rather from the viewpoint of the serious threat that even one disloyal person constituted to the security of the U.S. government. The FBI investigated (under the Hatch Act) federal employees only if there were definite and substantial indications that they were members of one of the 47 organizations declared subversive by the attorney general or allegations that they personally advocated the overthrow of the government or belonged to an organization advocating such. Also, the FBI maintained files on those who, after lengthy investigation, were shown to be members or, affiliated with, so-called subversive organizations and, in addition, were either important or influential functionaries in such organizations or very active, influential, or longtime members, or they occupied important or strategic positions outside the subversive organizations to which they belonged.

The final TCEL report, submitted to Truman on March 2, 1947, recommended that all federal employees, as well as all future applicants, be investigated, with the standard for "refusal of employment" to be that "on all evidence, reasonable grounds exist for believing that the person involved is disloyal to the government of the United States." Truman accepted the TCEL's major recommendation.

On March 21, 1947, President Harry S Truman signed Executive Order No. 9835, "Prescribing Procedures for the Administration of an Employee Loyalty Program in the Executive Branch of the Government," which established the first peacetime federal employee loyalty program in the history of the United States. As part of the executive order, the government established a Loyalty Review Board under the direction of the Civil Service Commission. Although Truman privately expressed doubts that there was any substantive danger of subversion within the federal government, he agreed to support the establishment of a loyalty board in response to growing political pressure from conservative groups.

It applied not only to the Department of State but to nearly every agency in the executive branch of the government; its purpose was threefold: (1) to ensure the absolute loyalty of all federal employees, (2) to ensure that no disloyal persons would infiltrate the ranks of loyal federal employees, and (3) to protect loyal federal employees against unjust accusations of disloyalty. Each employee was granted the right to a hearing if "charged with being disloyal," as well as to written notice informing him or her "of the nature of the charges against him in sufficient detail, so that he will be enabled to prepare his defense." Charges needed to be "as complete as, in the discretion of the employing department or agency, security considerations permit" and that, in submitting information to government agencies, investigative agencies such as the FBI could, at their discretion, "refuse to disclose the name of confidential informants," so long as they provided "sufficient information" so that the employing agencies could make "an adequate evaluation of the information furnished them." In practice, most charges were based on FBI information, and the FBI would not divulge its sources and methods or make its agents or informants available for testimony. As a result, federal employees investigated under the loyalty program were usually provided only extremely vague charges, not told the sources of allegations against them, and denied the right to cross-examine their (unknown) accusers.

The previously secret AGLOSO was published in December 1947 in connection with Truman's so-called loyalty program. Although officially its major function was to provide guidance for federal civil service loyalty determinations, AGLOSO was quickly adopted by a wide variety of public and private groups, including state and local governments, the military, defense contractors, hotels, the Treasury Department (in making tax-exemption determinations), and the State Department (in making passport and deportation decisions), to deny employment or otherwise discriminate against listed organizations or persons alleged to be affiliated with them.

In effect, the publication of the list, originally designed to help screen federal employees for loyalty, effectively became an official government proscription blacklist.

Loyalty Program

The loyalty program was used as an umbrella against several types of federal employees. The first were individuals suspected as Communists, or with Communist sympathies, along with disclosures of Communist Party activity in cabinet departments, other executive agencies, and the staffs of Senate committees that were made witnesses in the course of several Congressional investigations. Although the best-known cases were in the State Department, there was also turmoil in agencies such as the Voice of America, where foreign-born employees, hired as broadcasters for their language and country expertise, turned on their U.S.-born bosses (and vice versa) by reporting them to McCarthy's Senate subcommittee or to HUAC.

As the U.S. public grew more concerned about Communist infiltration in the United States in the late 1940s and early 1950s, many local and state governments, educational institutions, and corporations adopted loyalty oaths that required an individual to swear that he or she was not a member of any organization that sought to overthrow the state or national government by force and to declare loyalty to the U.S. Constitution as well as to the state constitution. The ostensible purpose of the oaths was to deny employment to Communists, even though the organizations failed to take into account the possibility that true Communists would readily swear a false oath to keep their identity secret. Many of the individuals who refused to take loyalty oaths did so because they opposed the oaths on moral or religious purposes.

One of the most famous incidents of the loyalty program erupted when false charges were made by McCarthy, who charged in a speech in Wheeling, West Virginia, on February 9, 1950, that Communists in the State Department were shaping U.S. foreign policy and that he had "here in my hand a list of 205" names that were "made known to the Secretary of State." His statement was later disputed as not being original; much of his speech had been lifted verbatim from earlier attacks on the Roosevelt and Truman administrations by conservative Republicans and Democrats, but the timing of the attacks, less than three weeks after the conviction of Alger Hiss, together with McCarthy's claims that he had the documentation to prove his charges, produced sensational headlines and promoted McCarthy into sudden prominence. The State Department counterattacked by noting that the figures came from old information and that the individuals that McCarthy claimed to have discovered no longer worked in the department.

McCarthy repeated these charges on the Senate floor, but a Congressional investigation, chaired by Senator Millard Tydings (D-Md.), found no evidence to substantiate McCarthy's charges.

In a radio interview in Salt Lake City, Utah, on February 20, 1950, McCarthy continued his attack, stating that he had the "names of fifty seven card-carrying members of the Communist Party," another charge that the State Department proved false, noting that these figures were based on late 1940s information that McCarthy had received from "loyal" State Department employees who misled and deceived the Senate.

Follow-up investigations by Congress revealed that the loyalty program was considered to be of indispensable value in protecting both the employee and the security of the federal service and that it was efficiently administered, specifically that the FBI's loyalty investigations were comprehensive, that the State Department's Security Division and its Loyalty and Security Board were made up of individuals of unquestioned loyalty, and that the Loyalty Review Board provided an effective control over the functioning of the loyalty program. In fact, the loyalty employee program instilled an atmosphere of fear and paranoia throughout the State Department and in other government agencies. During the Eisenhower administration, Secretary of State John Foster Dulles used security reviews to force able officers out of the Foreign Service or to cripple their promising careers.

Federal Departments

The government department that was most affected by the loyalty security program was the State Department. In a speech before the Federal Bar Association (April 24, 1950), President Truman announced that "the loyalty program has rid the Government of all employees who were found to be disloyal—and they were only a tiny fraction of one percent. Not a single person who has been adjudged to be a Communist or otherwise disloyal remains on the Government payroll today." This was certainly the case with Alger Hiss, perhaps one of the best-known State Department employees who was forced out of government service by the climate of the times and his own suspected affiliations.

A Soviet spy ring, unearthed in 1946, led investigators to Hiss, who had been a wartime foreign policy adviser. He was accused of passing secrets to the Soviet Union by a former Communist, Whittaker Chambers. In August 1948, in a series of meetings before HUAC, Chambers and Hiss confronted each other. Chambers first accused Hiss of having been a fellow member of the Communist Party. On August 18, Hiss identified Chambers as a man he had known as George Crosley in the mid 1930s. Footage of this event provided one of the set pieces of the McCarthy period, even though the Wisconsin senator was not directly involved in the case. Hiss challenged Chambers to make his accusations in public—with the immunity from libel that statements made in Congressional proceedings received—and firmly denied that he had betrayed his country.

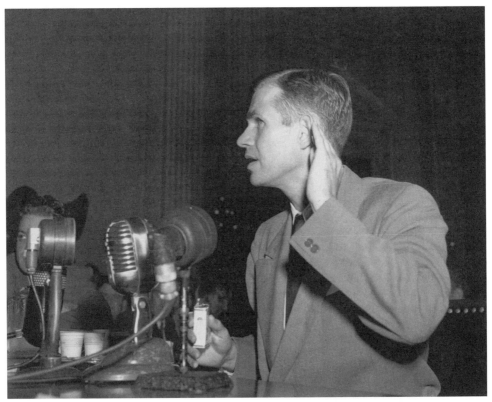

Alger Hiss testifies before the House Committee on Un-American Activities in 1948. (AP/Wide World Photos)

HUAC promised to reveal new evidence of Communist activities in government circles. Richard Nixon, then an ambitious young Republican California congressman, was convinced that Hiss was lying. Hiss was jailed for perjury, and Nixon's name was made; he turned his crusade against Communism into a weapon for Republicans. In 1952, he was chosen by Republican presidential candidate Dwight D. Eisenhower as his vice presidential running mate, and, in 1968, he won the presidency.

Further investigations by the Internal Security Subcommittee of the Committee on the Judiciary, under Senator Pat McCarran, resulted in the purging of the Far East Bureau of the State Department, prematurely ending the careers of several State Department diplomats, including John Carter Vincent, John Service, John Paton Davies, and O. Edmund Clubb.

In early 1950, McCarthy blamed so-called traitors in the State Department for the loss of China. He launched his own witch hunt, helped considerably by the efforts of Communist fighters, such as Alfred Kohlberg. Efforts to monitor the Loyalty Security Program among federal employees often involved the participation and cooperation of Americans who were supportive of McCarthy's efforts. Kohlberg was one of the best known of these McCarthy supporters; he was chairman of the American China Policy Association (ACPA), with considerable experience in China as a textile manufacturer. His name became synonymous with the China Lobby, an informal collective of individuals and of institutions that were highly critical of the loss of China to Communism and the supposed Communist sympathies of the Far East Bureau of the State Department.

In one case, McCarthy accused John S. Service, who was hounded out of the State Department; Service was cleared in six security or loyalty proceedings, but he was fired after the seventh. Congress gave the secretary of state the right to discharge anyone in the department with a hearing or other administrative procedures. In Service's case, he had trouble renting a home, renting an apartment in New York, and finding a job; companies that he previously had dealings with abroad were concerned about stockholders' reactions and refused to hire him.

McCarthy continued his attacks. In another of his 1950 speeches that helped his rise to prominence, he said: "One communist, one communist in the faculty of one university is one communist too many. One communist among the American advisors at Yalta was one communist too many. And even . . . even if there were only one communist in the State Department, even if there were only one communist in the State Department that would still be one communist too many."

Hiss and Service were two of the better-known State Department employees who lost their jobs in the glare of media attention, but there were others who were not so high profile. In charges he made on the Senate floor, February 20, 1950, McCarthy also publicly named and levied charges against Gustavo Duran, Haldore Hanson, and Philip C. Jessup. Two others, Owen Lattimore and Harlow Shapley, were consultants to the State Department, but never employees.

In the case of the overseas libraries, administered by the State Department until the creation of the U.S. Information Agency (USIA) in 1953, it was the program that came under attack, but the Foreign Service Officers (FSOs) who administered the libraries often came under scrutiny.

Information Centers and Libraries

The purpose of the investigation and hearings on the information centers was presumably to determine the extent of Communist influence in these centers. The method was to examine witnesses whose books were in the libraries of the centers in an attempt to connect the authors with the Communist movement, where such a connection existed. For U.S. embassy libraries, the period was a particularly unpleasant one for the U.S. officers and their staffs who had to deal with the barrage of scrutiny from Washington, D.C., headquarters, as well as from McCarthy supporters, such as Alfred Kohlberg and his wife, who showed up unannounced at the Berlin library (USIA Airgram, PAO John E. McGowan, Berlin, to USIA, April 27, 1954) and, in a rather demanding encounter, identified themselves as "friends of Senator McCarthy" who were "very much afraid that USIA is not doing its job overseas." In the course of their short visit, the Kohlbergs spoke to embassy official John E. McGowan and two other U.S.

staff officers attached to the information center and demanded answers to questions about the "Americanism" of certain authors, with intent to report their findings to McCarthy.

The overseas libraries came under attack in the early 1950s, with McCarthy's charge that they contained at least 30,000 volumes (not titles) by Communist authors in a deliberate attempt to encourage foreigners to side with the Russians. This was untrue. Most of the admittedly objectionable books were inherited from the Office of War Information (OWI) during wartime, when the libraries were trying to whip up support—at a time when the Soviet Union was either an ally or a co-belligerent against the Axis powers and a favorable opinion for the Russians was not considered a bad thing. This changed in 1946, when the Soviet Union started criticizing the United States as a "capitalist country without culture" and closed all U.S. libraries behind the Iron Curtain.

There was an attempt at headquarters not to purchase any books by authors with Communist or other suspicious leanings in their background. The individual case that comes to mind was that of Howard Fast; his books were in quite a few of the overseas libraries, and library staff were supposed to pull them. At the Agency Library in Washington, the reference staff had FBI investigation forms that were used for background checks of all these authors. In 1954, books by 238 persons were banned from these libraries. One of the reasons for McCarthy's actions seems to be USIA's counterattack: banning two of the Wisconsin senator's books from USIA shelves. A direct attack by McCarthy was the so-called tour of the USIA libraries by Roy Cohn, representing McCarthy's Senate Permanent Subcommittee on Investigations, and David Schine, another subcommittee staffer, in April 1953, on a tour that was to include discussions with FSO personnel in Europe (Munich, Vienna, Belgrade, Athens, Rome, and Paris) on the operations of these libraries and their information centers and their adherence to pro-American values. Except for instilling fear into the embassy staff who had to deal with the tour group, the trip was more a farce than a witch hunt: it uncovered no new facts about the information centers and libraries that McCarthy did not already know. However, on May 10–11, 1953, in what was approximately a 24-hour trip, McCarthy went to Havana, Cuba, accompanied by Cohn and Schine, and visited a USIA office to see for himself how such an operation actually worked.

Voice of America

Another major investigation of government employees took place at the Voice of America (VOA), when hearings by the Senate Permanent Subcommittee on Investigations began on February 16, 1953 (U.S. Congress. Senate. Committee on Government Operations. Permanent Subcommittee on Investigations. *State Department Information Program—Voice of America*). Charges of an anti-American conspiracy at the U.S. government's official broadcasting service started over the location of two powerful transmitters (Baker East, Baker West) and their audiences, which McCarthy claimed were possible targets of jamming by the Russians. This expanded to further

Joseph McCarthy is shown discussing the Voice of America, a radio broadcasting agency he accused of promoting Communist propaganda, with reporters in 1953. (Library of Congress)

charges against VOA employees in some of the language services (e.g., French, Latin American)—mostly foreign employees on special visas that allowed them to be language broadcasters—on alleged "anti-American" broadcasts. The Hebrew Service was of particular interest to McCarthy. There was trouble over an order (December 5, 1952) to suspend broadcasts to Israel because of budget considerations. McCarthy's implication, which he made to a witness during the hearings, was that Communist sympathizers were choking the life out of the service and that the suspension decision was the fault of Reed Harris, then acting administrator of the International Information Administration (USIA's immediate predecessor) in the State Department. An ugly subplot of the VOA investigations was that it gave a chance for employees and supervisors to turn against each other. Unhappy and disgruntled VOA staffers who had lost arguments with superiors over policy, lived in a rivalry of hateful tensions, or were likely to lose jobs over administrative decisions, took their concerns to McCarthy's committee, and many were called as witnesses to answer these charges.

Oppenheimer Case

Another controversial case that tested loyalty security involved J. Robert Oppenheimer, who worked on the Manhattan Project that developed the first atomic bomb. Oppenheimer was a pioneer in the field of quantum mechanics, the study of the energy of atomic particles, and a charismatic teacher and effective administrator, who directed the laboratory at Los Alamos, New Mexico, where the atomic bomb was developed during World

War II. In the postwar years, however, Oppenheimer staunchly opposed the proliferation of nuclear weapons. This stance brought him before Congress during the McCarthy era and cost him his security clearance as a government consultant.

In 1946 Oppenheimer became chair of the general advisory committee of the Atomic Energy Commission and continued to advocate controls on the development of nuclear power. As the 1940s drew to a close, President Truman decided that it was in the country's best interest to develop the hydrogen bomb. Oppenheimer's position was clear; he did not believe in the proliferation of nuclear weapons, and he did not hesitate to express his opinion in public. In November 1953, William Borden, former executive director of the Joint Atomic Energy Committee, sent a registered letter to J. Edgar Hoover of the FBI, stating that he had considerable evidence to show that Oppenheimer was a Soviet agent. In December, Oppenheimer was informed that his security clearance, which he needed to have access to classified information, was revoked on suspicion of unpatriotic activities on his part. Congress gave Oppenheimer the opportunity to clear himself, but Oppenheimer's association with Communists during the 1930s, never a secret nor an obstacle to his receiving clearance when he was director of Los Alamos, was now presented as a blot on his character and a challenge to his patriotic commitment. After many grueling hours of testimony, the majority of a three-man panel found that Oppenheimer was a loyal citizen but still denied him clearance on the basis of certain defects of character.

These were probably the most scrutinized cases affected by the Loyalty Security Program and the long arm of McCarthy and his subcommittee, but incidents at other agencies abounded; no agency was really free from the climate and atmosphere that prevailed. During the last two weeks in August 1953, a series of hearings were held on individuals deemed to be suspicious or dubious in their loyalties. One, Edward Rothschild, was a bookbinder at the Government Printing Office (GPO), who was cleared by the agency loyalty board four times and then pleaded the Fifth Amendment when asked by McCarthy's subcommittee about possible Communist associations. Rothschild was accused of stealing secret documents from GPO. In August 1953, a U.S. Air Force lieutenant, Milo Radulovich, was asked to resign for what was actually guilt by association. He was accused of harboring allegiance to his father and to his sister, who were considered to be subversives. He refused, and a board was called and heard his case. At the end, it was recommended that he be discharged from the Air Force, although it was also stated that there was no question of Radulovich's loyalty. His case became part of the public record when Edward R. Murrow broadcast it as a segment of his *See It Now* television program (aired October 20, 1953).

U.S. Army

The event that finally brought McCarthy down was his investigation of alleged Communists in the U.S. Army. During the 1952 presidential election, the senator supported Republican candidate Dwight D. Eisenhower, the Army general who was Supreme Commander of U.S. Forces in World War II, but Eisenhower had no use for McCarthy. However, when Eisenhower's old wartime commander, General George C. Marshall, was accused by McCarthy of treachery, the intimidated presidential candidate dropped words praising Marshall from an election speech that he gave in McCarthy's home state—an action that Eisenhower later regretted and for which he was roundly criticized because it seemed to indicate that he was influenced by McCarthy.

However, the senator then denounced senior Army officers as Communist sympathizers.

Most of the hearings, which came to almost 3,000 pages of record and took six weeks to compile, had nothing to do with the Communist movement, but a great deal to do with questions of fact and assertion about McCarthy and his staff by Army spokesmen (U.S. Congress. Senate. Committee on Government Operations. Special Subcommittee on Investigations. *Charges and Countercharges Involving: Secretary of the Army Robert T. Stevens, John G. Adams, H. Struve Hensel and Senator Joe McCarthy, Roy M. Cohn, and Francis P. Carr*).

In 1954, McCarthy's committee investigated allegations of spying and of sabotage within the Army Signal Corps at Fort Monmouth, New Jersey, but the scope of charges expanded. The important confrontation took place at the end of the Army-McCarthy hearings in 1954, after the senator discovered the case of Major Irving Peress, an Army dentist stationed at Camp Kilmer, New Jersey. The "Fifth Amendment dentist," as the senator called Peress, refused to answer questions on an Army form concerning membership in organizations labeled as subversive, but he was routinely promoted while awaiting discharge. McCarthy demanded to know who had promoted Peress. It was General Ralph Zwicker, commander at Fort Kilmer and a decorated war hero, who was insulted by McCarthy during televised hearings. When the Zwicker transcript was published, opinion started to turn again McCarthy. Secretary of the Army Robert T. Stevens called for a "showdown" with the senator over his treatment of Army officers. The Army retaliated by publicizing McCarthy's unethical practices, including efforts to get one of his staff (David Schine) a deferment from military service. In the Army-McCarthy hearings, attorney Joseph Welch confronted McCarthy with putting forward flimsy charges in a now classic exchange during which McCarthy accused an attorney in Welch's law firm of harboring leftist sympathies.

ATTORNEY JOSEPH WELCH: Until this moment, Senator, I think I never really gauged your cruelty or recklessness . . . Little did I dream you could be so cruel as to do an injury to that lad.

SEN. JOE McCARTHY: May I say that Mr. Welch talks about this being cruel and reckless . . . he has been baiting Mr. Cohn here for hours.

WELCH: You've done enough. Have you no sense of decency, sir, at long last? Have you left no sense of decency?

The disgust in Welch's voice—and McCarthy's obvious embarrassment because he had no answer for the attorney—amounted to a national exposure of the senator's cruel and crass investigatory methods. After this, the Senate reprimanded McCarthy for his conduct, and he was censured. He died in May 1957, a broken man.

"Lavender Scare"

In his speech in Wheeling, West Virginia, there was no doubt that McCarthy was referring to both Communists and homosexuals when he alleged that Communists were working for the State Department. The "lavender scare" was the period of political repression during the Cold War when homosexuals in the federal government were forced out of jobs for their alleged perversions and other violations of the loyalty oaths. Instead of being challenged with the question "Are you now or have you ever been a member of the Communist Party?" security officials posed another question: "Information has come to the attention of the Civil Service Commission that you are a homosexual. What comment do you care to make?" Like the purges of their counterparts in other parts of the federal government who were accused or suspected of being Communists, the homosexual purges ended promising careers, ruined lives, and pushed many to suicide.

Assistant Secretary of State John Peurifoy set off a "lavender scare" within the State Department when he revealed, before a Senate appropriations committee in February 1950, that among those ousted from the department as security risks were 91 homosexuals. In June 1950, the Senate authorized a full investigation into the employment of homosexuals and what it designated as "other sex perverts in government"; it was headed by Senator Clyde Hoey (D-N.C.), who was first elected to Congress in 1898. The Hoey Committee issued an interim report in December 1950; it stated rather emphatically that all of the intelligence agencies of the U.S. government that testified "are in complete agreement that sex perverts in Government constitute security risks" and that Russian intelligence agents had been given orders to find weaknesses in the private lives of U.S. government workers (U.S. Congress. Senate. Committee on Government Operations. Permanent Subcommittee on Investigations. *Employment of Homosexuals and Other Sex Perverts in Government*).Through the Hoey Committee's report, the notion that homosexuals threatened national security became accepted as official fact. A second, broader justification for removing homosexuals from government was that they were vulnerable to blackmail, exerted a "corrosive influence" on their co-workers, and might entice young men and women entering government service into acts of perversion. The report was sent to U.S. embassies and foreign intelligence agencies around the world, became part of federal security manuals, and continued to be quoted for years by the U.S. government and its allies as justification for excluding homosexuals.

With the Hoey Committee investigation, the "lavender scare" came to enjoy bipartisan support and became part of standard, government-wide policy. At the U.S. Department of Labor, Bruce Scott lost his job in 1956, after 17 years of service, when security clearances were upgraded and he was suspected of homosexuality, after the government learned that he lived with a homosexual and had been arrested for loitering in Lafayette Park. Probably the most significant case was that of Franklin E. Kameny, who was fired from his job as an astronomer with the U.S. Army War Service in 1957; he fought his dismissal all the way to the U.S. Supreme Court, which declined to hear his case. When his legal efforts failed, he organized the Mattachine Society of Washington, which held a series of pickets in front of federal government buildings to call attention to the exclusion of gays and lesbians from both civilian and military jobs.

Franklin Edward Kameny

One of the pioneers in the gay movement in the United States, Frank Kameny was a Harvard-educated astronomer in the Army Map Service, whose scientific career abruptly ended in the late 1950s when he was fired for being a homosexual. He promptly challenged the federal government's ban on the employment of homosexuals and later took on federal policies on security clearances for homosexuals, among other battles, and the nation's perception of gays as sick people. His 1968 slogan "Gay Is Good" helped change the gay movement's self-perception, paving the way for gay pride.

In 1945, he served in an armored infantry battalion in Germany. After returning to the United States in 1946, he earned his bachelor's degree in physics. In 1957, a year after earning his PhD from Harvard, he landed a civil service job with the Army Map Service in Washington, D.C., where he received superior performance ratings.

At the end of that year, however, he was discharged because of homosexuality. He contested the dismissal through every possible channel; Kameny personally petitioned the U.S. Supreme Court, but the high court refused to hear his case in 1961.

With a few supporters, he started the Mattachine Society of Washington (MSW), the nation's first "civil-liberties, social-action organization

dedicated to improving the status of the homosexual citizens through a vigorous program of action," according to an MSW brochure. The group targeted employment discrimination in the government, and Kameny, recognized as the authority on security clearances for gay people, personally worked on hundreds of cases against the Civil Service Commission and the Pentagon during the next three decades.

In 1971, several friends persuaded Kameny to become the first self-declared gay man to run for the U.S. Congress. He campaigned against five other candidates for the District of Columbia's non-voting post in the House of Representatives, championing personal freedom and gay rights in every appearance; he finished fourth.

His activist achievements include the reversal of the Civil Service Commission's anti-gay policy on July 3, 1975, and the repeal of Washington, D.C.'s sodomy law on September 13, 1993. The latter feat represents a three-decade battle for Kameny, who personally drafted the new law at the request of a city council member.

The Franklin Kameny archive, at the Library of Congress, includes thousands of pages of letters, government correspondence, testimony, photographs, picket signs, and other memorabilia.

Aftermath

What was the aftermath of the Loyalty Security Program and the employees affected by it? This was the most human issue of McCarthyism. In the first four years of the program, nearly three million employees were cleared, but about 212 employees were dismissed as potentially disloyal or security risks. In January 1954, President Eisenhower reported that approximately 2,200 federal employees had either resigned or been dismissed from their jobs as security risks. However, a later Senate study discovered that only 343 federal employees had actually been dismissed as security risks by the Eisenhower administration between May 1953 and June 1955, and another 662 had resigned after being informed that they were considered disloyal.

The effects of the Loyalty Security Program were still felt years later, as employees who had been fired or forced out of their jobs sued the U.S. government or came back into government service. Some got vindication in their lifetime. Such a case was Reed Harris, who was brought back into government service by USIA director Edward R. Murrow, who appointed him a special assistant in 1961. This was considered an act of courage, a move that did much to restore morale. The longest case against the U.S. government from a fired employee came in 1996, when the estate of the late Beatrice Braude received a check for $200,000, 45 years after she was fired for allegedly talking to a Communist and for visiting a leftist book store. Braude filed for wrongful firing, among other things, and won her case a few weeks after she died.

References and Further Reading

Belfrage, Cedric. *The American Inquisition, 1945–1960: A Profile of the "McCarthy Era."* New York: Thunder's Mouth Press; St. Paul, MN: Distributed by Consortium Book Sales and Distribution, 1989.

Bontecou, Eleanor. *The Federal-Loyalty Security Program.* Ithaca, NY: Cornell University, 1953.

Caute, David. *The Great Fear: The Anti-Communist Purge under Truman and Eisenhower.* New York: Simon and Schuster, 1978.

Clifford, Clark. *Counsel to the President: A Memoir.* New York: Random House, 1991.

Corker, Charles, ed. *Digest of the Public Record of Communism in the United States.* New York: New York City Fund for the Republic, 1955.

Fitzgerald, Brian. *McCarthyism: The Red Scare.* Minneapolis, MN: Compass Point Books, 2007.

Freeland, Richard. *The Truman Doctrine and the Origins of McCarthyism: Foreign Policy, Domestic Politics, and Internal Security, 1946–1948.* New York: Schocken, 1974.

Fried, Albert, ed. *McCarthyism—The Great American Red Scare: A Documentary History.* New York: Oxford University, 1997.

Fried, Richard. *Nightmare in Red: The McCarthy Era in Perspective.* New York: Oxford University, 1990.

Friedman, Andrea. "The Smearing of Joe McCarthy: The Lavender Scare, Gossip, and Cold War Politics," *American Quarterly* 57, no. 4 (December 2005): 1105–1129.

Goldstein, Robert J. "Prelude to McCarthyism: The Making of a Blacklist," *Prologue* 38, no. 3 (Fall 2006): 22–33.

Goodman, Walter. *The Committee: The Extraordinary Career of the House Committee on Un-American Activities.* New York: Farrar, Straus and Giroux, 1968.

Griffith, Robert. *The Politics of Fear: Joseph R. McCarthy and the Senate.* 2nd ed. Amherst: University of Massachusetts, 1987.

Griffith, Robert, and Athan Theoharis, eds. *The Spector: Original Essays on the Cold War and the Origins of McCarthyism.* New York: New Viewpoints, 1974.

Harper, Alan. *The Politics of Loyalty: The White House and the Communist Issue, 1946–1952.* Westport, CT: Greenwood, 1969.

Johnson, David K. *The Lavender Scare: The Cold War Persecution of Gays and Lesbians in the Federal Government.* Chicago and London: University of Chicago, 2004.

Johnson, Haynes. *The Age of Anxiety: McCarthyism to Terrorism.* Orlando, FL: Harcourt, 2005.

Kretzmann, Edwin M. J. "McCarthy and the Voice of America," *Foreign Service Journal* (February 1967): 26–27, 44–45.

Latham, Earl. *The Communist Controversy in Washington from the New Deal to McCarthy.* Cambridge, MA: Harvard University, 1966.

The McCarthy Hearings. Jesse G. Cunningham, book editor; Laura K. Egendorf, assistant book editor. San Diego, CA: Greenhaven, 2003.

Office of the Secretary of the Army (Record Group 335) National Archives. Washington, DC.

Office of Personnel Management [OPM] (Record Group 478) National Archives. Washington, DC.

Reeves, Thomas C., ed. *McCarthyism.* 3rd ed. Malabar, FL: R. E. Krieger, 1989.

Rosteck, Thomas. *See It Now Confronts McCarthyism: Television Documentary and the Politics of Representation.* Tuscaloosa: University of Alabama Press, 1994.

Rovere, Richard H. *Senator Joe McCarthy.* Berkeley: University of California, 1995.

Temporary Committees, Commissions, and Boards (Record Group 220) National Archives. Washington, DC.

Thompson, Francis. *The Frustration of Politics: Truman, Congress, and the Loyalty Issue, 1945–1953*. Rutherford, NJ: Fairleigh Dickinson University, 1979.

United States Senate. (Record Group 46) National Archives. Washington, DC.

U.S. Congress. Senate. Committee on Foreign Relations. *State Department Employee Loyalty Investigation;* report of the Committee . . . pursuant to S. Res. 231. Washington, DC: Govt. Print. Off., 1950.

U.S. Congress. Senate. Committee on Government Operations. Permanent Subcommittee on Investigations. *Employment of Homosexuals and Other Sex Perverts in Government;* interim report submitted pursuant to S. Res. 280, 81st Congress. Washington, DC: Govt. Print. Off., 1950. [Hoey Committee Report]

U.S. Congress. Senate. Committee on Government Operations. Permanent Subcommittee on Investigations. *State Department Information Program— Information Centers.* Hearings before the Permanent Subcommittee on Investigations of the Committee on Government Operations, United States Senate, 83rd Congress, 1st session; hearings held March 24–July 14, 1953. Washington, DC: Govt. Print. Off., 1953.

U.S. Congress. Senate. Committee on Government Operations. Permanent Subcommittee on Investigations. *State Department Information Program— Voice of America.* Hearings before the Permanent Subcommittee on Investigations of the Committee on Government Operations, United States Senate, 83rd Congress, 1st session, pursuant to S. Res. 40; hearings held February 16–April 1, 1953. Washington, DC: Govt. Print. Off., 1953.

U.S. Congress. Senate. Committee on Government Operations. Special Subcommittee on Investigations. *Charges and Countercharges Involving: Secretary of the Army Robert T. Stevens, John G. Adams, H. Struve Hensel and Senator Joe McCarthy, Roy M. Cohn, and Francis P. Carr;* report. Washington, DC: Govt. Print. Off., 1954.

U.S. Congress. Senate. Committee on Government Operations. Special Subcommittee on Investigations. *Special Senate Investigation of Charges and Countercharges Involving: Secretary of the Army Robert T. Stevens, John G. Adams, H. Struve Hensel and Senator Joe McCarthy, Roy M. Cohn, and Francis P. Carr;* hearings, 83rd Congress, 2nd session. Washington, DC: Govt. Print. Off., 1954

U.S. Congress. Senate. Committee on Government Operations. *State Department Information Program; Information Centers;* report of the Committee on Government Operations made by its Senate Permanent Subcommittee on Investigations pursuant to S. Res. 40. Washington, DC, U.S. Govt. Print. Off., 1954.

U.S. Congress. Senate. Select Committee to Study Censure Charges. *Report of the Select Committee to Study Censure Charges, United States Senate, Eighty-third Congress, second session, pursuant to the order on S. Res. 301 and amendments, a resolution to censure the Senator from Wisconsin, Mr. McCarthy.* Washington, DC: U.S. Govt. Print. Off., 1954.

U.S. President's Temporary Commission on Employee Loyalty. *Report.* Washington, DC: 1947.

U.S. Subversive Activities Control Board. *Reports of the Subversive Activities Control Board.* Washington, DC: Govt. Print. Off., 1966. 3 v.

Weisberg, Jacob. "Cold War without End," *New York Times Magazine* (November 28, 1999): 116–123, 155–158.

McCarthy's Forgotten Defenders: Political and Social Conservatism in 1950s Pop Culture

3

Bryan E. Vizzini

Between 1945 and 1960, Cold War politics decisively shaped U.S. popular culture. During this period, conservative activists waged war against the purveyors of pop culture—writers, filmmakers, and even comic book publishers—who, they charged, were guilty of promoting anti-American social and political values. Although much of the conservatives' battle to reclaim U.S. pop culture coincided with Senator Joseph McCarthy's highly publicized investigations, they both predated and outlived his brief yet meteoric ascent. Historians continue to debate whether pop culture ever possessed the leftist bias that its critics in the 1940s and 1950s alleged, but a consensus of sorts does exist over its subsequent embrace of political and social conservatism.

The historical literature long has commented upon the extent to which conservatism dominated the United States in the early 1950s, but only recently have scholars begun to pay attention to the explicitly right-wing political and social agendas driving much of that era's pop culture. Their research underscores the extent to which science fiction, comics, and pulp fiction, for example, implicitly vindicated not only the sentiments and actions of men like McCarthy and FBI director J. Edgar Hoover, but the entire conservative agenda as well. It is ironic, given Peter Nicholls's conclusion that, in the case of science fiction, "Because it was deemed socially insignificant, it could play host to political criticism of a kind which might elsewhere have attracted the attentions of Joseph McCarthy and his Un-American Activities Committee" (Clute and Nicholls, 1992, 946). The same might be said of the burgeoning postwar comic and pulp fiction industries, which, despite their "under the radar" status, repeatedly reflected and reaffirmed the conservative spirit.

To be sure, the pop culture industry hardly invented the social and political paranoia upon which it subsequently capitalized. Were it not already widespread, fear of internal subversion and monolithic external enemies likely would have drawn few consumers of the era, and, in the 1950s, as in the present day, profitability and marketability ultimately determined the success or failure of pop culture media. Rather, writers, filmmakers, and artists created works that became instantly popular precisely because their worlds and the issues within them proved so readily recognizable (and frightening) to their audiences.

Indeed, given the events between 1945 and 1952 alone, one reasonably might ask why the general population would *not* feel paranoid and frightened. Americans could cite cases where high-ranking U.S. government officials—Assistant Secretary of the Treasury Harry Dexter White and State Department official Alger Hiss, among others—had been found guilty of passing secrets to the Soviets. By 1953, Americans could add Julius and Ethel Rosenberg, convicted of selling nuclear secrets, to that list. The courts found another 300 or so Americans guilty of passing sensitive information to the Soviets during World War II (Lichtenstein, Strasser, and Rozenzweig, 2000, 562).

Worse still was the notion that, despite all the Communist agents or sympathizers already discovered, many more might have escaped notice. Thus, when the Chinese Communist Party won control of China in 1949, Republican legislators charged their opponents with having "lost" China. Historian David Caute notes that Senator Joseph McCarthy, quickly sharpened the right-wing critique, alleging that the loss had resulted from Communist infiltration of the U.S. State Department, an old claim that dated back to 1938, when HUAC concluded that two thousand Communists held jobs in Washington, D.C. McCarthy subsequently dubbed Secretary of State Dean Acheson the "Red Dean." The senator went on to accuse the State Department, the Truman administration, and even the U.S. Army of harboring Communist sympathizers and subversives. McCarthy's eventual censure did little to abate the anti-Communist hysteria that the senator had helped foment. Up and coming politicians from both parties—future presidents Richard M. Nixon and John F. Kennedy among them—built their careers on reputations as hard-liners with respect to anti-Communism at home and abroad.

Pop culture, and especially the film industry, likewise faced scrutiny. Congress held 84 hearings on the topic of Communist subversion, the most highly publicized of which—HUAC—in 1947 set its sights on the motion picture industry. When, as Historian Tino Balio noted, the committee set out to prove that "card-carrying party members dominated the Screen Writers Guild, that Communists had succeeded in introducing subversive propaganda into motion pictures, and that President Roosevelt had brought improper pressure to bear upon the industry to produce pro-Soviet films during the war," the public took notice. Stunned Americans subsequently watched as Screen Actors Guild President Ronald Reagan supplied HUAC with list after list of suspected Hollywood socialists. Although many of the suspects were virtual unknowns, others, like bigger-than-life pop icons Charlie Chaplin and Lucille Ball, were very well known.

Whether as a carefully calculated response to the intense political scrutiny, a cynical attempt to capitalize on it, or both, the 1950s entertainment industry subsequently exploited popular fears of internal subversion. The Western classic *High Noon* and director Elia Kazan's *On the Waterfront*, for example, urged audiences to confront domestic Communism and to cooperate with the government. In *High Noon*, audiences quickly identified director Fred Zinnemann's outlaw thugs as "stand-ins" for domestic Communists; the timid townspeople served as the Americans who failed to stand up to them, thereby necessitating the final showdown between the former and Gary Cooper's sheriff. In *On the Waterfront*, Kazan used corrupt union officials (especially their leader, played by Lee J. Cobb) to represent the Communists among us (Briley, 1990, 228). More openly anti-Communist offerings came courtesy of John Wayne (*Big Jim McClain*, 1952) and director Leo McCarey (*My Son John*), who earlier had chosen to cooperate with HUAC. To the growing list of right-wing films, we might also add *The Red Menace* (1949), *Conspirator* (1952), *I Was a Communist for the FBI* (1951), and *I Married a Communist* (1950) (Leab, 1984, 59–88). The waning of McCarthy's popularity had little impact on the continued success of stories that focused on subversion and paranoia. As mainstream films and novels gradually turned to other subjects, popular science fiction writers and filmmakers picked up the proverbial ball and ran with it.

Science fiction writers in the 1950s repeatedly played upon their audiences' paranoia over domestic subversion, a paranoia that Senator McCarthy and his supporters had bred and disseminated successfully for political gain. Robert A. Heinlein's *The Puppet Masters*, Jack Finney's *Body Snatchers* (filmed in 1956 as *Invasion of the Body Snatchers*), and John Wyndham's *The Midwich Cuckoos* all featured stories that turned on the notion of deadly doppelgangers successfully having infiltrated the American family. Should Americans fail to protect their traditional family values, the authors suggested, the subversion would metastasize and spread to the broader society.

Heinlein affirmed, as did many social conservatives of his time, that only a thorough commitment to American values (in the form of the patriarchal society) would enable humans to resist the alien invasion. Thus, Heinlein cast his protagonist's loyalty to his boss in distinctly familial terms. Theirs was a father-son relationship in which both characters fulfilled their traditional obligations and roles. Subservient both to the protagonist, Cavanaugh, and his boss, the Old Man, and playing in part the damsel in distress, the heroine Mary fell madly in love with Cavanaugh, despite her status as a professional operative. In the course of the story, Heinlein treated his readers to the requisite rescue scene—when aliens seized control of Mary's mind. As *The Puppet Masters* progressed, Cavanaugh and Mary (with the Old Man's encouragement and blessing) spoke increasingly of marriage and a family. The death of Cavanaugh's father at the hands of the aliens allowed Heinlein to pass the proverbial torch. Cavanaugh married Mary and assumed his father's former position.

To be sure, Heinlein viewed the son's ascent to the position of the father as a victory in the war being fought. On one level, Cavanaugh's marriage to the subservient Mary (her trademark line throughout the novel is a soft "Yes, dear" that is completely bereft of sarcasm), and their subsequent efforts to produce a family enabled the patriarchal status quo to reproduce itself. On another level, Cavanaugh's ascent ensured that, at the novel's end, he was capable of leading an interstellar attack on the aliens' home world.

Even though the decision to end the story with preparations being made for further battle against the enemy clearly had Cold War and McCarthy-esque overtones, equally telling was Heinlein's social commentary on gender roles and their part in combating domestic Communism. Michael Rogin, in his study of motherhood and domesticity in Cold War films, showed that, from 1943 through 1964, filmmakers often equated strong-willed or independent women and mothers with threats to the fabric of U.S. society. Whether as seductresses (e.g., *Kiss Me Deadly*, 1955; *Jet Pilot*, 1957) or as domineering wives and mothers capable of emasculating the men in their lives (e.g., *My Son John*, 1952; *The Manchurian Candidate*, 1962), women who strayed from the traditional norms that U.S. society had set for them either led good men astray or raised sons too weak to avoid conscription into the ranks of domestic Communists.

Just three years later, novelist Jack Finney revisited the themes that Heinlein had developed earlier. Unlike *The Puppet Masters*, however, Finney's *The Body Snatchers* made the transition to Hollywood's big screens almost immediately. Equally impressive, the film version differed very little from its textual origins. Director Don Siegel, who later attained fame with the *Dirty Harry* films, produced a very successful B-grade science fiction film in 1956, one that cashed in big on the decade's anti-Communist hysteria. That both

The 1956 film *Invasion of the Body Snatchers* used science fiction to portray the dangers of alien infiltration of victims' bodies and psyches. (Photofest)

Finney's story and the resulting film bore such a strong resemblance to Heinlein's tale apparently evoked little comment.

Like *The Puppet Masters*, Siegel's *Invasion of the Body Snatchers* turned on the realization of its protagonist, Dr. Miles Bennell, that aliens were taking control of the people around him. Beginning with Santa Mira, California, the pod people—so-called because the alien spores kill their hosts only after producing clones of them in what look like giant pea pods—planned to take over the United States and, presumably, the entire planet. The problem, of course, was that nobody took Bennell seriously.

Santa Mira's residents fell—one by one, family by family—to the alien spores, which wasted no time seizing control of the town government and police force. They took control as well of the town's telephone operators, thereby ensuring an effective lockdown on communications with the outside world. Although the loss of Santa Mira and all those familiar to Bennell and Becky was devastating enough in its own right, matters went from bad to worse when they discovered the pod people loading fresh pods onto vehicles that were headed to other towns in California. Having conquered Santa Mira, the aliens were extending the lines of battle.

When the doppelgangers of Jack and Dr. Kaufman finally cornered them, Bennell and Becky learned that the aliens had "no need for love . . . desire . . . ambition . . . faith." Without them, the pod people sighed, "life is so simple." Unfortunately for Becky, her dreams of marriage and family were dashed when the aliens took control of her. The film ended with a disheveled, frantic Bennell standing in the middle of a busy highway screaming to drivers and viewers alike, "Look, you fools. You're in danger. Can't you see? They're after you. They're after all of us. Our wives, our children, everyone. They're here already. YOU'RE NEXT!"

Interestingly enough, considerable debate exists over whether Siegel's film implicitly embraced the McCarthyist position or merely lampooned it. According to the Internet Movie Database's trivia for the film, Siegel maintained, until his death in 1991, that the film contained no political message of any form—that it was simply an invasion story and intended as entertainment. Siegel's motives notwithstanding, *Invasion of the Body Snatchers* played very well as a vindication of anti-Communist hysteria and a prescription of sorts for how to deal with the enemies among us. It serves as another excellent example of the political and social conservatism that characterized *The Puppet Masters*.

Politically speaking, *Invasion of the Body Snatchers* was little more than a restating of what HUAC and McCarthy had been saying all along—i.e., that subversives had infiltrated all of the most cherished social and political institutions of the United States. That the pod people eschewed human emotions, desires, and ambitions, making all of their decisions collectively, only reinforced for the audience the sense that Bennell and Becky were dealing with Communists or, at the very least, with aliens bearing a striking resemblance to common U.S. stereotypes of Communists. Likewise, the notion of well-placed townspeople—the town physician, the police, and the telephone operators—serving as a vanguard, squashing inquiries before they could threaten the conspiracy, echoed McCarthy's most extreme claims regarding Roosevelt and Truman (and their respective underlings) providing cover for Communist infiltrators. Finally, Bennell's failure to stop the conspiracy's spread sent a strong message regarding the need for greater vigilance and action.

Rogin's earlier observations on the roles that U.S. filmmakers assigned women in the 1950s prove equally sharp with regard to Becky. Throughout the film, Becky's actions and desires remained well within accepted societal constraints (the fact that she is divorced hardly registers in the film). Once the spores gained control of her, however, she transformed into the classic seductress, a threat to all things American.

Although one could perhaps argue that the film's over-the-top quality suggests that Siegel intended it as a satire on McCarthyism, the evidence against such an interpretation is fairly compelling. Even when taking into account factors such as tone and presentation (rather than plot or narrative), the film never fails to take itself seriously, even if viewers today do not. To argue persuasively that Siegel was subtly targeting McCarthy and anti-Communist hysteria necessitates evidence of the director's tongue being firmly in cheek. The closest Siegel comes to this is in his casting of actor Kevin McCarthy as Bennell.

Viewers scarcely had left the cinema when British science fiction author John Wyndham added his own take on what was fast becoming a staple story. Already famous for his 1951 tale *The Day of the Triffids*, Wyndham in 1957 published *The Midwich Cuckoos*. Three years later, a faithful film adaptation, *The Village of the Damned*, appeared in theaters. Both the novel and the film added a creepy twist to the now familiar storyline, making unborn children the hosts for Wyndham's alien invaders. As the children were born and grew up, they threatened those around them, explaining to the protagonist at one point, "You cannot afford *not* to kill us, for if you don't you are finished" (Wyndham, 1976, 172).

The story's political implications could not be any clearer or, by this point, less original. For the third time in seven years, a major work of science fiction argued that subversives had infiltrated society and would wreak havoc until the public acknowledged and confronted the threat's existence. Failure to face down the threat would lead to defeat. In story terms, the townspeople's unwillingness to face the proverbial truth, despite the evidence mounting, would enable the alien presence to take root and grow strong.

The use of human women as incubators for the aliens provided Wyndham with an opportunity to explore at length social mores and expectations with respect to family. In each of the cases where the alien doppelgangers were born to single women, they quickly gained control of their mothers' minds. Married couples, by contrast, proved far more difficult to control. Matters really spun out of control when the people of Midwich removed the children from their home environments, where the married couples could at least exert their own influence over the children, and placed them in the special school. In short, the further removed from the nuclear family, the more powerful and dangerous the cuckoos (i.e., the alien children) became. Wyndham's conclusion surely set well with the social conservatives in his audience.

Just as filmmakers and science fiction writers came to embrace conservatism, so too did comic book publishers, who faced much the same intense scrutiny as their aforementioned counterparts. The odyssey began in 1947, when the Fraternal Order of Police concluded that the increasingly popular genre of true crime comics, filled with gun-toting anti-heroes and lascivious molls, were pathways to the most malignant attack on family values and the patriarchal order—juvenile delinquency. The Daughters of the American Revolution, along with other social activist groups, soon joined in condemning the popular medium. The tipping point came in 1954, with psychologist Frederick Wertham's *Seduction of the Innocent*, which brought the issue national and, ultimately, Congressional attention. Every bit as terrifying as Wyndham's cuckoos, Wertham's specter of juvenile delinquents undermining law, order and all things American demanded immediate action.

Under heavy fire, comic book publishers rushed to counter the criticism. First up was the showcasing of romance comics that had been made popular three years earlier when *Young Romance* debuted. No bodice-rippers these—rather, the romance stories used G-rated cautionary tales as a means of promoting good values (and virtues) in U.S. women. Once again, the pop culture industry defined women's roles in the most black-and-white terms imaginable. Assertive women or those willing to engage in seduction or sexual activity were threats and were not to be emulated. Elsewhere in the industry, the few female superheroes, such as Wonder Woman, Bat Woman, and Black Canary, subsequently found themselves subordinated to male co-stars, whose regular rescues of the heroines reaffirmed the patriarchal order. Gone entirely were the lusty and headstrong women who previously had made such a splash in the crime comics genre.

Still, not all publishers proved content to tighten the reins and wait out the criticism. William Gaines's EC Comics, immensely popular with the teenage crowd, pushed back—with titles such as *Tales from the Crypt* and *Weird Science*, which featured graphic violence and sexuality. Their anti-segregation and anti-war plots merely increased the opposition's ranks. When, in 1954, the Senate Subcommittee Investigation of Juvenile Delinquency got underway, Gaines quickly found himself on the stand. When asked to defend a particular strip that featured a gruesome dismemberment, ending in an ad hoc baseball game using the victim's body parts, Gaines demurred. Rather than face Congressional oversight, comic book publishers subsequently formed their own self-censoring committee—the Comics Magazine Association of America. Gone were the lurid violence, wanton sexuality, and anti-heroes of the crime comics. In their place were seemingly asexual nonconfrontational heroes who, as often as not, solved crimes with a dash of humor and a notable absence of death.

Comic strips, for their parts, largely escaped notice, having already committed to socially and politically conservative characterizations almost from their inception decades earlier. Blondie, for example, enjoyed a very brief stint as a flapper before settling into the role that 1930s society assigned her. With minor variations, she remained there for the duration of her career. Likewise, Mary Worth hardly challenged societal expectations of the stereotypical wealthy elderly widow. The characterizations of good and bad in

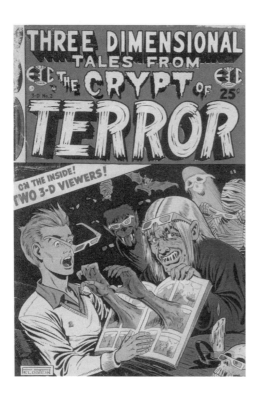

Three-Dimensional Tales from the Crypt of Terror comic book, 1953. (Photofest)

Dick Tracy were sufficiently straightforward for even the youngest of readers. Even the far future and distant past offered little respite from increasingly consensual assumptions—Buck Rogers, Flash Gordon, and Prince Valiant were, in effect, present-day Americans who viewed themselves as bearers of civilization and progress.

Although characters such as Blondie, Popeye, and the Gasoline Alley gang continued to avoid provocative issues, as did newcomers such as *Beetle Bailey*, *Hi and Lois*, and Charles Schultz's *Peanuts*, the age of comic strips as simple affirmations of the social and political status quo was fast coming to an end, thanks in part to cartoonist Walt Kelly. Kelly's decision to attack McCarthyism in the panels of his daily *Pogo* marked an important shift in the cultural landscape of comic strips—one that paved the way for future strips, such as Gary Trudeau's *Doonesbury* and Berke Breathed's *Bloom County*. When conservative viewers complained of Kelly's decision to depict Senator Joseph McCarthy as a wildcat named Simple J. Malarky, Kelly subsequently drew the character with a bag over his head, leading to additional complaints that the notorious senator now resembled a member of the Ku Klux Klan, an image that Kelly apparently found appropriate. Together with artist Al Capp (of *Li'l Abner* fame), Kelly challenged the conservative views that dominated the comic strip industry.

The pulp fiction market, by contrast, remained firmly in the grasp of social and political conservatism. Rooted largely in the crime noir that authors such as James Cain had made popular during the Depression, pulp fiction tropes had long featured independent women as dangerous and subversive. Just as the femme fatales of 1950s films such as *Jet Pilot* had led good men into the clutches of Communism, the adulterous women in Cain's *Double Indemnity* and *The Postman Always Rings Twice* led men to murder on their behalf. In the late 1940s, pop writer Mickey Spillane upped the ante. Under Spillane's direction, women no longer led men to turn the proverbial coat or murder; instead, Spillane transformed the women themselves into turncoats and murderers.

In the 1947 classic *I, the Jury,* detective Mike Hammer set out to solve the murder of an old army buddy. Along for the ride was his buddy's ex-drug addict girlfriend. Hammer himself was the epitome of the conservative hero. He lived in a world of moral blacks and whites, where the ends always justified his brutal acts of violence and bloodshed. In what fast became the blueprint for 1950s pulp fiction heroes, Hammer boozed, womanized, beat, and killed his way through nearly two hundred pages of type. Neither his conscience nor the law impeded his rampages. When he discovered, at the book's end, that the killer was in fact his buddy's ex-girlfriend, Hammer gut-shot her with his .45. She asked how he could do it. He replied, "It was easy." Cut and print—Hammer was off to his next adventure, the 1950 potboiler *My Gun Is Quick*.

Spillane continued to equate active women (especially with respect to sex) with danger. Nearly all of Hammer's most dangerous adversaries proved to be duplicitous and murderous women with whom he had explicit sexual relationships. Near caricatures of the dangerous women featured in the stories of James Cain or in the crime comics, Spillane's women reaffirmed in the strongest terms the connection between "good" and the increasingly antiquated roles of domesticity and motherhood for U.S. women. Lest readers somehow miss the point, Spillane provided in Hammer's secretary Velda a counterpoint to the dangerous dames that filled the pages. Every bit as beautiful and alluring as the women who repeatedly led Hammer astray, Velda served as the epitome of the pure, virtuous, hard-working country girl come to the city. Although she and Hammer shared a mutual attraction, Velda never graced the detective's bed sheets. And, in what became yet another standard part of each story, Hammer repeatedly took the time to reflect that Velda was the kind of woman that a guy marries and that, until such time that they could promise themselves to one another in matrimony, their relationship would remain platonic. In short, Spillane explained for the sake of his reading audience that the idea was to sleep with bad girls and marry good girls. The difference between the two, moreover, was crystal clear—the latter conformed to the most conservative of social mores. The former did not.

The social conservatism that Spillane preached found its equal in the author's political conservatism. Vehemently anti-Communist (yet with little apparent understanding of Communism), Spillane wasted no time cashing in on the anti-Communist fervor of the early 1950s. In *One Lonely Night*, Mike Hammer set out to destroy an insidious Communist plot that was no less ridiculous than the premise of Finney's *Body Snatchers*. One might even argue that Finney's doppelgangers possessed more depth than Spillane's paper-thin caricatures of Communist agents. Educated coffee-house intellectuals—likely the kind of folks who denounced McCarthy's witch hunt in the first place—comprised the menace threatening to erode the foundations of U.S. liberty. In a soliloquy that would have made McCarthy himself proud, Hammer declared, "I had one good, efficient, enjoyable way of getting rid of cancerous Commies. I killed them." And kill them he did, without remorse and without running afoul of anything more substantial that the amorphous bleeding heart establishment against which Hammer spent the better part of his career railing.

Although on a different level altogether than that of Spillane and his pulp fiction counterparts, author Ian Fleming offered a similarly conservative commentary with respect to women's roles and geopolitics in the 1950s. In the first of his immensely popular James Bond stories, *Casino Royale* (1953), Fleming drew heavily from the noir masters of old, offering readers a sadistic murderer, a femme fatale, and a nebulous supporting cast of characters who might or might not have been more than their appearances suggested.

The first of Bond's many literary conquests, Vesper Lynd offered readers a far more subtle, although equally clear, commentary on the role of women in the 1950s. Introduced as a British agent sent to assist Bond, Vesper was the seeming antithesis of what became the stereotypical "Bond girl." Intelligent, resourceful, and all business, she successfully rattled the notorious womanizer, whose physical attraction to her conflicted with an uncharacteristic intention to pursue the relationship more seriously once the assignment ended. Like Spillane's Velda, Vesper's qualities made her the kind of woman that one married. Indeed, at the mission's conclusion, Bond became sufficiently involved with Vesper to resign from Her Majesty's Secret Service and contemplate marriage.

A scene from Terence Young's 1962 James Bond film, *Dr. No*. Shown from left: Joseph Wiseman, Sean Connery, and Ursula Andress. (Photofest)

James Bond

James Bond first appeared in author Ian Fleming's 1953 *Casino Royale*. Over the course of the next 13 years, the immensely popular character appeared in 11 further novels and two collections of short stories. Assigned a Double-O rating, Bond literally had license to kill in the line of duty. Bond's 1962 cinematic debut—*Doctor No*, starring Sean Connery—catapulted Fleming's creation to international fame.

Fleming drew largely upon firsthand experiences in his depictions of Bond's covert activities. The author, who served first as a naval commander in World War II, later organized British special forces operations in Europe. When he began writing *Casino Royale*, Fleming chose to place Bond in the contemporary setting of the Cold War. Interactions with Soviet agents thus became commonplace in *Casino Royale* and the aptly titled *From Russia with Love*.

Although novels such as *Thunderball*, *On Her Majesty's Secret Service*, and *You Only Live Twice* featured less overt Soviet involvement (Bond's nemesis over the course of the series increasingly became the international criminal organization SPECTRE and its leader Ernst Blofeld), Cold War tropes continued to appear in full force. Stolen nuclear weapons drove the plot of *Thunderball*. In *Moonraker*, Bond raced to save London from nuclear destruction at the hands of madman Hugo Drax. *The Man with the Golden Gun* dealt in part with the phenomenon of brainwashing, which attracted considerable public attention after the 1962 cinematic debut of *The Manchurian Candidate*.

United Artists' successful film series departed considerably from the novels on which the studio based the films. Even films such as *The Spy Who Loved Me* (1977), however, which shared only the novel's title, continued to feature Cold War plotlines and characters—the theft of nuclear missiles and a joint mission involving Bond and a Soviet agent, Anya Amasova.

Then, with his career staring into the abyss of premature demise, Bond discovered that Vesper was a Communist double agent. After her suicide, the shell-shocked Bond coldly remarked to his superiors, "The bitch is dead now," having now erected the impenetrable façade that characterized him in the adventures to come. Fleming's shock ending neatly tied together the many strands of social and political conservatism woven into the story, the genre, and the character of Bond.

The revealing of Vesper as a Communist agent illustrated the Right's belief that the subversion of U.S. or Western civilization began with attacks on its core—i.e., the nuclear family. Had Bond married Vesper, the act would have constituted a victory for the Communists, who then might have had access to national security secrets. At the very least, Bond's marriage would have removed a valuable chess piece from the board. In short, Vesper's successful yet subtle seduction of Bond represented the perversion of what underlay freedom and democracy. Her success would have been equivalent to that of the pod people in Finney's *Body Snatchers*, the aliens in *Puppet Masters*, and the sirens in films such as *Jet Pilot*.

By 1960, McCarthyist fears had begun to loosen their grip on popular culture. Thereafter, engagement and coexistence, rather than confrontation, increasingly became the new Cold War paradigm. Mainstream films such as

Fail-Safe, Doctor Strangelove, and *Seven Days in May* all reflected popular culture's slow rejection of political conservatism. Social conservatism's stranglehold on pop culture similarly faced a mounting challenge from feminist science fiction writers Alice "Andre" Norton, James Tiptree, Jr. (the pseudonym of Alice Hastings Bradley Sheldon), and Marian Zimmer Bradley, all of whom challenged the traditional patriarchal society. Even Ian Fleming increasingly took a more nuanced approach to women and the Cold War, relying less and less upon the stock stereotypes that he drew upon in *Casino Royale.*

One very clear bellwether of the pop culture paradigm shift appeared on network television on the night of March 4, 1960. Set in small-town America, the *Twilight Zone* episode "The Monsters Are Due on Maple Street" revisited fears and themes that had been made all too familiar over the course of the previous decade. Once again, aliens were using their mind control devices to create a domestic fifth column in anticipation of a full-fledged invasion, and once again they were targeting the nuclear family— or were they?

The story centered on the people of Maple Street who, following the opening credits, saw *something* flash through the heavens and crash off-screen. The power and communications immediately went out, effectively cutting off Maple Street from the outside world. Tommy, a young science fiction buff, was convinced that the power loss was the work of aliens. "They don't want us to leave. That's why they shut everything off," he notes. "It's always that way, in every story about a ship landing from outer space."

Tommy's mother and the other adults enjoyed a good laugh at the idea before suggesting that someone go into town to see if the power was out there too. Young Tommy, however, persisted, stating, "You might not be able to get to town. It was that way in the story. Nobody could leave. Nobody except . . ." "Except who?" his neighbor Steve asked. "Except the people they'd sent down ahead of them," Tommy quietly replied.

With the seeds of doubt and suspicion now planted, the neighbors' growing paranoia soon bore fruit. In a matter of minutes, the good people of Maple Street observed that Mr. Grossman has no difficulty starting his car. When they confronted him, tempers flared and recriminations flew, as neighbor accused neighbor. Mr. Grossman spent many late evenings on his porch, staring into the sky; he worked on a strange radio apparatus in his basement, and so on. Eventually, the panic-stricken residents killed an innocent man, whom they mistook for an alien. From a nearby field, two aliens watched the mayhem.

At this point, one might easily forgive *Twilight Zone* viewers for feeling a collective sense of déjà vu. The episode's political and social sensibilities were old hat by 1960. Yet again, the metaphorical Communist threat came not from without but from within, and yet again it found sanctuary in the nuclear family. Moreover, as pop culture writers and filmmakers had suggested earlier, the belated action taken by the townspeople might well have proved to be too little, too late.

The episode's conclusion quickly showed, however, that this was a new era and one with new sensibilities. As Maple Street's inhabitants turned on one another, the first alien said to the second, "Understand the procedure now? Just stop a few of their machines and radios and telephones and lawn mowers . . . throw them into darkness for a few hours and then you just sit back and watch the pattern." In an inversion of viewers' expectations, Americans' irrational fear of enemies (internal or external) proved far more destructive than the realities upon which they were allegedly based. The Soviets, Sterling suggested, did not have to attack or infiltrate our communities to defeat us. Our own suspicion, fear, and hatred would do their work for them.

Although "The Monsters Are Due on Maple Street" explicitly criticized the assumptions that underlay conservative 1950s pop culture, it could never have succeeded without them. What makes Sterling's tale work (like all recursive fiction) is the viewers' familiarity with the basic plot elements and their conditioned expectations with respect to how they typically unfold. As a result, *Twilight Zone* viewers had little reason at first to believe that Sterling was mocking, not mimicking, the social and political conservatism with which they had become familiar. Sterling's straight-faced approach further lowered the audience's guard. For the first 25 minutes, "The Monsters Are Due on Maple Street" led viewers to believe that the monsters of the title referred to the aliens rather than to themselves. Having been dramatized countless times already, the possibility of domestic subversion hardly needed introduction, although the character of Tommy was there to ensure that the audience and characters alike realized that "they" could look just like "us." His example of aliens controlling "a mother and a father and two kids" reconfirmed increasingly tired themes involving the role of the nuclear family in both preventing and proliferating subversive ideas. Finally, the first two suspects, Mr. Grossman and Steve, had failed to maintain the gender expectations associated with the traditional family—each had a wife who complained and gossiped about her husband.

With the realization that the characters' unfounded fears threatened the very society that they fought to protect, viewers likely understood that, even though they might not be entering the Twilight Zone, they were indeed entering a new era. Social and political conservatism remained part of U.S. pop culture, but thereafter it had to compete with alternative political and social visions, which, by the late 1960s, threatened to eclipse the conservatism that characterized the period from 1945 to 1960.

References and Further Reading

Alves, Teresa. "'Some Enchanted Evening': Tuning in the Amazing Fifties, Switching Off the Elusive Decade." *American Studies International* 39:3 (2001): 25–40.

Balio, Tino, ed. *The American Film Industry.* Madison: University of Wisconsin Press, 1985. Accessed August 18, 2005. http://www.thirdworldtraveller.com/McCarthyism/HUAC_Rise_AntiCommun.html.

Berger, Roger A. "'Ask What You Can Do for Your Country': The Film Version of H. G. Wells's *The Time Machine* and the Cold War." *Literature/Film Quarterly* 17:3 (1989): 177–187.

Biskind, Peter. "Pods, Blobs, and Ideology in American Films of the Fifties." Georg Slusser and Eric S. Rabkin, eds. *Shadows of the Magic Lamp: Fantasy and Science Fiction in Film*. Carbondale, IL: Southern Illinois University Press, 1985: 58–72.

Briley, Ron. "Reel History: U.S. History, 1932–1972, as Viewed through the Lens of Hollywood." *The History Teacher* 23:3 (May 1990): 228–229.

Caute, David. *The Great Fear*. New York: Simon and Schuster, 1978. (accessed August 18, 2005) http://www.thirdworldtraveller.com/McCarthyism/HUAC_Rise_AntiCommun.html.

Clute, John, and Peter Nicholls, eds. *The Encyclopedia of Science Fiction*. New York: St. Martin's Press, 1992.

Davis, Ronald L. *Celluloid Mirrors: Hollywood and American Society since 1945*. Fort Worth, TX: Harcourt Brace College Publishers, 1997.

"Film Trivia for *Invasion of the Body Snatchers*." (accessed August 16, 2005) http://www.imdb.com/title/tt0049366/.

Fleming, Ian. *Casino Royale*. New York: Signet, 1964 [repr. 1953].

Fuller, Linda K. "The Ideology of the 'Red Scare' Movement: McCarthyism in the Movies." Loukides, Paul, and Linda K. Fuller, eds. *Beyond the Stars*. Bowling Green, OH: Bowling Green University Popular Press, 1990, 229–248.

Gilbert, James B. "Wars of the Worlds." *Journal of Popular Culture* 10:2 (1976): 326–336.

Hardin, Michael. "Mapping Post-War Anxieties onto Space: Invasion of the Body Snatchers and Invaders from Mars." *Enculturation: A Journal for Rhetoric, Writing, and Culture* 1:1 (Spring 1997).

Heinlein, Robert A. *The Puppet Masters*. New York: Signet Books, 1979 (repr. 1951).

Hendershot, Cyndy. *Paranoia, the Bomb, and 1950s Science Fiction Films*. Bowling Green, OH: Bowling Green State University Popular Press, 1999.

Invasion of the Body Snatchers. Dir. Don Siegel. Allied Artists, 1956.

Kirshner, Jonathan. "Subverting the Cold War in the 1960s: *Dr. Strangelove, The Manchurian Candidate*, and *The Planet of the Apes*." *Film & History* 31:2 (2001): 40–44.

Leab, Daniel J. "How Red Was My Valley: Hollywood, the Cold War Film, and *I Married a Communist*." *Journal of Contemporary History* 19:1 (January 1984): 59–88.

Leab, Daniel J. "Hollywood and the Cold War, 1945–1961." Robert Brent Toplin, ed. *Hollywood as Mirror: Changing Views of "Outsiders" and "Enemies" in American Movies*. Westport, CT: Greenwood Press, 1993.

Lichtenstein, Nelson, Susan Strasser, and Roy Rosenzweig. *Who Built America? Working People and the Nation's Economy, Politics, Culture, and Society*, v. 2. New York: Worth Publishers, 2000.

Lucanio, Patrick. *Them or Us: Archetypal Interpretations of Fifties Alien Invasion Films*. Bloomington, IN: Indiana University Press, 1987.

Murphy, Brian. "Monster Movies : They Came from Beneath the Fifties." Marsden, Michael T., John G. Nachbar, and Sam L. Grogg, Jr., eds. *Movies As Artifacts : Cultural Criticism of Popular Film*. Chicago, IL: Nelson-Hall, 1982.

Neve, Brian. *Film and Politics in America: A Social Tradition*. London and New York: Routledge, 1992.

O'Donnell, Victoria. "Science Fiction Films and Cold War Anxiety." Peter Lev, ed. *Transforming the Screen, 1950–1959*. New York: Charles Scribner's Sons, 2003.

Quart, Leonard, and Albert Auster. *American Film and Society since 1945*. London: Macmillan, 1984.

Rogin, Michael. "Kiss Me Deadly: Communism, Motherhood, and Cold War Movies." *Representations* 6 (Spring 1984): 1–36

Seed, David. *American Science Fiction and the Cold War: Literature and Film*. Chicago, IL: Fitzroy Dearborn, 1999.

Serling, Rod. "The Monsters Are Due on Maple Street." *The Twilight Zone*. March 4, 1960.

Spillane, Mickey. *I, the Jury*. New York: E. P. Dutton, 1947.

Spillane, Mickey. *One Lonely Night*. New York: New American Library, 1951.

Village of the Damned. Dir. Wolf Rilla. MGM, 1960.

Wyndham, John. *The Midwich Cuckoos*. New York: Ballantine Books, 1976 (repr. 1957).

McCarthy and the Media: How the "Red Scare" Affected Radio, TV, and Film

4

Donna L. Halper

In early February 1950, Senator Joseph McCarthy made a startling assertion. The Republican senator from Wisconsin gave a speech in which he claimed to have a list of 205 members of the Communist Party who were working in the U.S. State Department. He followed up a week later by informing the press of a letter he had written to President Truman, demanding that the president fire 57 Communists who he said were actively shaping State Department policy. Not many people had been aware of Senator McCarthy prior to that point, but in the next few years, his name would seldom be out of the media spotlight, and his actions affected the lives of thousands of people, including many members of the entertainment industry.

In addition to average citizens, who suddenly found themselves accused of being traitors, there were also celebrities whom McCarthy and his colleagues declared to be subversive. Thanks in large part to a book called *Red Channels* (June 1950), which purported to identify those in the media who had ties to Communism, a number of writers, performers, filmmakers, and radio stars lost their livelihood; many had to leave the United States, and several committed suicide. Some of the entertainers who were accused had at one time expressed an interest in Communism, especially during the Great Depression; but many others were guilty of no more than having pro-union or anti-war views, attitudes that conservative Republicans like McCarthy considered too liberal and, thus, unpatriotic.

Years later, the fear and suspicion that Joe McCarthy wrought lived on in the term "McCarthyism," which came to refer to such tactics as making false and inflammatory assertions about political opponents and attempting to stifle dissent by branding anyone who disagreed with the government as anti-American. McCarthyism is usually associated with the 1950s, but there were similar efforts by conservative politicians of the 1920s, 1930s, and early 1940s to demonize people with left-wing political views and accuse them of being Communists.

When commercial radio first came along in 1920, there were few rules about the content of the programs. Stations filled their time on the air with live music, educational talks, religious services, and special programs aimed at homemakers, children, or sports fans. But as the radio craze swept the country in the early 1920s, it didn't take long for politicians to realize the benefits of addressing the "invisible audience." A radio speech could reach thousands of people and make a politician's views better known. Soon, candidates were hard at work mastering the difficult art of discussing politics in a concise yet personable style.

For the most part, the early political coverage featured members of the two major parties, the Democrats and the Republicans. But by the mid-1920s, Socialist Party leader Norman Thomas was asking to be included, only to find that some radio station managers did not want any speaker they perceived as outside the mainstream. Several New York station managers denied Thomas permission to broadcast, or they limited his appearances; this continued even after he became a presidential candidate in 1928. Then, in the mid-1930s, there was a controversy over whether Earl Browder, the leader of the Communist Party of the USA, should be given network time. In May 1936, John Shepard III, president of the Yankee Network, refused to broadcast a speech that Browder had planned to deliver, telling the *Christian Science Monitor* that, because the aim of the Communist Party was to overthrow the American form of government, he could see no reason to provide Browder any air time ("Banned," 1936, 9). He was not the only station executive to prevent Browder from broadcasting.

During radio's formative years, many newspapers and magazines began hiring critics to comment on the programs and evaluate the performances. But political analysis was not on the radar screen for most of them. They might discuss which candidates were good speakers and which ones were boring, but they seldom evaluated the content of the speeches. In fact, the most common complaint the critics had was that there was too much advertising on the air. The critics were also upset about announcers who didn't speak proper English, and they disliked the fact that most stations played popular dance music rather than opera and the classics.

It wasn't until the mid-1930s that the focus of the critics began to change, which was undoubtedly a response to current events. By the time of the era often called the "Golden Age of Radio," the medium was becoming more essential to everyone's daily life—not just for radio dramas or the latest hit songs. With the worsening situation in Europe and the rise of Adolf Hitler, stations increased their news coverage and added commentators. The public came to rely on radio for information about what the major news makers were doing and even to hear them speak.

Hitler himself frequently used radio to spread the Nazi message, and, in the United States, President Roosevelt was an equally strong proponent of broadcasting; the public found his Fireside Chats very reassuring. But the United States had its share of demagoguery too, most notably from a priest named Father Charles Coughlin. He used his weekly radio show not just to give sermons, but to rail against the Jews, the New Deal, Communism, greedy corporations, and various others that he believed were to blame for the problems of the United States.

There had been bigots on the air before, but the popularity of Father Coughlin puzzled many sociologists and academics. They raised questions about the effect that some of the religious and educational programs were having on the audience. The critics had taken notice as well. They worried that too many news stories about war or too many radio shows about crime could frighten children. And after Orson Welles's 1938 broadcast of "War of the Worlds" terrified so many people and convinced them that Martians had actually invaded, the critics also expressed great concern about radio's ability to persuade.

In 1937, an organization called the Institute for Propaganda Analysis (IPA) was founded, to offer analysis and research on the techniques of political persuasion. IPA issued books and educational materials so that teachers could help impressionable students recognize and reject manipulative speech and demagoguery whenever they heard it. In addition to the critics, who continued to write about whether radio was a bad influence on impressionable listeners, some conservative political figures also joined in with a critique of their own.

As they saw it, the U.S. media, especially radio and film, were in danger of being infiltrated by radicals, Nazis, and Communists. Given the tendency of most stations to prevent speakers like Norman Thomas and Earl Browder from getting on the air, the politicians probably had nothing to worry about, but that didn't stop many of them from using the alleged threat in their campaign speeches. Colonel Frank Knox, the Republican nominee for vice president, exemplified this tactic. He gave a radio talk in July 1936 in which he warned station owners to be vigilant so that "the wrong ideas" would never be heard on the air ("Knox Demands," 1936, 4).

But this so-called vigilance was easier said than done; because the constitution guaranteed freedom of speech, broadcasters had a genuine dilemma as they chose which groups could express their views and which ones were too inflammatory. There had to be a balance between the mandate to keep the public informed and the desire of most sponsors (and many listeners) to avoid controversial topics, such as birth control or racial discrimination. Unfortunately, the decision-making process was often arbitrary, and some of the groups who were excluded accused the major networks of censorship. And that leads us to Martin Dies, considered by many to be the forerunner of Joseph McCarthy.

Representative Martin Dies was a conservative Democrat from Texas, and he was convinced that those on the political left, including Socialists, Communists, members of organized labor, and most liberals, were disloyal and unpatriotic. He also believed that Communists had already infiltrated education, labor unions, and the media and that, if they were not stopped, they would destroy our way of life. In 1938, he formed a committee to investigate so-called un-American activities, and, within a year, he was going after those he considered traitors, getting much media attention in the process, while winning the support of conservative groups such as the American Legion.

As the first chairman of the House Committee on Un-American Activities, from 1938 to 1945, Martin Dies endeavored to discredit New Deal programs and labor unions by exposing alleged Communist infiltration. (Library of Congress)

At the height of his committee's power and influence, Dies accused hundreds of government employees of being Communist sympathizers; even though his evidence was questionable, many lost their jobs. He had an ongoing feud with the American Civil Liberties Union (ACLU), which he believed was a Communist front (historically, the ACLU had defended the free-speech rights of unpopular groups, including Communists, which Dies saw as proof the ACLU comprised "fellow travelers"). Dies was even able to get Communist Party leader Earl Browder sent to prison ("Browder Indicted," 1939, 1).

As Joseph McCarthy did later, Martin Dies often claimed that he had lists of names of people who were subversives; in 1941, for example, he said he could identify 1,124 of them, many of whom held important positions in the federal government. Dies also questioned the patriotism of any politician or government figure who dared to challenge his tactics. That included even President Franklin D. Roosevelt and his wife. The Dies Committee told the press that the League of Women Shoppers was a Communist front, determined to destroy the U.S. free-enterprise system. The League, which was founded in 1935, stated that its mission was to encourage women to "use their buying power for social justice, so that the fair price which they pay as consumers will also include an American standard of living for those who make and market the goods they buy" ("Matthews Meets," 1939, 14). And among its members were female celebrities such as playwright Lillian Hellman (who was later blacklisted during the McCarthy era) and actress Tallulah Bankhead, a number of Congressional wives, and the First Lady, Eleanor Roosevelt. She took an especially dim view of being called a Communist, as did President Roosevelt, who berated Dies. But Martin Dies persisted with his hunt for Communists.

Although Dies was never as famous as McCarthy, it is certainly safe to say that the Dies Committee, also known as HUAC, set the stage for McCarthyism. By the time Joe McCarthy came to power, there were already companies demanding loyalty oaths from employees, and some of the more conservative newspapers had begun publishing essays about the danger that Russia posed to the U.S. way of life. The Cold War had begun, and the "Red Scare" would quickly follow.

And even though Dies had been a conservative Democrat, the issue of fighting Communism and identifying U.S. traitors was taken up by the Republican Party, which began making it a talking point in radio speeches and in interviews with the press. The issue was framed with an "us versus them" focus: the United States was godly, Russia was atheistic; the United States wanted peace, Russia sought to destroy us.

McCarthy's speeches also called for greater scrutiny over those with the wrong views, most notably the usual groups that conservatives disliked, such as members of labor unions or the ACLU. And using Dies's technique, McCarthy began saying that he knew of a specific number of card-carrying Communists in the government, and he was ready to point them out. Unfortunately, the press did not always fact-check his claims, and some members even agreed with them. When the networks had begun hiring radio commentators, the men and women they chose came from a variety of political views.

But one of the most ultra-conservative was Fulton Lewis, Jr., who was widely syndicated by the Mutual Radio Network beginning in the late 1930s. Known for his sweeping generalities and accusations directed at people that he perceived as liberal, Lewis continued to be a strong supporter of Dies and then of Joe McCarthy ("Fulton Lewis, Jr.," 1966, 33).

In September 1947, HUAC opened a series of hearings and began to focus its attention on the entertainment industry, especially radio and movies. The committee was chaired by New Jersey Republican J. Parnell Thomas and included a young Republican from California named Richard M. Nixon. It also included a man who became one of the committee's most visible members—John Rankin, a well-known conservative Democrat from Mississippi, whose views were both racist and anti-Semitic. HUAC started summoning various writers, performers, and producers, nearly all of whom had views that the committee saw as left-wing and the majority of whom were Jewish. In November 1947, it was discovered that, among the 35 people in the State Department who were arbitrarily dismissed for allegedly being disloyal, 33 of them were Jewish. For those who still didn't trust Jews, this only proved that there was good reason, whereas for those who were convinced the government was still dominated by anti-Semites, such purges only showed that Jews were being singled out and fired, whether guilty of anything or not (Lewis, 2000, 9, 13–14).

As the committee summoned a growing number of entertainers, many were puzzled as to why they were called. Yes, some had been members of the Communist Party, but that was back in the 1930s and not so much because they planned on overthrowing the government. Rather, the American Communist Party had a history of fighting against racism and supporting workers' rights, and that was very appealing at a time when neither the Democrats nor the Republicans were speaking out about racism or income inequality. But if the Communist Party ever had any influence in the past, by 1950, its membership was down to fewer than 10,000 members. Yet HUAC continued to see its existence as a major threat to the United States. Anyone who had been a member—even back in the 1930s—was an object of suspicion.

And even for those who didn't officially join the Communist Party in the 1930s, visiting Russia or studying Russian was treated with just as much scorn by the committee, as well as by a subcommittee set up to investigate internal security within the government. Julia Older had been a well-respected radio critic at the *Hartford Courant* for nearly five years before she left to study in Moscow in the mid-1930s. She got a job working for an English-language newspaper there, the *Moscow Daily News*, which was run by an ardent supporter of Communist ideals, Anna Louise Strong ("Julia S. Older," 1935, 9). She returned to the United States in 1937, and, by the early 1940s, she was working for the Office of War Information, helping produce pro-U.S. broadcasts to be transmitted overseas. Martin Dies believed that, because of her past experiences in Russia, she shouldn't work for the U.S. government, and he tried to have her fired, but her work was excellent and his efforts were unsuccessful ("Julia S. Older," 1942 1).

However, by the time the Red Scare was in full force, attitudes about having worked in Moscow had become more negative. Older (by then known by her married name of Julia Bazer) was working at the United Nations, and this time she was dismissed. She challenged her dismissal and won; the United Nations reinstated her, with back pay. But being in the spotlight made her the target of a number of accusatory articles by conservative news columnists such as Westbrook Pegler, as well as several visits to answer questions from the Senate subcommittee about whether her three years in Russia meant that she was a subversive.

Meanwhile, as the public heard repeatedly about Communists infiltrating the government and the media, their attitude about the crime of treason had also hardened; a Gallup poll in early 1953 revealed that 73 percent of those surveyed believed that the death penalty was a suitable punishment for anyone convicted of being a traitor. Fortunately for people like Julia Older, accusations of treason were not the same as being convicted.

But the country seemed increasingly willing to believe McCarthy, J. Edgar Hoover of the FBI, and others who insisted that there were secret Communists everywhere and that their identities had to be revealed. Often, as in the time of Martin Dies, the evidence was no more than an affiliation with a group or a cause that the conservatives had branded as subversive. The difference was that in the early 1940s, during World War II, Russia was still our ally, and the Cold War had not broken out. By the 1950s, Russia was the enemy, and politicians were playing the patriotism card relentlessly. And although Julia Older had been inconvenienced and insulted, at least she wasn't imprisoned. Others caught up in the HUAC net were not so fortunate.

As mentioned earlier, the hearings in 1947 focused on radio to some degree, but the main focus was on the film industry, which was supposedly dominated by Communists and their sympathizers. The committee had an interesting weapon—a publication called *Counter-Attack*, published by three former members of the FBI, all of whom had ties with conservative groups. Theodore (Ted) Kirkpatrick was the dominant figure in the four-page weekly, which claimed to be a newsletter with the facts to help combat the spread of Communism. Kirkpatrick and his colleagues, along with a right-wing TV producer named Vincent Hartnett, then published the infamous *Red Channels—the Report of Communistic Influence on Radio and Television* in June 1950.

The committee relied on the information in *Counter-Attack*, as well as on interviews with more than 40 people who worked in Hollywood. Among those whom the committee interviewed and who, by all accounts, was co-operative with the committee's investigations was then-actor Ronald Reagan. HUAC then identified a number of writers, actors, and directors who were allegedly involved in Communist activities. Ten of them, the so-called "Hollywood Ten," were indicted. They included novelist and screenwriter Alvah Bessie, playwright (and union activist) Lester Cole, publicist and screenwriter Ring Lardner, Jr., and screenwriter Dalton Trumbo.

The members of the Hollywood Ten believed in the First Amendment, and, were it not for the way that politicians had stoked the fears of the U.S. public, that argument might have sufficed. But, during the height of

The "Hollywood Ten" stand with their attorneys on January 9, 1948, outside of a district court after being charged with contempt of Congress for refusing to cooperate with the House Committee on Un-American Activities. (AP/Wide World Photos)

McCarthy's reign, refusing to answer the committee's questions or rejecting its central premise that Hollywood was a haven for Communists was enough to cast suspicion upon an individual's loyalty. Surprising as it seems today, the Hollywood Ten were all found guilty of contempt, for refusing to answer the committee's questions, and all were fined and imprisoned; the majority received 1-year sentences (Bradlee, 1950, 16; "New Review Asked," 1950, 20).

This period of time led to the practice of blacklisting, which meant refusing to hire anyone suspected of Communist ties, even if the charges had not been proved. Among those blacklisted were actors Larry Parks, Peter Brocco, Phil Brown, and Zero Mostel; actresses Lee Grant and Marsha Hunt; screenwriter Paul Jarrico; and Director Jules Dassin. Some of those who were blacklisted decided to "name names" in the hopes of being able to find work again, but the majority refused to co-operate, and, in a number of cases, the only way they could find work was to leave the country, which is what Jules Dassin (France) and Phil Brown (England) did. A few of the Hollywood Ten, Ring Lardner, Jr. and Dalton Trumbo, for example, were able to find work again only by using pseudonyms. It was not until a new generation took over in Hollywood in the 1960s and early 1970s that some of those who were blacklisted were finally able to get hired again.

Blacklisting also affected the music industry: folksinger Pete Seeger was perhaps the best-known musician to be refused the opportunity to work. Seeger, a longtime political activist who proudly espoused left-wing views and worked for a number of pro-union and anti-war groups, as well as for the environment and for civil rights, was a member of the Communist Party in the 1930s, but, years later, he claimed to have severed ties with it. The FBI considered him a radical, and his group, the Weavers, found itself unable to get hired for concerts or for television appearances. Seeger eventually stood trial—the wheels of justice turned slowly, and his case didn't come up till 1961; as the Hollywood Ten had done, he too refused to answer the committee's questions. He was convicted of contempt and sentenced to jail, but his conviction was eventually overturned. Still, it wasn't until the mid-1960s that his career took off again, and he was allowed to appear as a guest performer on U.S. television shows ("Breaking the TV Blacklist," 1967, 18).

Another performer affected by the blacklist was African American actor and singer Paul Robeson, whose outspokenness about U.S. racism, coupled with his praise of Russia, where he had traveled as a performer and had spent some time, was enough to get the attention of HUAC and Senator McCarthy. Accused of being pro-Communist, Robeson found it increasingly hard to make a living, despite his excellent voice and his long career as a performer. The State Department revoked his passport, making it impossible for him to work overseas, and, when he tried to perform in the United States, conservatives often picketed, or riots ensued. He finally got his passport back, but, in poor health, he was not able to regain his professional momentum (Payne, 1975, 6).

Another African American victim of the blacklist was stage and film actor Canada Lee, who, like Robeson, continued to speak out forcefully against racism at a time before the subject was being discussed openly by the mainstream media. As a result, Lee gained a reputation for being too controversial, even though today his remarks read as early examples of what was expressed during the civil rights movement of the 1960s. The FBI tried to get Lee to testify against Robeson, but Lee would not.

Larry Adler, a talented harmonica player who often performed with the tap dancer Paul Draper, was accused of being a Communist sympathizer in 1948, and, when his livelihood dried up, he sued the woman who had accused him (the wife of one of *Time* magazine's editors) for libel; however, he was never fully vindicated, and he could only find work by moving to England. He was nearly forgotten in the United States, but he was able to have considerable success writing and performing in his newly adopted country.

Television was still relatively new as a medium, but it too was affected by McCarthy and the blacklist. John Henry Faulk was a humorist who had a successful radio show for CBS and then appeared on TV. He was also active in his union, AFTRA, the American Federation of Television and Radio Artists. But Faulk's career came to an end when Vincent Hartnett, who headed an anti-Communist group called AWARE and was the co-author of *Red Channels*, accused him of being a Communist in 1956. The evidence against Faulk included his having performed at a club that was supposed to be a favorite venue for Communist activities. He was let go by CBS in 1957, after some of his sponsors had pulled out from his shows; he then sued AWARE for libel. It took until 1962 for him to win his case, although he never collected much of the $3.5 million that he was awarded (Deeb, 1975, C10). Many historians believe that his trial and the publicity that it received brought the evils of blacklisting out into the open and resulted in the end of this practice. Faulk's story was dramatized by CBS in an acclaimed documentary called "Fear on Trial" in 1975.

Other performers, such as Jean Muir, who had been on radio but lost the chance at a role on the TV version of the *Aldrich Family* when her name came up in *Red Channels*, were not able to gain vindication, nor did they get their job back. But perhaps the most tragic case resulting from the blacklist was what happened to Philip Loeb, a popular character actor on the stage before getting the opportunity to play the role of Jake on the TV version of the longtime radio hit *The Goldbergs* in 1949. But in 1950, his name appeared in *Red Channels*, and several of the "friendly witnesses" who testified before HUAC, including director Elia Kazan, said that Loeb had been a Communist, a charge that he always denied.

The sponsors of the show, General Foods, told the show's creator and star Gertrude Berg that Loeb had to be fired. Berg seems to have been unwilling to do so. She told a newspaper that she believed him when he said he had never been a Communist. But at the height of McCarthyism, Loeb had few options. Being accused was as good as being found guilty. Loeb ultimately agreed to leave the show, and Berg paid him a $40,000 settlement. But with his reputation in ruins, Loeb was unable to get hired anywhere. In debt and suffering from depression, he committed suicide in 1955.

Lucille Ball Beats The Blacklist

Although numerous radio, television, and film stars found themselves blacklisted for long-ago flirtations with Communism, one notable exception was Lucille Ball. She had starred in a CBS Radio comedy called *My Favorite Husband* in the late 1940s, and, when it moved to television in 1951, it was renamed *I Love Lucy*. On television, Lucy played the scatterbrained housewife Lucy Ricardo, who wanted to be in show business; her real-life husband Desi Arnaz played bandleader Ricky Ricardo, who was constantly getting Lucy out of trouble. Even though it was somewhat sexist by today's standards, the comic genius of Lucy and Desi carried the show, and it became one of early television's biggest hits.

But in 1953, at the height of the Red Scare, gossip columnist Walter Winchell printed an item that accused Lucille Ball of being a member of the Communist Party. As it turned out, back in the mid-1930s, Lucy had registered as a Communist, at the urging of her grandfather, who was a member.

Lucy and Desi decided to come up with a strategy to counteract the possible bad publicity. He first denied that his wife had ever registered as a Communist, and he then expressed outrage that anyone would think his wife could sympathize with Communism.

Then, before a live studio audience, Desi defended his wife in a very emotional speech. He said that his wife was 100 percent pro-American, that she hated everything the Communists stood for, and that what was being said about her was a pack of lies. He concluded by referring to Lucy's trademark red hair, which she had been coloring for years: " . . . I want you to meet my favorite wife—my favorite redhead—in fact, that's the only thing red about her, and even that's not legitimate—Lucille Ball!"

Perhaps because Lucy's popular character seemed incapable of doing anything nefarious, or perhaps because of Desi's impassioned defense of her, the cloud of suspicion passed, and her sponsors stood by her. So did the public, which saw her as a talented comedian and forgave her for what was framed as a momentary, foolish mistake from many years before. And HUAC believed her when she testified that she had never attended a Party meeting. Even the critics were glad that she had been treated so courteously by all concerned. After all, everyone did love Lucy.

Although some historians believe that no one central event brought the reign of Joe McCarthy to an end, it is generally accepted that a very important person who contributed to McCarthy's downfall was the respected radio and TV journalist Edward R. Murrow. By the early 1950s, Murrow had cast his lot with TV; having been a news reporter and anchor during World War II, he then did a radio show called *Hear It Now* in 1950. Murrow renamed it *See It Now* and went on the air in 1951 on CBS TV, where the program won many awards. But the most memorable show in this series was probably on March 9, 1954, when Murrow courageously took on Joe McCarthy. At the end of the broadcast, which was mainly McCarthy in his own words, Murrow said to the viewers, "We will not walk in fear, one of another. We will not be driven by fear into an age of unreason if we dig deep in our history and doctrine and remember that we are not descended from fearful men, not from men who feared to write, to speak, to associate, and

Edward R. Murrow is seen following the broadcast of *See It Now* showing Senator Joseph McCarthy, April 6, 1954. (AP/Wide World Photos)

to defend causes which were for the moment unpopular. We can deny our heritage and our history, but we cannot escape responsibility for the result. There is no way for a citizen of the Republic to abdicate his responsibility" (Bliss, Jr., 1997, 247–248).

By many accounts, that program helped to de-mythologize McCarthy and demonstrate for the audience what a bully and demagogue the man was. McCarthy tried his best to discredit Murrow, accusing him of being a Communist sympathizer, but this time, the tactic that had worked so well for the senator seemed to have no effect. And even though some media critics felt that Murrow had been unfair to McCarthy, the show definitely had had an effect. Gradually after that, McCarthy's power began to wane.

In the end, it was the media that helped make Joe McCarthy popular— by quoting him and giving him endless publicity and not asking the tough questions until it was too late and the United States was caught up in the fear and the terror that enabled him to do his job. Perhaps it's fitting that the media also helped bring him down, with Edward R. Murrow in the lead.

But another factor may have been when TV began to broadcast some of the hearings in 1954, and the public was able to see, over and over again, the bullying and the browbeating that were typical of how McCarthy operated. An educational organization called the Fund for the Republic (created by the Ford Foundation) issued a two-volume refutation of *Red Channels* in 1956; when the editor, John Cogley, formerly with the Catholic publication *Commonweal*, was called before HUAC to testify, he refused to back down, even when the committee threatened to investigate both the Fund and Cogley. More journalists began to speak out and challenge what the conservatives had been saying, and McCarthyism was weakened even further.

In the end, Joseph McCarthy was censured by the Senate in December 1954, and he never did produce any list with the names of 205 known Communists (which sometimes became 57 or some other number, depending on whom he was speaking to). By 1957, his drinking problem had escalated, and he died in early May of that year.

A painful reminder of the harm that occurred during the McCarthy era took place in 1998, when the Academy of Motion Picture Arts and Sciences decided to present Director Elia Kazan with a Lifetime Achievement Award. Although Kazan certainly had an admirable career that included several Oscar nominations, he also earned the scorn of a number of blacklisted entertainers because he was one of those who "named names" to HUAC. Thus, the 1998 award was very controversial; many in Hollywood agreed that he deserved an award for his long and distinguished career, but others felt that Kazan had ruined the lives of other people to save himself and did not deserve to be honored.

As for McCarthy, to this day, he still has his supporters, who insist that he had good intentions and was very sincere about fighting Communism. But, as a result of his crusade and as a result of the actions of the FBI under J. Edgar Hoover and the HUAC that Martin Dies had created and McCarthy perpetuated, thousands of innocent men and women lost their jobs and reputations, often on very flimsy evidence. And the media learned the hard way that being skeptical and questioning those in power often gets reporters accused of being unpatriotic—but such skepticism is essential if the United States is to avoid another McCarthy era.

References and Further Reading

Alwood, Edward. *Dark Days in the Newsroom: McCarthyism Aimed at the Press.* Philadelphia: Temple University Press, 2007.

"Banned: Communist Speech over Yankee Network." *Christian Science Monitor*, March 5, 1936, p. 9.

Bliss, Jr., Edward, ed. *In Search of Light: The Broadcasts of Edward R. Murrow 1938–1961.* Cambridge, MA: DaCapo Press, 1997.

Bradlee, Ben. "Six Film Writers Fined, Jailed for Contempt." *Washington Post*, June 30, 1950, p. 16.

"Breaking the TV Blacklist." *New York Times*, September 4, 1967, p. 18.

"Browder Indicted in Passport Case," *New York Times*, October 24, 1939, p. 1.

Carini, Susan M. "Love's Labors Almost Lost: Managing Crisis during the Reign of 'I Love Lucy'" *Cinema Journal* 43(2003): 1, 44–62.

Deeb, Gary. "CBS Turns a Baleful Eye to One of Its Own Mistakes." *Chicago Tribune*, March 12, 1975, p. C10.

"Fulton Lewis, Jr. Is Dead at 63." *New York Times*, August 22, 1966, p. 33.

"Julia Older Has Become Columnist on Moscow Daily." *Hartford Courant*, March 23, 1935, p. 9.

"Julia S. Older Is Reinstated." *Hartford Courant*, October 9, 1942, p. 1.

"Knox Demands Press and Radio Stay Free," *New York Times*, July 13, 1936, p. 4.

Lewis, Jon. "'We Do Not Ask You To Condone This.' How the Blacklist Saved Hollywood." *Cinema Journal* 39:2 (2000); 3–30.

"Matthews Meets Denials, Attacks," *New York Times*, December 11, 1939, p. 14.

Navasky, Victor S. *Naming Names*. 3rd ed. New York: Hill and Wang, 2003.

"New Review Asked by Convicted Reds." *New York Times*, September 28, 1950, p. 20.

Payne, Ethel L. "Robeson Remembered." *Pittsburgh Courier*, March 8, 1975, p. 6.

Reeves, Thomas C., ed. *McCarthyism*. Malabar, FL: Robert E. Krieger, 1985.

Storrs, Landon R. "Left-Feminism, the Consumer Movement, and Red Scare Politics in the United States, 1935–1960." *Journal Of Women's History* 18:3 (2006):40–67.

Wicker, Tom. *Shooting Star: The Brief Arc of Joe McCarthy*. New York: Harcourt, 2006.

An Unlikely Team: The Social Aspects of the Ground Observer Corps

5

David Mills

"Aircraft Flash," Mrs. Jane Prohosky called into the telephone. Within seconds, the receiver crackled, "Air Defense, go ahead." Prohosky continued, "Two aircraft, very high, heading west, Golf Alpha Five Zero Black" (Wilson, December 1954, 3). This transmission was not taking place during wartime, nor was it even made by a professional soldier. Prohosky was a volunteer at the Ground Observer Corps (GOC) post in Grant, Montana, calling her counterpart at headquarters in Helena during the Cold War in 1954. The GOC was an organization charged with searching the skies for Soviet aircraft that might try to sneak into the United States to bomb U.S. cities or other strategic sites—at the height of the Cold War, the period of tension between the United States and the Soviet Union.

Prohosky and hundreds of thousands of others just like her made up the first line of defense against nuclear attack. These volunteers ranged in background from Boy Scouts and Girl Scouts, to hardened criminals who were serving time in the nation's prisons; from newly arrived immigrants, to the Daughters of the American Revolution; from Native Americans, to members of the U.S. military; and from Hollywood stars, to homemakers. The volunteers were as different as any cross-section of a society could be, but they watched the skies every minute of the day, serving unselfishly from 1952 to 1959.

The Cold War intensified during the late 1940s, and many feared a Soviet attack in the 1950s. The Soviets had more than one thousand bombers and three thousand troop transport aircraft stationed at new air bases in northern and eastern Siberia, ready to strike into the United States through several routes. Military officials estimated that the Soviets could launch an attack over the Pacific Ocean and strike the West Coast, or fly over the North Pole, targeting the northern portion of the United States and perhaps Alaska. These planes could drop nuclear bombs or paratroopers, depending upon their mission. Military planners understood this threat and settled on three defensive measures to combat the possibility of attack. An array of radar systems could track incoming bombers or troop transports, although few operational radar existed by 1952. The U.S. Air Force maintained fighter aircraft on a high state of alert, routinely patrolling U.S. skies, ready to intercept any Soviet threat that ventured into U.S. airspace. As a final measure, the U.S. Army stood ready, with anti-aircraft weapons, including first-generation surface-to-air missiles.

Radar was the most problematic of these options, because low-flying aircraft were invisible to radar, and the small number of radar systems created holes in the radar coverage, meaning that Soviet planes could get through the early warning net undetected. Analyzing the problem, the secretary of the Air Force remarked, "Radar . . . is not completely effective in spotting low-flying aircraft, and it is not completely immune to jamming by enemy counter-radar" (Wilson, March 1957, 2). The Air Force relied on volunteers of the GOC to bridge this gap, watching the skies at remote observation posts and reporting aircraft sightings to officials for evaluation.

The military had formed the GOC during World War II, but it was disbanded at the end of the conflict. Air Force General Ennis C. Whitehead, responsible for the defense of North America during the early Cold War period, officially reconstituted the GOC in February 1952, although civil defense officials had organized hundreds of posts before this time, during a test phase. The Air Force initially estimated that it required 160,000 volunteers to operate the 8,000 observation sites throughout the north of the United States. This plan encompassed only 36 northern states prior to 1955, but increasing reliance on the GOC to supplement radar coverage led the Air Force to establish GOC stations in all of the lower 48 states and Alaska. Just prior to when the Air Force disbanded the GOC in early 1959, some 350,000 active observers stood watch at 16,000 observation posts throughout the United States.

Observers occupied old buildings, rooftops, or observation towers and scanned the sky for low-flying aircraft. Once an aircraft was spotted, volunteers tried to identify its altitude and direction of flight and then called their headquarters via commercial telephone and reported this specific information. This message, called an "Aircraft Flash Message," went to a headquarters, known as a Filter Center (FC), where officials consolidated information. Aircraft that observers could not positively identify as friendly required the nearest airbase to scramble jets, meet the unidentified aircraft, and confirm its identity. The observers served an important role, ensuring that only friendly aircraft occupied U.S. airspace. As General James W. McCauley, an Air Force official charged with defense reiterated in 1953, "If the skywatchers help alert the Air Defense Command of just one plane carrying just one atom bomb, that alone would justify the work of the GOC" (Wilson, October 1953, 7).

It was a matter of pride for many communities to build an observation post out of donated funds, labor, and materials and then operate the post with volunteers. The Air Force paid for the telephones and the cost of the calls, but the volunteers had to pay for the observation towers, their furnishings, and all utilities. It was amazing that some towns even organized a

Spotter looking out during Ground
Observer Corps training exercise, 1950s.
(Mark Kauffman/Time & Life Pictures/
Getty Images)

Pamela Burr

Pamela Burr was born around the turn of the twentieth century in the Bryn Mawr Hospital, located on the outskirts of Philadelphia, Pennsylvania. On the day that she was born, no one could have guessed that she would one day perch high on the roof of that same hospital building, keeping an eye out for aircraft and reporting their location to Air Force headquarters.

That is exactly what she did, however, for four hours each week, between 1954 until the end of the Ground Observer Corps (GOC) mission in 1959. Burr was one of hundreds of thousands of volunteers at the height of the Cold War who hoped that they were not wasting their time watching for Soviet aircraft that might never appear, but that might try to target U.S. cities.

Burr had seen many posters and heard many appeals on the radio for volunteers, and she answered the call as soon as the Air Force established a GOC post in her neighborhood. As she recalled some years later, she would rather work than worry and did not mind giving up a few hours each week. Burr worked many lonely shifts at the GOC posts, becoming more familiar with the different types of aircraft and reporting each with a confidence that grew with experience.

She often spoke to friends and neighbors about volunteering their time at the GOC post and received many different reactions. Some complied; others admired her dedication but did not have the time to volunteer. Others openly mocked her. The Soviets would never attack the United States, they argued. "No," she countered, "and I don't think my house will catch fire either, but I'm glad there is a fire station right around the corner, just in case."

post at all. New Hradek, North Dakota, for example, a town of 35 residents, accomplished the nearly impossible by establishing an observation that required one hundred volunteers. Residents recruited volunteers from out-lying areas and swelled the ranks of observers to 125. In other areas, some posts consisted of a single family, with one member home at all times to per-form spotting duties.

Volunteers were continuously in short supply because observation posts and the FCs required so many people to meet commitments. One hundred volunteers at an observation post meant that a volunteer could expect to work a four-hour shift every eight days. President Truman pled for volun-teers in 1952 to meet national requirements, and, early in his presidency, Dwight Eisenhower issued a statement on Soviet nuclear capabilities, also hoping to increase the number of volunteers in the GOC. Numerous state and local officials constantly reiterated the need for more volunteers throughout the tenure of the GOC, especially as the Air Force continuously increased the required number of GOC posts.

Radio broadcasts helped recruit volunteers, as did ice cream socials held at the FCs and observation posts. Creativity, however, was the most impor-tant element in a successful recruiting effort. "Target Sacramento" was a two-week recruiting effort to raise awareness of the GOC in 1953 and to remind citizens that the Soviets had targeted California's capital city with nuclear weapons. A week of community awareness through radio and press releases got the campaign underway; Boy Scouts distributed over 150,000 GOC leaflets to every home in the Sacramento area. Two shopping cen-ters hosted mobile displays of B-29 bombers, almost identical to the Soviet TU-4 bomber, driving home the realization that over one thousand Soviet bombers stood ready to attack the United States. Throughout the campaign, radio and television stations aired more than 1,400 GOC announcements and carried 15 live interviews with GOC workers. The drive ended with a meeting at the local fairgrounds, where at least one thousand citizens listened to presentations, participated in discussions, and watched Air Force officials present GOC workers with awards and medals.

The Baltimore GOC was also quite creative, collaborating with televi-sion station WMAR, which televised a scavenger hunt in December 1953, using GOC volunteers as contestants. The five participants wore GOC plac-ards, and each of the contestants received one of the following instructions: (1) a woman with handcuffs must return with a sailor locked to her; (2) a man with a hand mirror must return with a woman's wig; (3) a woman with a leash must return with a dog; (4) a man with a dress must return with a mannequin; (5) a woman must return with at least one GOC volun-teer. All of the contestants returned within 45 minutes, all successful.

In what has to be one of the first and most successful telemarketing campaigns, 150 civil defense workers from various organizations in Manchester, New Hampshire, called over 20,000 potential volunteers in July 1954, explaining the various organizations that needed help. Many civil defense organizations netted a number of volunteers, and over 300 vol-unteered for service with the GOC. Other creative ideas included a "bomb-ing raid" in Minot, North Dakota, where a local flyer dropped balloons over the city with requests for volunteers. Each balloon carried a free ticket to see *Invasion USA*, a popular movie viewed throughout the country that illustrated what might happen if Soviet bombers struck a U.S. city. Nationally, newspapers and magazines also helped in the recruitment effort. An advertisement in *Newsweek* depicted three observers at an observation post looking at the sky; the caption read: "Another town is safer tonight because these trained civilian members of the Ground Observer Corps are scanning the skies to warn against possible enemy attack" (*Newsweek*, November 28, 1955, 28) The advertisement proclaimed that many towns did not have such protection and encouraged concerned citizens to volunteer for the GOC. Other creative ideas for raising awareness of the GOC included beauty pageants—crowning an FC or GOC queen—and large numbers of floats entered in Independence Day or Veterans Day parades.

Many Hollywood actors lent their time and prestige to raise awareness for the need of the GOC and volunteers. Liberace, a popular concert pianist at the time, met with Mrs. Anne Hammer, a GOC volunteer in Chicago, offering congratulations on her selection as one of Chicago's "Volunteers of the Year" in 1954. Screen star Alan Ladd donated several hours of his time at a Chicago GOC post in 1956 while filming a movie, and actor Jimmy Stewart even had a GOC post operating on his ranch in Nevada. Stewart, perhaps best known for his role as George Bailey in *It's a Wonderful Life*, was a bomber pilot during World War II and held a reserve officer's commission in the Air Force after the war, attaining the rank of brigadier general. When Stewart got the chance, he liked to chat with volunteers like those in Reno, Nevada, in 1956. He was in town to receive an award for his film *Man from Laramie* and could not help stopping by the FC to observe the proceedings. "Never before in my life have I been so impressed," Stewart remarked. "It is amazing to see the extent to which this organization has developed" (Wilson, September 1956, 2).

Many women, homemakers for the most part, volunteered to help GOC operations; in fact, more than 65 percent of all GOC volunteers were women. In the 1950s, the world was a different place from today: women were not encouraged to find employment outside the home, and family expectations weighed heavily on a person's career choice. Margaret Orr, for example, planned to join the army like her brother, but family objections forced her to reconsider, and she found satisfaction volunteering at a GOC post. There were probably as many reasons that women joined the GOC as there were women, but two consistent themes emerged. First, many women had lost loved ones in World War I, World War II, or the Korean War and felt the need to serve in their place. Second, many women simply felt the need to serve their country for the same patriotic reasons that men served in the military, and the GOC was a respectable alternative to military service.

Other women had reasons that are more personal. "I haven't forgotten how frightened we were at the time of Pearl Harbor," recalled Florence Bilyeu of Bremerton, Washington (Wilson, August 1954, 4). When she heard GOC members asking for volunteers in her area, she immediately offered her time and effort to aircraft spotting duties. Mrs. Helen Shaffer of

Hutchinson, Kansas, was working as a journalist in the Philippine capital of Manila and became a prisoner of the Japanese when they overran the island. As a prisoner, Shaffer learned the value of freedom and later remarked, "What we civilians of the allied nations had not done was to help in preparedness of an attack" (Wilson, August 1954, 4). Shaffer served many hours in the GOC as an aircraft spotter during the Cold War, believing that security was its own reward.

In addition to spotting and reporting aircraft, women carried out a number of administrative and recruiting efforts. One such woman was Mrs. Lila Hall, supervisor of the post at Grand Marais, Minnesota, who wrote a number of articles for the local newspaper about the necessity of air defense and was largely responsible for the fact that 450 of her fellow residents were members of the GOC. Whatever their reasons for volunteering, women GOC members gave freely of their time, talent, and energy to help their local communities and their nation prepare for the unthinkable.

Many Americans had their personal stories, but newly arrived immigrants had their own reasons to volunteer. "I know what it means to lose my country—don't lose yours," advised Julius Szakats, who worked in the FC in Sioux Falls, South Dakota (Wilson, October 1953, 3). Szakats was born in Budapest, Hungary, and was the son of a Supreme Court justice when the Soviets invaded his homeland and forced his family to flee in 1940. His family spent five years in a displaced persons camp in Germany before making their way to the United States. Mrs. Janina Lehr was an active GOC volunteer in her native Poland in the 1930s, listening for airplanes and reporting sightings to her government. When the Germans invaded her country in 1939, she and other members of her family hid in caves until the Germans captured them. They deported Lehr to a slave labor camp, and she never saw her family again. When officials organized the GOC in her hometown of Kinsley, Kansas, she immediately volunteered, hoping to prevent an invasion of her adopted country. Mrs. Ingerid Braenne of Trondheim, Norway, understood what it was like to lose her country, but she was lucky enough to reclaim her native land after the allies defeated the German Army, who had occupied the Norway area for over five years. When she came to visit her brother in Connecticut, Braenne explained that Norway had a similar GOC organization, lest the country suffer a similar fate under the Soviets.

One of the attractions of the GOC was the opportunity to serve the nation regardless of physical ability; citizens with physical challenges found they could serve effectively despite their limitations. One such young man was John Anspauch, a polio victim who wanted to volunteer at the GOC post in Walla Walla, Washington. The difficulty was the location of the post—high in a former airport control tower; the climb up the stairs was difficult, even for those without disabilities. Anspauch was undeterred. He decided he could still assist with administrative duties, helping to write letters to potential volunteers and paying utility bills in the office located on the ground floor. He never saw the inside of the observation tower.

William Swayze was another volunteer who did not let his physical condition deter him from duty. Swayze, who lost both of his legs in an industrial accident, spent much of his day organizing the shifts at the GOC tower at Lapeer, Michigan, by using his bedside telephone to call volunteers to fill in where needed. Post supervisor Sherry Rinn told reporters that Swayze "was nearly as indispensable to our program as one man can be" (Wilson, September 1953, 7). The Freedom Foundation, a nonprofit and nonpolitical organization that awarded cash and medals to Americans who contributed to the U.S. way of life, awarded the George Washington Honor Medal to Swayze on behalf of the GOC.

An unlikely pair of observers in Roylston, Massachusetts, proved themselves capable of contributing to their nation's defense, despite their limitations. Mrs. Alice Clark, who was partially deaf, handled the aircraft spotting duties, while her son Richard, who was blind, used the telephone to pass communications to the FC. Richard, however, did a fair amount of "spotting" as well. He could hear planes that others could not, and he could tell—by sound—the number of motors and the direction of the aircraft's flight—talents that proved necessary on many cloudy days and at night. For their contributions to the Roylston GOC, the Air Force awarded each of them the Meritorious Service Award.

Some older Americans also felt a strong desire to serve their country, and many of the volunteers at GOC posts were veterans of the nation's many wars. Examples of veterans who volunteered their time included the observers at the Custer National Monument in Montana. Seven veterans of three U.S. wars, all of whom lived and worked on the battlefield grounds, kept watch for enemy aircraft throughout each night, while other volunteers kept watch during the day. Not far away, in Columbia Falls, Montana, 40 veterans at the State Soldiers Home, some of whom saw action in the Spanish-American War in 1898, organized a GOC post. The post operated from 6 a.m. to 8 p.m. daily and occupied a strategic location, only 15 miles from the Canadian border. The veterans were meticulous in their tracking and reporting, sometimes reporting dozens of aircraft in a single day. Even a Civil War veteran was not too old to contribute to the GOC. Bill Lundy of Crestwood, Florida, was 109 years old and a Confederate veteran of the Civil War, earning a GOC Certificate of Achievement in 1956. Although Air Force officials noted that the award was more for honorary purposes than it was for achievement, Lundy's positive attitude and desire to help was an inspiration to many other volunteers at the post.

Although Lundy had the distinction of serving in the Confederate Army, another member of the GOC had the honor of being the first observer ever to send an "Aircraft Flash Message." A. W. Drinkwater of Durham, North Carolina, was present at the first flight of the Wright brothers' plane on the wind-swept dunes of Kittyhawk and immediately sent a telegraph reporting the event. Interestingly, no one believed him when he reported that an aircraft had made a short flight under its own power. Another GOC member of distinction was John Nance Garner, a former vice president, who served two terms under President Franklin D. Roosevelt. At age of 87 in 1956, Garner volunteered for duty with the GOC, saying, "I have been an American all my life; the American people have made me what I am, and the least I can do is to help keep the country what it is" (Wilson, February 1956, 11).

Many disabled and mature citizens contributed significantly to the security of the nation through the GOC, but many younger Americans served as well. The GOC sought out conscientious Americans, regardless of age, who would donate their time and enthusiasm, working to protect their nation from Communism. Perhaps no other organizations fit this mold as well as the Boy Scouts, the Girl Scouts, and the Explorer Scouts. The Explorer Scouts were an organization headquartered under the Boy Scouts of America, but it included older boys, usually in their teens. The Explorer Scouts included Explorer posts, Sea Explorer ships, and Air Explorer squadrons; each group affiliated itself with a branch of the military.

Regardless of the scouting organization, Boy Scout, Girl Scout, or Explorer Scout, two major watchwords of each group were selflessness and service. The manuals stated, "Service is as much a necessity of life as food, clothing, and housing. Without it, the progress of neighborhoods, communities, and whole countries would bog down." Furthermore, the manuals noted that one could not just talk a project to completion—achievement came only through action. Thus, the GOC and the Scouts made a natural alliance. The GOC needed volunteers committed to preserving the nation,

Boy Scout delivers message to amateur radio "ham" operators during a civil defense exercise in Binghamton, New York, in 1957. (Binghamton [NY] Press/National Archives and Records Administration)

and the Scouts needed projects with a similar goal. The Scouts began standing watches at observation posts as early as 1951 and began working in FCs less than a year later. Over 9,000 Explorer Scouts, Boy Scouts, and Girl Scouts regularly worked as part of the GOC in concert with their entire scout unit or as individuals.

Teenagers comprised all of the volunteers at the GOC post in Stockholm, Maine. The boys and girls obtained an old skating rink and, through their hard work, converted it into a GOC post, but the transition was not easy. They borrowed binoculars, cut their own wood for heat in the winter, patched the walls of the building with cardboard, and went without lights—until the local newspaper ran a story reporting their amazing effort. Adults in the community pitched in, contributing money and material, and fixing the lighting system. The post seemed luxurious after its humble beginnings, but the effort helped bring the adults and the teens closer together for a worthwhile cause. Similarly, a group of teenage boys in Westerville, Ohio, became interested in plane spotting through television and radio advertisements. They organized a post in an old barn, and, for nearly a year, they detected and recorded aircraft but had no telephone with which to make reports to the FC in Columbus, Ohio. The FC, in fact, had no knowledge of the boys' activities, until a story in the Columbus newspaper sparked an interest and pushed officials into action. Within a few days, the Air Force had installed a phone, and the boys were in business, operating the post entirely by themselves.

Another group of teenagers who showed an incredible amount of initiative lived in Grand Rapids, Michigan. Those young people agreed to work in the local FC, but they soon discovered that there was a serious shortage of volunteers. They joined forces with a local amateur movie club and produced a 5-minute color film entitled, *Operation Teenager*, targeting other young people and encouraging them to join the GOC. The teenagers bore the cost of making the movie, which was shown in school assemblies and around Grand Rapids, resulting in a number of other teens volunteering their time at a GOC post or the FC.

The GOC affected many people during the 1950s, but no one could have imagined that the program would have such a positive influence upon the nation's criminals, including the Minnesota State Reformatory for Men, located three miles south of St. Cloud. When W. F. Mero first suggested using inmates as GOC volunteers, prison officials were not enthusiastic about the proposal. Many thought it would not work, because the inmates were too unruly, and that allowing the inmates to stay on the roof of the prison at night was simply inviting trouble. Mero persisted and finally won approval for his plan in February 1952. Officials selected ten inmates initially—all trustees from among hundreds of applications—and began operations around the clock. New volunteers replaced the released prisoner-observers, 35 by 1954, and only two inmates returned to prison, a 50 percent improvement over the average parolee. Other prisons adopted observation posts and used inmates as observers, including the notorious San Quentin prison in California and the Detroit House of Corrections.

Although many posts operated effectively throughout the United States, prudence dictated that the GOC needed outposts as far to the north as possible, where the Air Force could intercept enemy bombers before they reached their targets. One of the northernmost posts was in Minnesota, in a strip of land called the Northwest Angle, a peninsula off the Canadian land mass and separated from the rest of the United States by water. There, a pulpwood camp for the Minnesota and Ontario Paper Company operated an observation post from the 80-foot fire lookout tower. Once observers spotted an aircraft—a rare occurrence in the isolated forest—one of the spotters would radio the State Division of Forestry office in Warroad, Minnesota, and forward the information to the Minneapolis FC. The company had seven other lumber camps that performed GOC duties throughout northern Minnesota and a number of trucks with radios that also performed GOC functions.

For 17-year-old Larry Gray, his summer job in 1953 was to perch high aloft in the Wolf Creek Lookout Tower in the eastern California forest. He kept a sharp eye out for forest fires, but he kept watch for airplanes as well. The Wolf Creek Tower was one of 1,300 federal, state, county, and private towers throughout the nation that performed the double duty of fire watch and aircraft spotting. Most of these towers operated only in the summer months, when the chance of fire was at its peak, but these towers and their observers boosted the overall number of aircraft spotters on duty. With very little organizational effort or cost, the GOC gained 1,300 posts; the people who staffed the towers usually welcomed the additional responsibility, because it provided a distraction from an often-monotonous task. As one U.S. Forestry official put it, "We are glad to be of service to our air defense system. Skywatching fits perfectly into our fire lookout program . . . since both are designed to provide protection against destructive enemies" (Wilson, August 1953, 3–4).

Remote sites seem to make good GOC sites. Television engineers staffing a transmitter site for a station in Burlington, Vermont, also served as GOC observers, and only four men provided continuous surveillance throughout the year. Their post was located on Mt. Mansfield, which was also well known for the ski resort that shared the mountain's slopes. In fact, in order to get to their post, the engineers had to ride the chair lift to the top of the mountain and then ski or hike the rest of the way in. Accommodations were comfortable, even though trucks delivered most supplies during the summer months.

Many ethnic groups volunteered their time to the GOC, including a number of members of Native American tribes, "doing as much for their country as if they were in the Air Force," observed one government official (Wilson, May 1956, 11). The Papago Indian Reservation in Tucson, Arizona, hosted a GOC post, staffed by Native Americans, Franciscan priests, and government schoolteachers. They lacked a reliable telephone system, with only a few party lines coming into the reservation, and had one of the largest areas to cover, as large as some eastern states. Despite these obstacles, they performed admirably. Members of the Blackfoot tribe in Montana staffed several GOC posts, including one at a school on their reservation known as the Star School. Phillip Sellew, whose father was one of General Custer's scouts at the Battle of the Little Big Horn and managed to escape the battlefield alive, was an advisor to the students and worked as a special officer of the Blackfoot tribe. Sellew helped organize the post but noted that the students kept it going.

Another reservation school in South Dakota was active as a GOC post. Mr. Manahan, principal of the school on the Lower Brule Reservation and supervisor of the post, reported that students and tribal members not only served their country, but learned other important lessons; many members of the tribe had never used a phone before the post went into operation. Each post that the Native Americans staffed earned high marks in evaluations and rarely missed reporting aircraft flying over its area. Not all of the Native Americans associated with the GOC posts were helpful, however. Post Supervisor Keith L. Donohoo of Pearl, Illinois, reported that his community had constructed a GOC post on the site of an ancient Indian burial ground, and apparently, some of those spirits still frequented the area. Several times, binoculars or other items came up missing, only to reappear after a thorough search.

A float entered into the Billings, Montana, "Western Day" parade portrayed a Native American sending smoke signals, drawing a correlation between the GOC mission to detect and report enemies within their midst with that of the old Indian method. Continuing the analogy, an old Texas Ranger named Captain Tom Hickman said that he watched for smoke signals from Indian raiding parties around the turn of the century, but as an aircraft spotter for the GOC, he kept watch for vapor trails of enemy aircraft trying to penetrate U.S. defenses.

Having a GOC post close to the Soviet border was strategically desirable, and Alaska was a perfect spot. Only a few miles separated it from the Soviet Union, and an air armada might pass through the territory on its way to targets in the continental United States. The problems of establishing an effective GOC organization were formidable, because the weather was unfavorable for much of the year, there was no communication infrastructure, and many of the native people did not speak English. The location was too perfect and the benefits were too great, however, and the Air Force ordered the problems overcome. The Alaskan Air Command and the Alaska Civil Defense Office began recruiting volunteers and solving problems, and, within a few years, they had built a system covering the entire state. According to Air Force officials, the greatest attribute of the state was its people, who volunteered in great numbers to assist the United States in its defense. The people of Alaska made outstanding aircraft spotters, one Air Force official recalled, because they were acutely aware of changes in sight and sound because of their isolation. Additionally, airplanes were a common site throughout Alaska, and many citizens recognized different types of planes and were familiar with regularly scheduled flights and pilots. Alaskans quickly reported any strange aircraft flying at odd hours, earning the gratitude of the Air Force.

Even though the GOC had overcome many issues to establish an effective reporting system, many obstacles persisted. Few phones existed in the

Alaska wilderness, so GOC observers sent messages by dog sled when atmospheric conditions prohibited radio communication. Most GOC posts had no heating system, and, in a region where temperatures could reach 50 degrees below zero, this could prove a significant issue to the average volunteer. Native people in Alaska had two attributes to overcome the weather, however—a strong sense of patriotism and a hardy constitution. Alaskan observers regularly stood watch outside the GOC post, where few planes escaped their watchful eyes. The Alaska GOC was the only one in Air Defense Command that did not have an FC; instead, observers sent all messages directly to Air Force headquarters for evaluation. In a country one-fifth the size of the continental United States and given the incredible number of problems to overcome, it is difficult to imagine the magnitude of the highly successful GOC system within the state.

Throughout the United States, one of the benefits of having citizens staffing an official post with a wide view of the surrounding countryside was the assistance that these volunteers could render in time of emergency. When a U.S. Navy airplane exploded and crashed on a farm north of Odessa, Delaware, the two observers in a nearby GOC post called a report to officials in the FC, who requested rescue personnel from the Air Force, even as the crew's parachutes were visible in the air. Rescue personnel found the downed pilots, shaken but uninjured. In nearby West Virginia, torrential floods destroyed several communities because of the spring thaws, creating a situation that called for GOC help. Observers around the state called in weather reports to other civil defense centers and helped coordinate rescue efforts, leading to Post Supervisor D. F. Tabor's Distinguished Achievement Award for his assistance in Logan, West Virginia.

Another natural disaster that could have had disastrous results occurred in Oklahoma, in 1956. On the evening of April 2, observers at the GOC post in Cushing, Oklahoma, observed a funnel-shaped cloud formation, outlined by flashes of lightening, and noted that the community of Drumright lay in the path of the forming tornado. The observers called the FC in Oklahoma City, who turned the information over to the U.S. Weather Bureau, who in turn notified authorities in Drumright. The entire communications effort took less than ten minutes, enough time for residents to take cover. "If the community of Drumright had not received this advance warning," noted state Civil Defense director Tom Brett, "we have no idea how many casualties would have resulted from this thing" (Wilson, June 1956, 5). Other GOC posts throughout the United States also prevented numerous casualties by using their communication system to warn citizens of approaching tornados, saving an unknown number of lives.

Most emergencies left little question as to what had transpired, but this was not always the case, as when the fishing vessel *Josephine* was lost at sea. Lucky for the crew, Mrs. Alberta Smith was on duty at the Cedar Key, Florida, GOC post, and reported sighting three red flares off the coast of the Gulf of Mexico. The FC relayed her report to the Coast Guard, which sent a plane to search the area. After several hours of looking at an empty sea and on the verge of abandoning the search, the aircraft sighted the fishing boat, missing for more than eight days after the Coast Guard had called off the previous search because of hurricane *Debbie*. The crew members of the

Josephine were delighted to see the plane and explained after their rescue that they had had no food or water and no flares. No one knows what Smith saw from her GOC post, but it was not the fishing boat sending distress signals, nor any other craft that the Coast Guard could find.

The Air Force spent time and money developing new radar and tracking techniques throughout the 1950s, but perhaps it should have been investing money into "stovepipe technology." According to GOC observers Mr. and Mrs. Bob Grant of Hooper Bay, Alaska, whenever an aircraft flew near their home, their stovepipe rattled. Numerous tests proved the device was infallible, and it began to rattle long before the aircraft was audible to human ears. As Pedro and Fi Fi proved, however, human ears or stovepipes were not always preferred. Pedro, a dog of mixed pedigree, and Fi Fi, a white duck of unknown species, traveled with their human companions nearly every day to the GOC post in Albuquerque, New Mexico. The animals soon learned to detect aircraft long before their human counterparts and sounded the alert in a noisy manner. Other animals received attention from the GOC community, although not always in a positive way. Twice observers at the GOC post in Kennebunk, Maine, started to call their FC to report a massive air armada coming in from the Atlantic, only to realize that the "planes" were actually large flocks of seagulls.

Many patriotic Americans could not serve in uniform during the Cold War, but the opportunity to serve in the GOC gave many citizens a sense of pride in serving their country. Radar improvements gradually reduced the reliance upon civilian volunteers by 1958 and eliminated the requirement

A Distant Early Warning Line station in Bullen Point, Alaska. (Library of Congress)

for 24-hour alert. Air Force authorities disbanded the GOC by early 1959; numerous closure ceremonies throughout the nation marked the end of the proud tradition of the GOC.

The growing scope and efficiency of new radar systems gave officials the assurance that they could detect an enemy strike before it reached the United States, without the assistance of the GOC. Specifically, radar of the Distant Early Warning (DEW) Line across the Arctic—and its extension through ships and airborne platforms—into the Atlantic and Pacific Oceans, coupled with a similar line across the midpoint of Canada, provided the United States with a technological alternative to human detection efforts. Furthermore, the new Semi-Automatic Ground Environment (SAGE) System, an early computer-based communication system, transmitted aircraft "sighting" from a remote outpost to Air Force installations almost instantaneously, making human communications outmoded. Finally, technological advances in jet aircraft allowed bombers to fly higher and faster than humans could detect them, permitting the Air Force to relieve GOC volunteers of the surveillance burden. In sum, the Air Force was entering a new phase of aircraft detection, relying on technology to counter any invasion threat.

Lieutenant General Joseph H. Atkinson, the Air Defense Commander responsible for the GOC and its deactivation, wrote a personal letter to each of the GOC post supervisors with this tribute:

> You have borne these duties well and faithfully and have provided invaluable assistance to the air defense of our country. We will be forever grateful for your sacrifices. A most significant aspect of your work in the GOC is that it shows what free and independent people can accomplish through voluntary association and spiritual unity in the cause of the nation's security. I salute and commend all volunteers for a job well done. The Air Force, the Air Defense Command, and, indeed, all American citizens owe you a great debt of gratitude for helping the air defense system deter aggression. I hope that the Air Force will continue to merit the confidence and support you have so generously given it in the past. (Wilson, January 1959, 3–4)

The purpose of the GOC was to detect, identify, and then report enemy airplanes invading U.S. airspace. Because the Soviet Union never attacked the United States, the GOC never fulfilled its ultimate mission. Volunteers might argue, however, that the Soviets never attacked the United States knowing that the GOC was standing watch. In this sense, the GOC was highly successful and served in other unforeseen roles as well. The GOC lent assistance to numerous commercial and military aircraft, sometimes calling for rescue teams when a plane went down. Volunteers also reported innumerable natural disasters, from tornado warnings, to communications during floods and fires, in all instances saving human life and valuable property. Hundreds of thousands of volunteers, from diverse backgrounds and economic circumstances, gave freely of their time and talent during the tenure of the GOC from 1952 to 1959. As John Milton, the blind poet once stated, "They also serve, who only stand and wait" (Wilson, August 1954, 1).

References and Further Reading

"Another Town is Safer Tonight. . . ." *Newsweek*. November 28, 1955.

Bond, Priscilla H. *Army Air Force Ground Observer Corps of Jefferson, Maine*. Jefferson, ME: Jefferson Historical Society, 1992.

Burr, Pamela. "I Am a Sky Sentry." *Saturday Evening Post*, July 9,1955.

"How Russia Can Strike: An Enemy Air Force Has the Power to Hit Us in Three Ways." *Life*. January 22, 1951.

Kew, George. "Defense: The Supersonic Shield." *Time*, December 20, 1954.

Morgan, Mark L., and Mark A. Berhow. *Rings of Supersonic Steel: Air Defense of the United States Army, 1950–1979*. San Pedro, CA: Fort MacArthur Press, 2002.

"New Hradec Sets Example." *Dickinson* (North Dakota) *Press*. March 5, 1953.

"Pilot to Bomb Minot with Balloons Saturday." *Ward County* (North Dakota) *Independent*, February 26, 1953.

Schaffel, Kenneth. *The Emerging Shield: The Air Force and the Evolution of Continental Air Defense, 1945–1960*. Honolulu: University Press of the Pacific, 2004.

Shalett, Sidney. "They Hope They're Wasting Their Time." *Saturday Evening Post*, September 26, 1957.

Wilson, Gill Robb. "Interview with General Chidlaw: Air Defense." *Flying: The World's Most Widely Read Aviation Magazine*, August 1955.

Wilson, Jeff, ed. *The Aircraft Flash: Official Magazine of the GOC*. Colorado Springs: Department of the Air Force, 1952–1959.

McCarthyism and the Cold War against Organized Labor in the United States

6

Saranna Thornton

Union Local 22 of the Food, Tobacco, Agricultural and Allied Workers (FTA) represented employees of the R. J. Reynolds Tobacco Company in Winston-Salem, North Carolina—with over 7,000 members in 1941. Through collective bargaining and well-timed strikes, the left-led FTA dramatically improved the working conditions of Reynolds' mostly female, mostly African American workforce. The FTA actions to help its members went beyond the factory walls. They encouraged the workers to vote in state and local elections and to join the National Association for the Advancement of Colored People (NAACP). In 1947, an African American was elected to Winston-Salem's Board of Aldermen, and improvements were made in the provision of public services to the city's black community.

Also, in 1947, HUAC arrived in Winston-Salem to investigate the Communist affiliations of Local 22's leadership. This local hearing was accompanied by a Red-baiting campaign in the local press, thus weakening support for the Union within the broader community. Reynolds struck additional blows by redesigning its manufacturing process to eliminate the jobs of many of the unskilled African American women, who were the backbone of the Union's membership. By 1950, Local 22 was no longer functioning, and the Reynolds' plant remained unorganized—to the great detriment of the remaining employees.

Similar purges of left-led unions, all over the country, during the McCarthy period had an enormously deleterious effect on the U.S. labor movement. It inhibited the ability of unions to challenge a social order that elevated the value of capital (machines and money) over the value of labor (people) and was a retarding force in both the nascent civil rights movement and the women's movement.

McCarthyism, as defined by historians, refers to much more than the actions of Wisconsin's Senator McCarthy during his ten years, and two terms, in the U.S. Senate. The period from 1946 to 1956 was one of the most widespread periods of political repression in U.S. history. Although the alleged goal of the movement was to protect national security, the movement directly or indirectly infringed on the civil rights of hundreds of thousands of Americans. In order to eliminate an overblown threat of domestic Communist movements, a broad coalition of politicians, bureaucrats, school boards, businessmen, and even leaders in competing labor unions hounded a generation of people who sought to change the economic and political status quo. Although just a small percentage of left-wing change agents were charged with crimes and sent to prison, the lives and careers of many more were destroyed. And institutions offering left-wing alternatives to the status quo, including civil rights groups such as the NAACP and the U.S. labor movement, were seriously weakened.

Labor unions, also known as "organized labor," are groups of workers who have joined together to achieve common workplace goals. Union leaders negotiate employment contracts on behalf of their members (i.e., collective bargaining). Topics of negotiation typically include wages; the employer's hiring, firing, and promotion policies; fringe benefits; and workplace safety. To understand the enormity of the impact of McCarthyism on organized labor in the United States requires an understanding of some earlier events in the history of the U.S. labor movement.

Labor unions became increasingly important in the wake of the Industrial Revolution. The Industrial Revolution changed workplace norms in the United States from a context in which most free people were self-employed—as farmers, shopkeepers, blacksmiths, shoemakers, etc.—to one in which most working people became the employees of others—working in coal mines, garment factories, steel mills, and slaughter houses.

Work was impersonal, and there was constant pressure to reduce labor costs. Work days were long, work conditions were dangerous, and employees were exploited through the payment of low wages for arduous, dangerous work. Because the number of people who wanted to work and needed to work was plentiful, it was easy for employers to replace a single employee who tried to bargain for better work conditions or higher wages. Very quickly, the "troublesome" employee was fired and replaced by another worker who was desperate to earn money to pay for food and shelter.

Individual, national unions of skilled craftsmen (e.g., printers, carpenters) concluded that they could increase their power to secure better working conditions if they jointed together, and so they formed the American Federation of Labor (AFL) in 1886. The AFL was a confederation of sovereign national craftsmen's unions that were allowed to be autonomous within their own jurisdictions. If the carpenter's union wanted to make job security the primary focus of its negotiations with the firm and the toolmaker's union wanted to make workplace safety its focus, each union had the freedom to do so. The unions within the federation represented workers who might have different employers, but who were in the same occupation. Thus carpenters working in a steel factory and carpenters working for a railroad would all belong to the same union. The role of the AFL was to coordinate the efforts of the individual unions in political and educational activities where their interests overlapped.

The AFL was an aggressive group led by Samuel Gompers and other men who were heavily influenced by the work of Karl Marx (e.g., *The Communist Manifesto, Das Kapital*). Ultimately, they abandoned most Marxist principles as time went on, but they held fast to the belief that the interests of workers were distinct from those of business owners—and that workers had to fight for better pay and working conditions. Although they began as Marxists, Gompers and the other AFL leaders did not advocate the overthrow of capitalism but concluded that workers should try to get as much of the pie as possible—through the process of collective bargaining.

The roots of U.S. anti-Communism also go back to the Industrial Revolution and tactics used to put a stop to the industrial unrest and working class movements of the 1870s and 1880s. Firms opposed to organized labor realized that anti-Communism was an effective rhetorical tool with which to disarm the labor movement. By publicizing their anti-union activities as merely anti-Communist activities. employers could legitimize their opposition to organized labor without even having to address the economic issues related to the exploitation of U.S. workers.

Despite some successes, from 1880 through the 1920s, union membership in the United States generally remained below 10 percent of the non-farm workforce. Then, in October 1929, the stock market crashed, and, like a tsunami, recessionary forces quickly toppled other sectors of the economy. Between 1929 and 1933, the national output of goods and services declined by 29 percent. The unemployment rate rose to 25 percent, and many who remained employed managed to find only part-time work. Families were evicted from their farms and homes. Cardboard settlements of homeless families were common. Although local charities attempted to provide relief, they were overwhelmed by the vast numbers of the unemployed and impoverished.

Labor activist and founder of the American Federation of Labor (AFL), Samuel Gompers served as president from the organization's inception in 1886 until his death in 1924. (National Archives)

The enormous depth and length of the Great Depression caused broad swaths of the U.S. population to question capitalism itself. The idea that businesses operating in a capitalist system could promote widespread economic prosperity was discarded by many. In enormous numbers, workers looked elsewhere for institutions to provide for their welfare more consistently. One of the institutions that some Americans turned to was the Communist Party (CP) and other Communist-led community organizations. The CP members didn't just talk about the ways in which they believed Communism would improve the welfare of Americans; they were active in dealing with the painful impacts of the Great Depression. They organized community organizations to fight the evictions of people who were being thrown out of their homes, and they organized people to march on their local city halls, demanding relief. CP members worked tirelessly to organize labor unions and then used their unions to bargain militantly for better working conditions.

When Franklin Delano Roosevelt (FDR) became president in 1933, he promised help from another institution. FDR offered Americans a "New Deal"—under which government would exercise a more active role in the economy—more heavily regulating business (e.g., banking and financial services), setting a wage floor by guaranteeing a minimum wage for workers in non-agricultural employment, providing social insurance programs (e.g., unemployment insurance, Social Security) that would help people who were in need.

Unions benefited dramatically from the rising doubts about capitalism—and there was substantial growth in union membership. Between 1933 and 1939, membership tripled. Although membership in the various AFL craft unions was growing, a different kind of unionization was becoming more prevalent. Specifically, the rise of industrialized mass production industries in autos, rubber and tires, electrical products, etc. had created an enormous workforce of unskilled and semi-skilled workers, most of whom were ignored by AFL drives to organize skilled workers. In 1935, leaders of seven AFL-affiliated unions that had been organized along industrial lines (e.g., United Mine Workers) created the Committee for Industrial Organization (CIO), which was to pursue union-building in mass-production industries. The AFL suspended the unions whose leaders had formed this committee, so, in 1938, they formed the CIO to focus on unionizing workers in unskilled and semi-skilled manufacturing jobs. By 1938, the CIO was composed of 35 industrial unions. Estimates are that the industrial unions gained 2 million members between 1936 and 1941—roughly a tripling of the membership.

The year 1935 was also particularly fruitful for the union movement because that was when the federal National Labor Relations (i.e., Wagner) Act was passed. Although the first labor unions had actually appeared during colonial times, U.S. law was generally unfriendly to unions and the whole concept of workers banding together to bargain collectively. Initially, unions were considered to be illegal cartels in which workers created a monopoly on the supply of labor to employers, with the end result being the fixing of prices (i.e., wages, which are the price of labor).

The Wagner Act effectively overturned case-law rulings that declared labor unions to be illegal cartels or criminal conspiracies. Employees were guaranteed the right to form unions, bargain collectively, and work collectively for the mutual benefit of members. Additionally, the law prohibited many tactics used by employers to prevent unions from being effective bargaining agents. Employers were disallowed from interfering in the formation or administration of labor unions, from discriminating against workers who sought to organize or join unions, to otherwise discourage employees from joining unions, or to refuse to bargain with duly elected union leaders. To be effective, a law requires efficient enforcement mechanisms. Thus, the National Labor Relations Board (NLRB) was created for two reasons: (1) to resolve questions surrounding a particular union's rights to represent a specific group of workers and (2) to adjudicate complaints of unfair labor practices by employers. The Wagner Act radically changed the economic environment, from one that was hostile to unions to one that was supportive of union organization and negotiation. From Kentucky coal mines, to the San Francisco waterfront, to tobacco plants in North Carolina and auto factories in Michigan, union membership and union power grew.

During World War II, unions and business leaders had an informal armistice, agreeing that their primary concern would be increasing domestic production in order to contribute to the war effort. In order to maximize domestic output, without setting off waves of inflation, FDR's administration imposed wage and price freezes, which prohibited firms from increasing either the prices of their products or the wages of their workers. So striking for higher wages was considered not only unpatriotic—but was also unlawful. When World War II ended in 1945, the informal armistice ended too. However, the Cold War had just begun.

Clearly, Soviet Communism posed threats for the United States. But one might ask how specific threats coming from specific places morphed into a national paranoia intended to find and root out the Communists who were supposedly lurking in every corner of U.S. society, just waiting for the opportune time to overthrow the government violently. Communist Parties and Communist sympathies were substantially greater in the democracies of Western Europe, but none of those nations experienced outbursts of accusation and repression equivalent to that experienced in the United States between 1946 and 1956.

Although there were many individuals in the private sector who were all too happy to jump on the anti-Communist bandwagon, the United States would likely not have made eliminating Communist influence such a high priority if government officials in Washington, D.C., had not made it such a high priority. Actions taken by the federal government in the late 1940s helped create the national anti-Communist consensus that drew so many U.S. citizens into behaviors that violated the civil rights of their neighbors. The federal government's anti-Communist actions were not directed from a single source. All three branches of government acted, often independently, in the anti-Communist crusade. Although the name of the paranoid anti-Communist movement drew its name from the junior senator from Wisconsin, Joseph McCarthy, the executive branch of government actually wielded more power in the anti-Communist campaigns. Executive agencies in the Truman administration wanted to build up popular support for the Cold War and generate substantial bipartisan support for its foreign policy. Republicans, eager to wrest power from the Democratic administration, used the anti-Communist movement as means to charge that Truman was soft on Communism and should not be elected president in 1948.

McCarthyism was not monolithic within the national government—nor was it monolithic in its private sector manifestations. There were a variety of anti-Communist movements during this period that had differing agendas and utilized different tactics. Some ultraconservative versions of McCarthyism marketed themselves as patriotic groups, organized to purge textbooks of favorable references to the Soviet Union, Communism, and the United Nations. There were segregationists who pinned the label of Communist on civil rights workers in order to prolong the dominance of white power in a post-World War II era that was increasingly characterized by a movement for racial equality. There were business leaders who sought to define the Communist-led labor movement as a form of industrial sabotage and so used anti-Communist strategies and tactics to reduce the bargaining power of their unions. And there were politically conservative union leaders who used the anti-Communist movement as a means to eliminate challengers for positions in union leadership who were either left-leaning or Communist.

The period immediately following the war was known as Reconversion. The enormous government regulation of virtually every aspect of the economy—from production, to distribution, to consumption of goods and services—was meant to maximize the amount of material, machine, and labor resources that could flow into the war effort. Clearly, once the war ended, various government regulations needed to be unwound. But there was much disagreement regarding the optimal way to do this. Organized labor sought to maintain rigid enforcement of price controls while eliminating government-imposed wage freezes. Firms wanted to retain wage freezes but eliminate price controls. As wages and prices were unfrozen together, firms responded by raising their prices, and union members once again sought to bargain for higher wages and improved working conditions. During the 12 months from August 1945 to August 1946, there were 4,630 strikes, involving 4.9 million workers and production losses of 119.8 million worker-days. Large strikes rippled across the auto industry, coal, rail transportation, mining, oil refining, and the production of electrical goods.

Public concern over the number and pervasiveness of union-organized work stoppages was partly responsible for the election of an anti-New Deal Republican majority to Congress in 1946, including the junior senator from Wisconsin, Joseph McCarthy. Republican candidates across the United States attacked their Democratic opponents, as supporters of New Deal socialism, as encouraging domestic radicalism, and as failing to contain Soviet aggression effectively in Eastern Europe. The deterioration of U.S.-Soviet relations, in the wake of World War II, provided a comfortable environment for Republican and other anti-union forces to attack organized labor for being soft on Communism and for stirring up trouble during the

Mounted police clash with strikers outside an electrical plant in Philadelphia, in 1946. (National Archives)

1945–1946 strikes in order to weaken U.S. industrial production and thus its ability to stand up to Soviet aggression.

In a Gallup poll conducted in December 1946, the question was asked: "Should Congress in this coming legislative session pass new laws to control labor unions?" (Orshinsky, 1976, 64). Only 12 percent of the respondents were undecided, 22 percent disagreed, and an overwhelming 66 percent supported the statement.

The National Labor Management Relations (Taft-Hartley) Act of 1947 was one of the early salvos in the Cold War against organized labor in the United States. Taft-Hartley was the outcome of the belief that labor unions had become too powerful an economic force and had to be constrained by government. This law, passed over the veto of President Truman, stipulated that the public had an interest in avoiding crippling national strikes in essential industries and, consequently, that government was entitled to scrutinize bargaining results as well as bargaining procedures.

Ultimately, one of the most devastating provisions of Taft-Hartley was inserted as an afterthought. Section 9(h) was part of the late 1940s movement to purge Communist and socialist influences from the U.S. labor movement. All union officials were required by this provision to sign an affidavit with the NLRB that they neither were in the CP nor had any sympathy for its doctrines. Unions that didn't comply with Section 9(h) were denied access to the NLRB. Therefore, a firm could utilize unfair labor practices to paralyze union forces, and the union would have no recourse to stop the employer's actions.

Ironically, unions led by Communists or their allies on the political Left typically were different from other unions. Communist- or left-led union leaders typically were more educated and more militant in their demands for better working conditions and in their willingness to strike to obtain their goals; they were more class-conscious and often more democratic in their unions' organizational structure. While they fought for better wages and working conditions, they simultaneously fought for a wide range of social reforms.

From the start, the CP of the United States considered organizing labor unions its most important activity. The elevation of union organizing over other goals stemmed from the application of Marxist philosophy. Specifically, CP members understood that it would be difficult to be the self-appointed vanguard of the working class without being involved in organizations that were central to improving worker's lives.

Although communist labor leaders worked to organize white collar workers, including screenwriters, teachers, journalists, social workers, clerical workers, etc., the CP's philosophy was to try to aid the most disenfranchised workers. This led to special efforts by Communist labor leaders to organize blacks, Mexican Americans, women, and others who had been overlooked by the AFL-affiliated unions. At a time when African Americans were segregated at work into the most arduous, lowest-paying jobs, with little or no opportunities for advancement, the Communist-led unions fought for racial equality. The leaders of New York's Transport Worker's Union (TWU) were initially hesitant to fight the racist beliefs held by their mostly Irish American membership. But, racial equality was such a core issue of the Communist movement that the leadership of the TWU eventually decided to fight for the hiring of black bus drivers and motormen (among the higher-paid jobs). During World War II, when massive demand for labor, combined with shortages of labor, had created conditions favorable to African Americans seeking to break into better paid jobs, some Communist-led unions negotiated for new definitions of workplace seniority that would allow the more recently hired black workers to keep their jobs after the war ended.

Communist- and left-led unions also paid more attention to women's issues than other unions. In the days when women were routinely paid less in the same jobs as men, these unions fought for equal pay for equal work. In the days when factory jobs were regularly categorized as either "men's work" or "women's work," these unions fought to get women hired into the better-paying men's jobs.

Communists did not "infiltrate" the U.S. labor movement but were welcomed into the CIO (albeit not the AFL) by the CIO's president, John L. Lewis. Lewis had a long history of Red-baiting in his own union—the United Mine Workers—but he agreed with the Communists on many tactical issues regarding the organization of labor. In contrast to Sidney Hillman of the Amalgamated Clothing Workers Union or Philip Murray of the United Steelworkers of America, Lewis believed that a substantial amount of militancy was critically important to a movement using mass organizational techniques. Lewis recognized that few organizations in the United States could identify with and motivate working-class militancy better than the Communists. So Lewis sought to harness their strengths to advance his goals of organizing labor and using union-bargaining power to improve wages and work conditions.

By the end of World War II, Communists or allied individuals were in the leadership of unions representing about 20 percent of the CIO's membership—including the United Electrical, Radio and Machine Workers of America (UE); International Longshoreman's and Warehousemen's Union (ILWU); National Maritime Union; NYC-based Transit Workers Union; Food, Tobacco, and Agriculture Workers' Union; Fur and Leather Workers' Union; United Furniture Workers, etc. Only a small number of the leaders of these unions were openly Communist—such as William Sentner of the UE. Most were not—although their political affiliation was often known by those who knew them personally.

The AFL presented a much smaller target for anti-Communists. The AFL was older and more politically conservative than the CIO. The AFL structure was more decentralized, and, with a few exceptions in the Hollywood unions (e.g., the Talent Guilds and Stagehands' Union), Communists made up a much smaller percentage of the membership and leadership of AFL unions. The majority of the AFL unions were actively anti-Communist and widely recognized as such by the U.S. public.

By the end of the 1940s, the labor leaders were less a force of Soviet penetration of the U.S. economy and more a force for improving domestic social welfare—in the context of a Marxist philosophy that would elevate the treatment of workers over the treatment of capital (machinery, equipment, buildings, etc.) and the profits of firms. Although their focus was more Marxist than Stalinist, the numbers of left-leaning and Communist labor leaders and the size of the unions that they controlled gave the Communists some influence in U.S. society. Consequently, the private sector's and the government sector's campaigns against them were particularly intense. Communist- and left-led unions simultaneously faced attacks from internal dissidents within their own unions, rival unions trying to eliminate the competition, employers, and government agencies.

Taft-Hartley's mandate that all union leaders had to sign affidavits swearing that they were neither members of nor had sympathy for the doctrines of the CP did not initially appear all that threatening to union power. The signed affidavit needed to be on file with the NLRB and re-signed every 12 months. Labor leaders on the political Left and the political Right both opposed the Taft-Hartley Act because of its many provisions to weaken union power, and they hoped that President Truman's electoral victory in 1948 would lead to the repeal of the law.

The AFL was much less affected by Section 9(h) because it had never been a very welcoming place for Communists. Thus, many fewer members of the AFL were negatively affected by Section 9(h) than was the case for the membership of the CIO. Dave Beck, president of the AFL-affiliated International Brotherhood of Teamsters, wrote, "It is not necessary to prove that a member of our union is actually a member of the Communist Party. If he advocates a philosophy of Communism . . . we throw him out" (Orshinsky, 1976, 113).

Although some labor leaders complied with Section 9(h) and signed the affidavit, a substantial number refused to sign. Even non-Communists, like CIO President Philip Murray, opposed the affidavit provision and refused on principle to sign one. Section 9(h) was vague, and its prohibition of a "belief in" and "association with" Communism appeared to many to be in violation of the U.S. Constitution. Cases against the law were brought to federal court, with the expectation that the U.S. Supreme Court would ultimately declare this portion of the law to be unconstitutional.

Ironically, this mere afterthought provision of Taft-Hartley was seized by the opposition to left-led unions as an almost ideal weapon. Although some non-Communist union leaders took oppositional stances toward Section 9(h) on principle, others launched or relaunched campaigns to take control of Communist- and left-led unions, or they led their followers out of the union altogether. Rival unions trying to establish themselves as the bargaining agent for a specific group of workers intensified their raids on the Communist- and left-led unions. AFL unions and CIO unions cannibalized the left-led unions.

Before 1947, such raids were typically rebuffed, but Section 9(h) made this impossible. The Wagner Act explicitly states that, in order to represent a group of workers, a union must show, through a secret ballot election, that it has the support of a majority of a group of employees. If the union gains majority support, it becomes the only union that can represent those employees (although employees can subsequently vote to decertify the union if they are displeased with the representation). The five presidential appointees who serve on the NLRB hear and decide cases in which violations of the Wagner Act are alleged. So a union headed by anti-Communists could come into the workplace and, in violation of the Wagner Act, recruit members of the certified union. The certified union then would have no recourse to enforce its authority because its leaders' refusal to sign the affidavits would deny the entire union the right to take its case to the NLRB. Local 22 of the Food, Tobacco, Agricultural, and Allied Workers (FTA), mentioned at the start of this chapter, was a victim of these tactics.

Likewise, employers used Section 9(h) to fend off union efforts to improve workplace conditions. They refused to negotiate with unions whose leaders had not signed the affidavits, whether the document was unsigned because the union leadership thought it unconstitutional or because the union leadership was Communist. Because of Section 9(h), unions were unable to use the resources of the NLRB to force employers to come to the bargaining table, as they had been allowed to prior to the passage of Taft-Hartley.

Business also responded creatively in using all the tactics of McCarthyism and Cold War paranoia to paralyze organized labor. In a pamphlet on Communist infiltration in the United States, the powerful lobbying group, the U.S. Chamber of Commerce, wrote: "The tremendous power of labor today permits no . . . complacency. When a businessman or industrialist finds that nothing he does can please his union, he tends to form a sour view of organized labor. But as he becomes more sophisticated, he realizes that his difficulties may not arise from his own workers, who usually understand his problems, bur from outside forces controlling his local union. The Communists' demands are insatiable because they thrive on trouble" (Oshinsky, 1976, 88). As the Soviets put Eastern Europe more heavily under their grasp and exploded a nuclear weapon and as the Communists took over China, domestic paranoia grew. And more and more domestic "Cold Warriors" did what they could to convince people in the United States that members of labor unions could not be trusted during this period of international crisis.

By 1949, it was clear that the U.S. Congress would not repeal Taft-Hartley and that the Supreme Court would not overturn it. In fact, the Supreme Court ruled in 1950 that considerations of national security justified imposing Taft-Harley's restrictions on Communist influence within the labor movement. With no weapons left to fight Section 9(h), Communists discontinued their membership in the CP, and Communist sympathizers discontinued their support. They signed the affidavits. But by then it was too late.

The NLRB was aware that many of the labor leaders who ultimately signed the affidavits had been Communists and refused to believe that they had all left the CP. The NLRB took steps to decertify the unions headed by these men. The NLRB also brought in the U.S. Department of Justice to indict some of the signers for perjury.

Although, in retrospect, it is clear that the Section 9(h) affidavits had an enormous effect on decimating the Communist-led and left-led labor movement, by 1954, Congress had become increasingly frustrated with what it perceived as the ineffectiveness of the affidavits. Congress passed the Communist Control Act of 1954, which authorized the Subversive Activities Control Board to register left-led unions as "Communist-infiltrated organizations."

By the late 1940s, the Communist- and left-led unions had lost the support of the rest of the labor movement and also the support of the U.S. public. At its annual 1949 meeting, the CIO voted to expel the Communist-led UE and authorized an official investigation into the Communist affiliation of ten other unions. The outcome of these investigations was never in doubt. The other nine unions, subsequently expelled from the CIO, were the American Communications Association, FTA, International Fishermen and Allied Workers of America, International Fur and Leather Workers' Union, International Longshoremen's and Warehousemen's Union, International Union of Mine, Mill, and Smelter Workers, National Union of Marine Cooks and Stewards, United Office and Professional Workers of America, and the United Public Workers. These expulsions weakened the aforementioned unions even further and enabled rival union raiders to step up their attacks.

Business successfully used Red-baiting tactics and the national paranoia of the McCarthy era to weaken unions—regardless of whether or not the unions actually had Communist affiliations. The United Autoworkers 248 was the designated union for workers at the Allis-Chalmers Company (manufacturers of farm equipment, etc.) outside Milwaukee, Wisconsin. Employee strikes, countered by the firm's Red-baiting attacks, were common even in the 1930s. During a 76-day strike in 1941, the company fabricated the story that the walkout had come on Moscow's orders. When the employees went on strike, late in 1946, the company launched a massive publicity campaign, including 59 articles published in the local paper alleging Communist connections of the local union leaders. The company also provided similar information to the FBI, outside journalists, and several Congressional committees. In March 1947, the House Labor and Education Committee brought in the president and past president of Local 248 for questioning about their ties to the CP. HUAC followed up, with a second set of hearings, and a third set of hearings was held in Milwaukee by a subcommittee of the House Labor and Education Committee. The strike was called off by the union one week after the last set of hearings. During this six-month period, the membership of Local 248 fell from over 8,000 members to 184.

Government-related Cold War battles against organized labor were widespread—and went well beyond the activities of Senator Joseph McCarthy. The Supreme Court in 1950 upheld the constitutionality of letting national security concerns trump people's First Amendment rights. Businessmen and officials at executive branch agencies used national security concerns to justify attacks on left-led unions. In 1948, the Atomic Energy Commission (AEC) ordered General Electric Corporation to refuse to allow the UE to represent workers at its nuclear facility in Schenectady, New York. The AEC also issued an order that barred the United Office and Professional Workers of America from representing workers at the AEC's

Harold Christoffel

Harold Christoffel was just 29 years old when he led 6,000 members of Local 248 of the United Auto Workers Union out on strike at the sprawling West Allis Works of the Allis-Chalmers Manufacturing Company. Christoffel led the workers out on April 30, 1946, on a 329-day strike to obtain better working conditions for the skilled and production employees, several ethnic groups, men and women, African Americans and whites that they represented. The plant, owned by this major World War II defense contractor, was located outside of Milwaukee, Wisconsin, and was the first battleground of the Cold War on U.S. labor. Christoffel, a militant leader who fought for his workers, became a casualty in that war.

At first, the campaign against Christoffel and his union was local and championed by the *Milwaukee Sentinel*, which reported: "The cancer of Red-Fascism here is a national disease far greater than is obvious." In February 1947, the campaign moved to Washington, D.C. Three Congressional committees—the Senate Labor and Public Welfare Committee, the House Labor and Education Committee, and HUAC—investigated the strike and Local 248.

From the outset, it was obvious that the House Labor and Education Committee was determined to set a perjury trap for Christoffel. The Committee questioned Local 248 opposition leaders, who claimed that Christoffel was a Communist. The Allis-Chalmers Co. responded by firing Christoffel. Congressman John F. Kennedy, a Committee member, recommended that the Department of Justice indict Christoffel for perjury.

As a result, Christoffel became the first union leader jailed in the Cold War Red Scare. He served three years in federal prison before being released on a technicality. Ultimately, the power and authority of the state succeeded in breaking the fighting spirit of Local 248.

own laboratories in Illinois. The government used security orders to make left-led unions across the defense industry impotent. Common practices included widespread denial of security clearances to shop stewards and other union activists, making it impossible to circulate among the factories or to ensure that workplace contracts were being enforced.

The federal government's Port Security program, instituted soon after the start of the Korean War in 1950, hit left-wing maritime unions hard. Ultimately, the Marine Cooks and Stewards Union was wiped out.

Although the alleged espionage activities of Julius and Ethel Rosenberg were damaging to U.S. interests in the Cold War and more recently released historical documents from the former Soviet Union show that Julius Rosenberg was implicated in espionage, being a rank-and-file member of a union with one or more Communist- or left-leaning officers did not make the worker, or the union, guilty of operating on Soviet orders. Making national enemies of all individuals who either were Communists or were associated with Communist- or left-led labor unions is analogous to profiling all Muslims as terrorist security threats because of the actions of a small number of Muslims on September 11, 2001.

The Immigration and Naturalization Service (INS) was drafted in the Cold War on U.S. labor. The Longshoreman's leader, Harry Bridges, was subject to a 20-year deportation campaign that actually began in the 1930s. Twice, when the initial deportation hearing decision went against him, he had to appeal to the Supreme Court. Although Bridges was ultimately exonerated of the charges against him, the 20-year fight took an enormous toll on him and on the Longshoreman's and Warehousemen's Union.

Congress used its powers to convene hearings and to subpoena witnesses to inflict fatal wounds on U.S. unions. From the start of the McCarthy period,

Longshoreman's Union leader Harry Bridges is shown leaving a San Francisco county jail in 1950. (AP/Wide World Photos)

the main Congressional investigating committees put the labor Left in their sights. A very small number of left-wing union leaders were not subpoenaed by HUAC, the House Labor and Education Committee, etc. Those who were subpoenaed were grilled about their connections to the CP. But, because of their power within their own unions, they typically did not lose their jobs— in contrast to many other witnesses—from Hollywood, government, etc.— who appeared before these committees. However, the costs in terms of negative publicity and loss of internal and public support for the union were extremely damaging. A secondary effect of the committee hearings was that union leaders summoned to appear might be charged with perjury or contempt of Congress, and some served terms in prison on these charges.

In conclusion, the crusade against organized labor between 1946 and 1956 was opportunistic. Many of the crusaders' primary goal was not to fight Communists, but to eliminate unions as a source of bargaining power for workers. These crusaders recognized that the anti-Communist paranoia of the period had created a perfect environment to paint labor unions as Communist-infiltrated enemies of the United States and thus to use a variety of means to eliminate or weaken organized labor in various sectors of the economy. The crusades by real anti-Communists and faux anti-Communists were so effective because they came from so many different sources within rival unions, among business leaders, from right-wing journalists—as well as from legislative, executive, and judicial agents of the U.S. government. Many of the crusaders had been fighting the CP for years, but never before did they have such overwhelming support from the federal government in their efforts.

The anti-Communist crusaders were so effective because they were able and willing to use a variety of weapons. Communist leaders of labor unions were required to testify before Congressional investigating committees and grand juries. They were subjected to criminal prosecution, put under constant FBI surveillance, had their tax records audited by the IRS, and, if they were born abroad, they were threatened with deportation.

Unions, as institutions, were likewise under constant attack. They had to contend with internal schisms over the best strategies and tactics for dealing with McCarthyism. They suffered from cannibalism, practiced by rival unions, and from employers who successfully refused to bargain with Communist- or left-led unions. They were denied the protections of the Wagner Act when they lost their ability to be heard by the NLRB. They were called to register and testify before the Subversive Activities Control Board and expelled from the CIO. During the McCarthy years, unions had to utilize so much of their emotional and financial resources to fight off the anti-Communist crusaders that they didn't have adequate resources to perform their primary function—improving workplace conditions for employees.

References and Further Reading

Budd, John W. *Labor Relations: Striking a Balance*. New York: McGraw-Hill/Irwin, 2005.

Cherny, Robert W., William Issel, and Kieran Walsh Taylor. "Introduction," in *American Labor and the Cold War*, Robert W. Cherny, William Issel, and Kieran Walsh Taylor, eds., Piscataway, NJ: Rutgers University Press, (2004) 1–6.

Honey, Michael K. "Operation Dixie, the Red Scare, and the Defeat of Southern Labor Organizing," in *American Labor and the Cold War*, Robert W. Cherny, William Issel, and Kieran Walsh Taylor, eds. (2004) 216–244.

Lee, R. Alton. *Truman and Taft-Hartley,* Lexington, KY: Lexington University Press, 1966.

O'Brien, F. S. "The 'Communist-Dominated' Unions in the United States since 1950," *Labor History* 9 (1968) 184–205.

Oshinsky, David M. *Senator Joseph McCarthy and the American Labor Movement*, Columbia, MO: University of Missouri Press, 1976.

Palmer, David. "An Anarchist with a Program: East Coast Shipyard Workers, the Labor Left, and the Origins of Cold War Unionism," in *American Labor and the Cold War*, Robert W. Cherny, William Issel, and Kieran Walsh Taylor, eds. (2004) 85–117.

Reynolds, Lloyd G., Stanley H. Masters, and Colletta H. Moser. *Labor Economics and Labor Relations*. Upper Saddle River, NJ: Prentice Hall, 1998.

Schrecker, Ellen. *The Age of McCarthyism: A Brief History with Documents*. New York: Bedford/St. Martin's, 2002.

Schrecker, Ellen. "Labor and the Cold War: The Legacy of McCarthyism," in *American Labor and the Cold War*, Robert W. Cherny, William Issel, and Kieran Walsh Taylor, eds. (2004) 7–24.

Schrecker, Ellen. *Many Are the Crimes: McCarthyism in America*. New York: Little, Brown and Company, 1998.

U.S. Department of Labor. "Work Stoppages Caused by Labor-Management Disputes in 1945" 6. (1946) 2:716–735.

"Racist Saints and Communist Devils": African Americans, McCarthyism, and the Cold War

7

S. Ani Mukherji

Two crowds converged outside Peekskill, New York, on August 27, 1949. One group came to attend an open-air benefit concert by Paul Robeson, a world-renowned black singer and actor who had also achieved prominence for his strong stands for civil rights in the United States and against colonialism in Africa and Asia. Robeson's performance was intended to raise funds for the Civil Rights Congress (CRC), an organization dedicated to supporting the rights and civil liberties of African Americans and sympathetic radicals. A second crowd, comprising American Legion members and local youths, gathered to prevent this event. Like many Americans, this group took Robeson's condemnation of U.S. racism and his expressed sympathy with the people of the Soviet Union as evidence of "un-American" attitudes in the context of the heightening Cold War. Wielding baseball bats and brass knuckles, these men set upon the concert grounds to drive away performer and attendees alike. Before Robeson's scheduled arrival, a series of confrontations between concertgoers and protestors led to numerous serious injuries. According to the *New York Times*, several fires were set, and two burning crosses—infamous symbol of the racist Ku Klux Klan—were erected. Because of safety concerns, the concert was cancelled.

Undaunted by this experience, however, organizers resolved to reschedule the event for early September and enlisted the help of local union members to protect Robeson and the attendees. Again, protestors lined the road to the concert, shouting racist epithets and accusing attendees of being Communists and traitors. But this time, the audience was protected by a ring of hundreds of supporters who kept the anti-Communists at bay. The concert went on as planned, with Robeson flanked by bodyguards on stage. After the performance, violence erupted again, as anti-Red crusaders hurled rocks at cars leaving the grounds, sending dozens to local hospitals with cuts, bruises, and fractured bones.

A policeman is helped to his feet after being hit in the head by a bottle at the Peekskill Riots in 1949. (AP/Wide World Photos)

These events typify the ways in which African Americans experienced political repression after World War II. Although the McCarthy period is commonly remembered for subversions of due process and encroachments on freedom of speech, the Peekskill Riots call attention to the intermingling of anti-Communism with a backlash against racial democracy. The attacks also underscore the particularly violent aspects of McCarthyism that were faced by black subjects and their allies. At the same time, the riots serve as a reminder of the strength of the postwar push for racial equality and civil rights, as thousands turned out to support Robeson and the CRC despite rhetorical attacks and the real threat of violence.

In fact, the events outside Peekskill came in the midst of many significant transformations in African American life. From 1910 to 1940, nearly one million black migrants moved from the rural South to northern cities. This period also witnessed a vast expansion in the numbers of black industrial workers, middle-class professionals, and small-business owners. Yet, even though the economic and social welfare of many African Americans was on the rise, stark inequities persisted throughout the country. In the North, black migrants faced continued segregation, inferior housing, and limited employment opportunities; those who remained in the South were denied voting rights and coped with the constant threat of racial violence. As such, a variety of African American social and political movements took hold across the country, including Marcus Garvey's black nationalist Universal Negro Improvement Association (UNIA), the reformist National Association for the Advancement of Colored People (NAACP), and integrationist trade unions, often organized by Communists and fellow travelers.

U.S. entry into World War II intensified these patterns. Even though Franklin D. Roosevelt's New Deal programs had mixed results in terms of alleviating the economic distress of African Americans during the Great Depression, the socioeconomic and ideological transformations concomitant with the mobilization for the war effort caused massive changes in racial order in the United States. Approximately 500,000 black men entered the military service, and another million African American men and women joined the home front, working in factories, often in skilled positions that had previously been unavailable to them. These advances were not merely the result of an increased demand for labor; rather, they followed an explosion of civil rights and trade union activism. As early as 1940, A. Philip Randolph, of the Brotherhood of Sleeping Car Porters, threatened a march on Washington if the federal government did not agree to take measures to prohibit racial discrimination. Consequently, Executive Order 8802 established the Committee on Fair Employment Practices and proscribed discrimination in defense-related industries. Another indication of the mounting movement for equal rights was the growing membership rolls of the NAACP; the leading civil rights organization in the nation had at least tripled its numbers since 1934.

A union organizer and socialist early in life, A. Philip Randolph became one of the country's best-known African American trade unionists and a nationally prominent leader in the struggle for civil rights during the early to mid-20th century. (Library of Congress)

The ideological transformation of the war years was just as remarkable as the changing socioeconomic conditions of African Americans. The rise of fascism in Europe provided civil rights activists with a convenient foil to U.S. discrimination. While the United States decried the racial policies of Adolf Hitler against the Jews, African Americans hammered at the contradiction of accepting Jim Crow racism at home while condemning bias abroad. In 1939, an editorial in the *Chicago Defender*—one of the most widely read black newspapers of the day—praised Indian nationalist leaders' refusal to cooperate with the British war effort without the promise of independence. Shortly after the bombing of Pearl Harbor, the black-owned *Pittsburgh Courier* sounded a similar note, calling for a "double-V campaign" of victory against fascism abroad and victory against racial discrimination at home. Most important, state-sponsored rhetoric decried racial prejudice as backward and detrimental to the war effort.

In the wake of the war, black veterans returned home to continue the fight, working through civil rights groups to apply increased pressure on the federal government for reforms. As a result of increased migration to the North and earnest efforts of voting rights organizers in the South, African Americans wielded increasing electoral power, demanding an end to discrimination in housing, transportation, and public education. At the international level, a number of black organizations took their grievances to the newly founded United Nations, which they envisioned as a world forum to protest injustices. Washington policymakers were particularly sensitive to such demands, because they wanted to maintain a positive image in the newly independent countries that emerged during the wave of postwar decolonization. Many of these countries had just thrown off the yoke of racialized colonialism, and officials feared they would be unlikely allies if the United States were perceived as racist.

And such alliances were an imperative, because the postwar world was increasingly bifurcated—into Soviet-controlled states and countries under the influence of the growing world power of the United States. Using their position in the United Nations, Soviet officials courted African Americans, along with the colonial world, and demanded that the U.N. charter include language calling for the cessation of racial discrimination. To undercut the appeal of the Soviet Union and Communism and to secure the electoral backing of African Americans, President Harry Truman, in late 1946, established the Committee on Civil Rights, with the stated goals of guaranteeing "domestic tranquility, national security, the general welfare, and the continued existence of our free institutions" (*To Secure These Rights*, 1947, 178). This changed political climate also helped usher in a series of legal decisions that chipped away at the legal precedent of the "separate but equal" doctrine established by the U.S. Supreme Court's *Plessy v. Ferguson* (1896) decision; these decisions included *Morgan v. Virginia* (1946), which outlawed segregation in interstate bus travel, and the prohibition of the enforcement of discriminatory housing covenants in *Shelley v. Kramer* (1948). By 1951, the U.S. armed forces were desegregated, and, in 1954, the U.S. Supreme Court ruled against ostensibly "separate but equal" public schools in *Brown v. Board of Education*.

Remarkable in the face of these sweeping governmental reforms was the general lack of concerted militant action, radical demands for socioeconomic improvement, or critiques of U.S. foreign policy that had been common to black politics in the 1930s and early 1940s. To explain this absence, one need explore the nature of the postwar political repression that is commonly referred to as McCarthyism.

The association of this repression with the figure of Senator Joseph McCarthy is, in many ways, misleading. McCarthy is most readily remembered for his frenzied, unsubstantiated attacks in the early 1950s. As such, the appellation is deceptive, because McCarthy's fervent push to rid the federal government of Communist influence only began in earnest in 1950, years after the first signs of intolerance of left-wing activism. The tag of McCarthyism creates an erroneous impression that such repression was an aberrant paranoid campaign, led by one particular devout anti-Communist. In contrast, a number of black progressives took McCarthy's sensationalism as a mere extension of the cruelties that they had faced since the close of the war, as the Truman administration sought to consolidate its power on the national and international levels.

As U.S. influence expanded across the globe, the government needed a means to secure its image as a pluralist democracy and to silence its critics. Key to this strategy was Truman's cooperation with the NAACP, under the direction of Executive Secretary Walter White. Throughout the 1930s and into the 1940s, White was a central figure in the development of black anti-Communist politics, in a period that has often been remembered for the deepening relationship between African Americans and Communism. Starting with the struggle against the CP over the defense of the so-called Scottsboro Boys—nine black youths who were falsely accused of raping two white women in Alabama—the NAACP's national leadership took a self-consciously anti-Communist stance in its advocacy for civil rights. Simultaneously, White tried to limit more strident local organizers and consolidate the politics of the NAACP at the national office. By the mid-1940s, the anti-Communist political tack, combined with the increasing centralization of decision-making, led a number of important NAACP organizers to split from the group.

At the same time, White's strong leadership of the largest organization of African Americans brought about a growth, both in numbers and in the political influence that he wielded. In exchange for Truman's limited support of civil rights reform, White, along with a number of other vocal black anti-Communists, lent their support to the Democratic Party and to U.S. Cold War objectives at home and abroad. It was a most effective strategy, when offered as an alternative to radical demands for racial democracy.

Although black anti-Communists curried the favor of the Truman administration, those who called for fundamental and immediate changes in the current racial order found their voices suppressed by an evolving set of repressive mechanisms. Two watershed developments before the war had paved the way for the stifling of black radicalism. In 1938, HUAC emerged from a special investigative committee, under the control of Texas congressman Martin Dies, a staunch anti-Communist, xenophobe, and reputed racist. This body—made into a standing committee in 1946—was originally charged with investigating extremism, particularly among those who sympathized with Nazi Germany. But under Dies's leadership, it quickly focused its efforts on scrutinizing the work of the CP and other leftist groups. More important, the Committee became a vehicle for anti-New Deal Democrats to criticize what they viewed as the excesses of the Roosevelt administration, including its relationship with African Americans. The second development that aided those seeking to quash dissent was the passage of the Alien Registration Act (Smith Act) in 1940, which required adult resident non-citizens to register with the federal government and prohibited advocacy of the overthrow of the state by force or violence, a charge commonly leveled against political radicals.

The establishment of HUAC and the enactment of the Smith Act instigated widespread monitoring of political activity throughout the war years and after. This surveillance was conducted for the most part by the FBI, under J. Edgar Hoover, with the assistance of other federal administrative bodies and privately organized right-wing anti-Communists. The leaders of this collaborative effort had first come together during the Red Scare that immediately followed World War I. Throughout the interwar years and into World War II, when there was little popular support for an anti-Communist crusade, these men and women quietly collected an archive of intelligence that connected fears of Communism with racial subversion; this work was compiled in right-wing journals, State Department reports, and voluminous FBI investigations.

Throughout this enormous collection of materials and in more popular anti-Communist tracts of the time, a conspiracy theory was constructed that conflated the civil rights demands of Communists and black leaders as part of one general subversive plot. Little attention was paid to the internecine battles between anti-Communist civil rights activists and Communists, who continually attacked each other as accommodationist lackeys and foreign agents, respectively. Instead, *National Republic* editor Walter S. Steele, a conservative white anti-Communist, assembled research files on a wide spectrum of civic organizations that encouraged improved racial relations; notably, he denounced the Society of Friends (Quakers) for their Communist sympathies, basing his case on the involvement of many followers in civil rights activism. For Steele, advocacy of racial reform was an indication of Communism. In this belief, he was not alone.

As the perceived threat of the expanding influence of the Soviet Union loomed in the minds of many Americans after World War II, these anti-Communist conservatives seized a long-awaited opportunity to squelch the combined threats of Communism, demands for racial equality, and the liberal gains made under Roosevelt's New Deal programs. And soon liberals joined the crusade, because they feared being labeled soft on Communism and were also eager to silence their more radical critics. Federal and state governments investigated any organizations or persons who criticized U.S. domestic and foreign affairs, applying the sweeping label of "subversive activities" to a large swath of the political spectrum. Those who were identified as possible subversives faced a number of possible disciplinary mechanisms, including intimidation, blacklisting, deportation, passport restrictions, imprisonment, and vigilante violence. It is not surprising that African Americans, already deprived of many of their civil rights, often faced the most severe repercussions.

The most effective tactic employed to mute black critics of racial inequality was the public humiliation of major figures. Such spectacles functioned not only to intimidate the particular person under scrutiny, but as educational theater, demonstrating to the public the dangers of Communism and the perils of collaborating with "Reds." The persecution of three towering figures in black life—Paul Robeson, W. E. B. Du Bois, and Langston Hughes—illuminates different elements of the postwar repression of progressive racial politics.

Before the war, Paul Robeson was perhaps the preeminent black performer of stage and screen. The New Jersey-native son of a preacher had been an all-American football player at Rutgers University before launching his career as a singer and actor in the 1920s. By the end of that decade, Robeson had settled in the London theater scene and came into close contact with anti-colonial students from Africa and Asia, as well as a number of Communists. Intrigued by the promise of socialism, Robeson traveled to the Soviet Union to witness the new society being built there and was so favorably impressed by the lack of racism and class inequalities that he later left his son there to be schooled.

These commitments to anti-imperialism and sympathy for the Soviet Union led Robeson to criticize strongly the direction that the United States was taking on the eve of the Cold War, as the country aspired to shape the future of the decolonizing world and sought to limit the role of the Soviet Union in global affairs. Furthermore, Robeson had hesitations about Truman's commitment to racial equality in the domestic sphere, rebuking the president for his failure to support anti-lynching legislation in 1946.

At the Paris Peace Conference of 1949, Robeson voiced his beliefs, stating that black Americans would not fight in an aggressive war against the Soviet Union, a confrontation that Robeson thought imminent. The press quickly condemned Robeson as a traitor, a "black Stalin" who was a threat to U.S. democracy. The entertainment industry blacklisted Robeson such that he could find little profitable employment for nearly a decade, and the State Department revoked his passport on the grounds that his presence abroad was detrimental to the international interests of the United States.

The media and government officials also pressured other black notables, including black baseball star Jackie Robinson, to denounce Robeson publicly and to proclaim their faith in U.S. democracy. At the peak of his career, with a large following both at home and abroad, Robeson was suddenly reduced to small performances supporting local causes and existing on a pitifully small income. And, as a result of the smear campaign directed against him,

Paul Robeson shaking hands with New York City Councilman Ben Davis, in Union Square, during May Day ceremonies. (Library of Congress)

Robeson faced the threat of violence from vigilantes, such as those at Peekskill, who no doubt felt that they were fulfilling their patriotic duty by hurling rocks at a turncoat.

Yet in the face of these pressures, Robeson never relented in his support for militant anti-racism or his denunciation of the encroachment on civil liberties imposed by McCarthyism. As punishment for this stand, he languished for nearly a decade without an audience, and, by the late 1950s, he had largely been written out of black social, cultural, and political life.

Like Robeson, W. E. B. Du Bois was a longstanding authority in the black community. Born in 1868 in the wake of the Civil War, Du Bois came of age at a time when the promise of emancipation and Reconstruction gave way to the segregationist backlash of the late 19th century. In the face of this disappointment, Du Bois dedicated his life to the betterment of African Americans, or the "uplift of the race," in the parlance of the day. In the half-century before the McCarthy period, Du Bois helped found the NAACP, edited its journal *The Crisis*, and wrote over a dozen books on the condition of Africans throughout the diaspora. By the 1940s, the great scholar and activist had come to perceive the twinned evils of capitalism and imperialism as the foremost impediments to the advancement of the race. Such a vision, of course, was not easily sustained in the repressive atmosphere of postwar politics.

First, Du Bois was forced out of the NAACP. The association had long been deemed by extreme anti-Communists as a possible Communist front, but this gratuitous charge gained credence when it was repeated in *Life* magazine by the young Harvard professor Arthur Schlesinger, Jr., in 1947. Such Red-baiting, in addition to Director Walter White's personal and political differences with Du Bois, led to the founder's ousting from the organization a year later. Yet, Du Bois, 80 years old, did not take his dismissal as an opportunity to exit the political stage. Rather, he continued to pursue his life's mission vigorously, stumping for Henry Wallace and the Progressive Party in the 1948 election, taking part in the work of the anti-colonialist Council on African Affairs led by Robeson, and criticizing Truman's Cold War policies from the chair of the Peace Information Center (PIC), an organization dedicated to nuclear disarmament.

In 1950, the Justice Department, invoking an act requiring the registration of "foreign agents," informed Du Bois that the PIC must immediately file paperwork with the government, because the center was a purported propaganda agency for Soviet interests. In 1951, Du Bois and four others were arraigned for failing to register, despite the fact that the organization had disbanded the previous autumn. The case, a weak one from the beginning and turning into a public relations nightmare for the government, was eventually dismissed. But attempts to silence Du Bois's growing criticisms of the U.S. government's failures at home and abroad continued.

In 1953, Du Bois, like Robeson, had his passport revoked. More hurtful, Du Bois was rebuked by the civil rights establishment, including many former colleagues who were looking to demonstrate their fealty to Truman's race-relations model, for his stands against U.S. foreign policy and economic inequities. Although the aging scholar was favorably impressed by the 1954 *Brown v. Board* decision, he found himself surrounded by a small circle of beleaguered victims of McCarthyism and castigated by the mainstream reformers.

Unlike Robeson or Du Bois, Langston Hughes was more tractable in the face of anti-Communist repression. The famed poet of Harlem, who had taken up progressive causes throughout the so-called "Red Decade" of the 1930s, had been under attack by private anti-Communists since 1940. By the mid-1940s, Red-baiting had been transformed from the obsessive hobby of a few determined individuals and administrators to a national craze supported by institutional power. As public and private forces united to stymie Hughes's successful writing career, the author recast his history of commitment to Communist-led struggles for black equality, establishing a narrative arc of his life—from youthful radicalism to a mature patriotic reformism.

Simultaneously, Hughes tried to forget as many details as possible from his past and distance himself from his former associates. When Hughes was subpoenaed by McCarthy in 1953, many assumed that he would follow the path of Robeson and Du Bois, pleading the Fifth Amendment and castigating the Committee's curtailment of civil liberties. In fact, Hughes had already stood up against the prosecution of Du Bois in 1951, calling the grand man of letters "a skyrocket for the great dreams of all mankind" facing unfair abuse. Instead, appearing before McCarthy himself, Hughes repudiated his past, heaped praise on the promise, if not the practice, of U.S. democracy, and even complimented McCarthy and his colleagues on their good manners. This tack allowed Hughes to stop short of "naming names" or outright excoriations of the CP—a duty commonly demanded by McCarthy and his cronies in exchange for exoneration. Hughes chose to negotiate a fine line of compromise that permitted him to continue his literary work as a writer and editor, rather than languishing on the black-list. While Robeson and Du Bois found themselves excised from the realm of legitimate politics, Hughes thus obfuscated his previous beliefs and inten-tionally muted his disappointments with the contemporary situation. But, in some sense, the impact of each of these three men was forcefully distorted by the anti-Communist crusade.

The overall effect of these targeted persecutions of black leaders was the delimiting of acceptable (and unacceptable) forms of black loyalty. In the cases of both Robeson and Du Bois, their purported transgressions were paired with expressions of proper, moderate civil rights activism and patri-otism in the figures of Jackie Robinson and Walter White. These couplings explicitly marginalized the political demands of Robeson and Du Bois as "subversive" and "extremist."

The lessons here were unmistakable. Hughes, on the other hand, main-tained a carefully carved-out place in black politics, but at the cost of an amnesiac-like re-scripting of his public persona. This white-washing could be seen as one model for former progressives who could not stomach a full repudiation of all their former compatriots and beliefs.

These well-publicized national spectacles then became models for inquiries by other government agencies, employers, and fellow citizens. And, indeed, trade unions, progressive organizations, newspapers, and colleges regularly scrutinized their members and employees for possible subversive elements. Because of the decentralized nature of these cam-paigns, it is difficult to discern the number of victims who failed to find work, were forced to resign, or were run out of organizations because of their beliefs or some past connection.

But the general patterns are clear. Within the unions of the CIO, federal officials pushed the leadership to exclude left-wing elements, especially those who had worked to establish a program of civil rights unionism and fought for an end to discrimination within trades. Despite the NAACP's growing influence at the national level, membership in many Southern branches plummeted, as they were assailed by local anti-Communists and received little support from headquarters.

The worst of the violent persecution of perceived racial subversion in the South can be seen in a rash of church burnings and mob attacks in the late 1940s and early 1950s. Major black newspapers that had taken up a critique of U.S. domestic and foreign policy during the 1930s shifted to the center and criticized former prized columnists who stood now accused of subversive radicalism. Colleges and universities routinely denied employment to instructors who advocated racial equality; according the distorted logic of McCarthyism, such attitudes reflected underlying Communist sympathies.

These actions were typically cued by the Justice Department, which uti-lized its enormous archive of anti-Communist surveillance to identify employees and members of private organizations as possible threats. FBI agents followed suspected Communists, questioning their employers, their landlords, and their associates, in order to ostracize the subject of surveil-lance. One scholar of McCarthyism has dubbed such harassment of suspected communists by FBI officials as *lanting*, a word that refers to the

19th-century agricultural practice of soaking seeds in stale urine to keep wild animals from feeding on the stock (Price 2004, 97). Unlike formal court proceedings, this technique of defamation and intimidation required no due process and was subject to no appeals. In order to avoid its wrath, many African Americans, along with the rest of country, simply avoided public expressions of discontent as a whole.

Yet, one group of activists was immune to the spoil of *lanting*. Self-professed, unapologetic members of the CP could hardly be made to fear a label that they proudly embraced. Bullying and blacklisting did not silence this group. Instead, the federal government instituted prosecutions of the leadership of the CP for violating the Smith Act, which prohibited the advocacy of violent overthrow of the government. According to Truman's Justice Department, the theory of Communism demanded revolution, and therefore all CP members could be subject to prosecution. The Attorney General started at the top. In the late 1940s, 12 leading Communists were arrested and put on trial for violation of the Smith Act, including two prominent African Americans, New York City Councilman Benjamin Davis and CP Administrative Secretary Henry Winston. Both men were convicted and served time in prison, although Winston initially went underground to continue CP work as a fugitive.

Shortly thereafter the trials of "second-string" CP leaders began, including James E. Jackson, a veteran of the Southern Negro Youth Congress, and the high-ranking black activist Pettis Perry. In 1954, William L. Patterson, director of the Civil Rights Congress, served five months in prison.

Foreign-born Communists were usually subjected to deportation rather than imprisonment, because the burden of guilt was lighter on immigration violation charges, and there were fewer legal protections available to non-citizens. The Internal Security Act of 1950 and Nationality Act of 1952 had codified U.S. fears of Communism as an external threat that could be removed from the body politic, enabling the deportation of non-citizens on grounds of political belief. By 1953, some three hundred "political" aliens had been arrested for deportation.

While these acts were used against Eastern Europeans and Asian Americans for the most part, they were also applied to black Americans of Caribbean descent. West Indian Secretary of the CP's Women's Commission Claudia Jones was arrested on deportation charges in 1948 and fled the country in 1955 after proceedings were started again. Jamaican-born Secretary of the National Maritime Union Ferdinand Smith, who had been fighting to preserve the left wing of the CIO, was forced to leave the country in 1951. Even the former Trotskyite from Trinidad, C. L. R. James, was arrested on deportation charges, despite his protests that he had been a staunch critic of the Soviet Union and the CP for over a decade. The anti-Communist repression did not make such fine distinctions among the varieties of Marxist ideology.

Such arrests, trials, and deportations of members of the CP crippled its work, because activists focused on defense campaigns. After the arrest of the CP leadership in 1948, the Committee to Defend Negro Leadership was quickly assembled, to rally support for black victims of McCarthyism. Chief among its organizers were the wives of activists who had been threatened with imprisonment, including Esther C. Jackson and Eslanda Robeson.

These women deftly manipulated early Cold War rhetoric about the threat of Communism to the nuclear family by underscoring the irony that McCarthyist persecution of black radicals was separating fathers from children and husbands from wives. Undoubtedly, there was a deep truth to the pain that families underwent as their children were hounded by FBI agents and as life partners were separated for long stretches of time. At the same time, the necessity of embracing the role of wife and mother must have rankled women who had been voices for women's equality and independence within the CP.

But these were the constrained choices of the period. As the CP went on the defensive, it was no longer able to build on the momentum gained in organizing African American workers in the 1930s and 1940s. One contemporary chronicler of the postwar repression, newspaper editor Cedric Belfrage, pointed out that the goal of McCarthyism was not the imprisonment of every last Communist, but to drain the resources—financial, intellectual and organizational—of progressive associations to the point where they could no longer function. And it worked. By the mid-1950s, after almost a decade of repressive measures, the CP and other left-wing

Claudia Jones

Claudia Jones was an extraordinary woman, whose persecution typifies a number of elements of the postwar repression. At the age of eight, the future Communist leader immigrated to the United States from Trinidad, settling in Harlem in 1924. By her own account, Jones had a tough childhood, beset by poverty and the daily indignities faced by African Americans in this era. Shortly after graduation from high school, the young Jones joined the Communist Party, attracted to its strong stand against racism and imperialism.

Throughout the 1930s and 1940s, she tirelessly organized conferences, recruited new Party members, and wrote for left-wing publications about questions of class, race, and gender. By the time of the postwar political repression, Jones had ascended to the upper echelon of Party ranks as a result of her established reputation as an activist and author.

Her prominent position attracted the attention of government officials seeking to limit the influence of the Party on black political life. Beginning in 1948, the federal government attempted to silence Jones through a variety of means: harassment by FBI agents, deportation proceedings under the Walter-McCarran Act, and criminal prosecution for violation of the Smith Act. Throughout this time, Jones continued undaunted what she considered to be her vocation—writing and speaking out against racism, inequality, and militarism.

Finally in 1955, after a nine-month stint in jail and facing another round of deportation proceedings and incarceration, Jones's health was failing, and she chose voluntary exile in Britain. In London, Jones resumed her calling, founding the progressive newspaper *West Indian Gazette* and establishing the annual Notting Hill Caribbean Carnival. Yet the toll of poverty, ceaseless labor, and imprisonment weighed heavily on Jones. She died in 1964, at the age of 49.

associations had almost no role in African American politics at the national level. There is some reason to doubt that Communists would have wielded any authority among African Americans after the war, even without the ascent of anti-Communism. A series of programmatic flip-flops throughout the war years and the abandonment of the Communist International during World War II had left the organization in disarray by the mid-1940s. But the role of the repression absolutely nullified any hopes of restored influence.

The effectiveness of the persecution of radicals was most apparent to black Communists. In 1961, longstanding black activist Cyril Briggs wrote to his comrade Ben Davis, counseling that the CP, if it hoped to revive itself, needed to make clear the ways in which McCarthyism specifically affected the struggle for black equality: "Why shouldn't we stress the role played by the Dixiecrats in promoting anti-Communism? Expose the U.S. demonology of racist saints and Communist devils?" (*Benjamin Davis Papers*, Schomburg Collection, New York Public Library. New York City).

The problem with such an approach was that it no longer accurately described the racial politics of anti-Communism. Even though the anti-Red crusade had been initiated by racial conservatives, over the course of a decade, a strong faction of anti-Communist racial liberals had developed. The triumph of anti-Communist civil rights was that it successfully marginalized both the racist saints and the Communist devils.

The case of Annie Lee Moss ably demonstrates this point. Moss, an African American civilian employee at the Pentagon, had been caught up in the federal loyalty reviews of the Truman and Dwight D. Eisenhower administrations almost from the beginning in 1947. A former participant and beneficiary of the wartime wave of civil rights unionism, Moss worked her way from a job as a dessert cook in the Pentagon cafeteria to a well-paid position as a clerk in the Department of the Army. Aware of Moss's background in a left-leaning union and her possible Communist connections—based on a subscription to the CP newspaper the *Daily Worker*—McCarthy saw an opportunity to demonstrate the laxity of the U.S. Army's anti-Red crusade. In early 1954, McCarthy himself brought Moss before his Senate Subcommittee and accused her of membership in the CP.

But when McCarthy and his top aide Roy Cohn slipped and were unable to identify Moss positively as a Communist, the senator's growing number of opponents collaborated with Moss to turn the tables and put McCarthy on trial—for an overzealous anti-Communism that threatened the promise of racial liberalism. Moss testified about her struggle to lift herself and her family out of poverty, which was made possible by the opportunities offered by the federal government after the war.

McCarthy's foes, in the Senate and in the media, capitalized on this narrative and painted McCarthy as a racist bully, beating up on an uneducated black woman who was too simple to pose the type of threat that the Wisconsin senator conjured. This episode was a key moment leading to McCarthy's downfall, because it provided liberals with the opportunity to broadcast their patriotic commitment to both anti-Communism and to anti-racism, a contrast to McCarthy's illiberal excesses.

While the racist anti-Communism of an older vintage continued to animate local politics, especially in the South, anti-Communist civil rights dominated at the national level. Bringing together black and white liberals with foreign policy adherents to realpolitik, it was a force that neither the supposed racist saints nor the Communist devils could defeat.

It is difficult to conclude with an estimate of the balance of gains and losses of the McCarthy period for African Americans. Statistically speaking, there is no evidence that African Americans were disproportionately represented among the victims of McCarthyism, although they likely faced the most violent expressions of the postwar repression. Yet, the benefits of federal support for civil rights and the colossal shift in racial ideology are unambiguous. Anti-Communist racial liberals effected the desegregation of many institutions, among them public schools, the military, and even professional baseball. As the civil rights movement of late 1950s and 1960s garnered support, it undoubtedly built on these achievements.

Yet one should not underestimate the injuries of the period in terms of the stifling of political dissent and intellectual freedom. The quashing of radical trade union activism and militant organizing in the South had radically retarded progress toward racial equality in the spheres of economic well-being and voting rights. The plight of poverty in the cities, which could no longer be ignored after the urban riots of the 1960s, was likely exacerbated by the inability of black leaders to address socioeconomic problems in the repressive atmosphere of McCarthyist America.

Into the early 1960s, the civil rights establishment was conspicuously silent on questions of U.S. foreign policy, even as U.S. involvement in the Vietnam conflict escalated. In the intellectual realm, an entire generation

Mrs. Annie Lee Moss, suspended government worker and suspected Communist, shown testifying before the Senate Investigating Subcommittee, 1954. (Library of Congress)

felt the loss of the artistic vision of Paul Robeson, the philosophical insights of W. E. B. Du Bois, and the feminist analyses of Claudia Jones, among other works excised from popular memory by McCarthyism.

Finally, there was the human cost of the postwar repression. Surely, anti-Communist racial liberals shrewdly played the hand dealt to them after the war to push forward a civil rights agenda. But it should not be forgotten that black radicals had paid the price to get into this game, sacrificing their freedom to secure these rights.

References and Further Reading

Aptheker, Herbert, ed. *A Documentary History of the Negro People in the United States*. Vols. 5 & 6. New York: Carol Publishers, 1990.

Benjamin J. Davis Papers. Schomburg Center for Research in Black Culture, New York Public Library, New York City.

Caute, David. *The Great Fear: The Anti-Communist Purge under Truman and Eisenhower*. New York: Simon and Schuster, 1978.

Davies, Carol Boyce, "Deportable Subjects: US Immigration Laws and Criminalizing of Communism," *South Atlantic Quarterly* (Fall 2001) 100:4: 949–966.

Dudziak, Mary. *Cold War Civil Rights: Race and the Image of American Democracy*. Princeton, NJ: Princeton University Press, 2000.

Friedman, Andrea, "The Strange Career of Annie Lee Moss: Rethinking Race, Gender, and McCarthyism," *Journal of American History* (September 2007) 94:2: 445–468.

Marable, Manning. *Race, Reform and Rebellion: The Second Reconstruction and Beyond in Black America, 1945–2006*. 3rd ed. Jackson: University of Mississippi Press, 2007.

Price, David. *Threatening Anthropologists: McCarthyism and the FBI's Surveillance of Activist Anthropologists*. Durham, NC: Duke University Press, 2004.

Schrecker, Ellen. *Many Are the Crimes: McCarthyism in America*. Boston, MA: Little, Brown, 1998.

To Secure These Rights: The Report of the President's Committee on Civil Rights. Washington, DC: U.S. Government Printing Office, 1947.

Sexuality and Gender in Cold War America: Social Experiences, Cultural Authorities, and the Roots of Political Change

8

Howard H. Chiang

In February 1950, when the Republican senator Joseph McCarthy publicly claimed to "hold in [his] hand" a list of 205 known communists who were working for the State Department, the moment consolidated the transformation of a kind of anxiety fostered by U.S. foreign affairs into one primarily concerned with domestic subversions. Since the beginning of the Cold War, roughly when World War II ended, the American people had increasingly felt a threat imposed by Communism, primarily because it was rather real: the Soviet Union began to develop an atomic bomb abroad; the Chinese government was taken over by Mao Zedong's political regime in 1949; and, in fighting both the Soviets and the Chinese, U.S. intervention in the Korean War appeared embattled. In turn, many began to feel that something must be wrong within U.S. borders. The rising domestic insecurity and frustration gained momentum in the postwar era and culminated in a nationwide crusade in the 1950s, with McCarthy acting as one of its most celebrated leaders, against those within the country who were believed to be Communists.

In the postwar years, issues of gender and sexuality were discursively embedded within seemingly unrelated policy decisions, the legal system, medical opinions, and scientific theories. In addition to the widely documented Cold War persecution of homosexuals (D'Emilio, 1989; Johnson, 2004), the 1950s witnessed, in various domains of professional expertise, an effort to stigmatize people with unconventional gender and sexual expressions. Going beyond the richly studied McCarthy witch hunts, the first half of this article traces various examples that illuminate how gender and sexual diversity was dealt with and handled in public policy, law, medicine, and science between the mid-1940s and the late 1950s. From public policies and laws concerning citizenship, the welfare state, and immigration, to the rising cultural authority of medical professionals (especially psychiatrists) on the subject of sexuality and gender, to the scientific theories and medical treatments of homosexuality and transsexuality, the first half of this article explores how different—sometimes competing—elite discourses worked together in powerful ways to regulate and shape the American people's sexual experience in the early Cold War era.

Emerging in tandem with these dominant forces of surveillance, other medical and scientific discourses promoted a more liberalizing understanding of gender and sexuality. The second half of this article begins with these alternative discourses of sexual medicine and sexual science and, from there, describes how they interacted with the gender and sexual subcultures that took shape within the same sociopolitical context. The participants of these subcultures, usually cast as deviants who challenged the normative gender and sexual order, included unwed women, women who sought or performed abortions, prostitutes, gays and lesbians, and transsexuals and others who had strong cross-gender identification.

Simply put, under the aegis of McCarthyism and its aftermath, any forms of gender and sexual expression that did not fit the Cold War ideal of heterosexual nuclear familial lifestyle were treated as domestic subversions that threatened the moral fiber and national security of mid-20th-century America; cultural authorities participated in myriad ways to reinforce and promote this Cold War ideology of normative gender and sexuality. At the same time, by targeting members of the gender and sexual subcultures and forcing them to establish publicly invisible but privately tighter and more supportive bonds with one another, the oppressive postwar ideal of anti-Communism and domesticity unexpectedly cultivated the early roots of the second-wave feminist and modern sexual liberation movements.

* * *

In the immediate years leading up to the 1950s, one of the ways in which U.S. citizenship got defined was through the legal framing of an individual's access to the economic benefits of the then-expanding welfare state. Most returning soldiers perceived the 1944 GI Bill, for example, as a positive public policy innovation that gave them the most highly regarded honor as citizens of the country. Yet, this recognition did not apply to all returning soldiers: the Bill stated that "a discharge or release from active service under conditions other than dishonorable shall be a prerequisite to entitlement to veterans' benefits" (cited in Cory, 1951, 278). On April 21, 1945, Frank Hines, the administrator of Veterans Affairs, interpreted this clause in specifying that "an undesirable or blue discharge issued because of homosexual acts or tendencies generally will be considered as under dishonorable conditions" (cited in Cory, 1951, 278). As such, soldiers discharged for homosexuality were prevented from the legal entitlement to the economic (and social) benefits that other veterans enjoyed. The GI Bill, in other words, generated both an expansion and contraction in U.S. citizenship by democratizing education and home ownership for working-class and middle-class people, while simultaneously securing the access to these benefits in a way that explicitly excluded certain veterans because of their association with homosexuality (Canaday, 2003).

This process of the legal denunciation of homosexuality both reflected and reinforced the pervasive post-World War II gender ideology, according to which women were expected to devote their time entirely to domestic life, as opposed to gaining economic independence. In the case of the GI Bill, it offered the most generous benefits to married men, bolstering their role as family providers through dependency allowances and survivors' benefits. Women's benefits were always inferior to men's, and the 2 percent cap on women's participation in the military force (until 1967) made women's overall access to the GI Bill even more restricted. These regulations therefore ensured that women experienced the expansion of U.S. social citizenship primarily through their husbands' benefits. The GI Bill did more than exclude those individuals who were believed to have engaged in homosexual acts or to possess homosexual tendencies. It also channeled many more governmental resources to men than to women, securing the economic incentives for women to enter heterosexual marriages. Simply put, the denunciation of homosexuality in federal policy and the legal normalization of heterosexuality were two sides of the same coin.

In addition to defining U.S. citizenship internally through the welfare state, the legal normalization of heterosexuality also occurred at the nation's borders, which were governed by anti-homosexual U.S. immigration law around the mid-20th century. The 1952 Immigration and Nationality Act, also known as the McCarran-Walter Act, contained two anti-homosexual provisions: one barred from entry immigrants who had committed "crimes of moral turpitude," and another barred those "afflicted with psychopathic personality." Although the former framed homosexuality in terms of conduct and behavior, the latter supported the notion that homosexuality referred to a distinct personality type. Based on these two provisions and in consultation with the Public Health Service, immigration officials deported those aliens who had received "Class A" certification after examination by the Public Health Service. The McCarran-Walter Act exemplifies a legal articulation of anti-Communist and anti-homosexual campaigns in the context of the early 1950s. The increasingly widespread equation of homosexuals with Communists, both of which were construed as specific types of people who could easily slip into U.S. borders undetected, constituted an important driving force behind the Cold War surveillance of the geographical boundaries of the United States (Canaday, 2003).

Because the "psychopathic personality" clause of the McCarran-Walter Act involved the overlap between law and health care regulation, it remained a nexus of expertise contention throughout the 1950s. In the early phase of the enactment of the McCarran-Walter Act, the federal courts heavily relied on psychiatrists' expert opinions for identifying the "psychopathic personality" of immigrants. But psychiatric experts gradually refrained from testifying in immigration cases about the legal association of homosexuality with psychopathic personality. When it was first introduced to the United States, the concept of psychopathy was not confined to sexual abnormality. Before the 1920s, U.S. psychiatrists preferred to describe psychopaths as egocentric, selfish, irritable, antisocial, nervous, and weak willed, and primarily applied the term to either "hypersexual" women or unemployed men (Freedman, 1987).

Psychopaths were sexualized, so to speak, only after the power and cultural authority of psychiatry expanded beyond its initial base in mental asylums into courts, prisons, and the military forces, and this was accompanied by the increasing influence of Freudian psychoanalysis on U.S. psychiatric practice from the 1930s onward. By the 1950s, psychiatrists interpreted sexual psychopathy as a distinctly male trait that was appropriate for describing violent sexual offenders, a group that came to be understood as neither exclusively nor necessarily homosexuals. Meanwhile, homosexuality was theorized by psychoanalysts as a more profound inadequate psychosexual development that represented one of the fundamental roots to many other psychopathological traits.

Facing psychiatrists' increasing dissenting voices regarding the meaning and treatment of sexual psychopaths, Immigration and Naturalization Service officials and federal judges eventually codified homosexuality and psychopathic personality as legal-political and not medical categories (Canaday, 2003). Despite the different meanings attached to the same expertise language, the sexual experiences of those people within and those hoping to cross U.S. borders were intensely regulated in a relatively similar way.

Rather than treating homosexuality as a legal matter, medical professionals preferred to characterize it as a form of mental illness. U.S. physicians first reported cases of homosexuality in the 1880s, borrowing medical and scientific theories of "sexual inversion"—the clinical phrase that was more widely used for describing homosexuality around the turn of the century—that were already popular in Europe (Hansen, 1992 [1989]). In his famous *Psychopathia Sexualis* (1892 [1886]), the Viennese psychiatrist Richard v. Krafft-Ebing first propounded the theory of homosexuality as a type of diseased neurotic degeneracy, hinting at some sort of hereditary component to it, but, at the same time, treating it strictly as a psychiatric disorder.

In explaining homosexuality, other medical doctors in Europe, followed by the ones in the United States, quickly adopted Krafft-Ebing's degeneration theory, in part because the theory struck a strong resonance with the then-popular framework of Darwinian evolutionary ideas. Gradually, doctors and the lay public began to view homosexuality as a clinical pathology that fell under the (exclusive) realm of medical expertise.

In 1905, Sigmund Freud published his *Three Essays on the Theory of Sexuality*, which substantiated the pathological view of homosexuality in the early 20th century and had a profound influence on how other medical and scientific experts conceptualized human sexuality in the subsequent years. Emphasizing childhood experience, Freud rooted the causality of male homosexuality in the psychosexual developmental model of the Oedipal complex. In the Oedipal complex, the boy child began his development by desiring his mother. However, as he soon discovered his mother's "lack of penis," he developed castration anxiety—the fear of his father, the totem figure. At this point, some boys inappropriately resolved the castration anxiety by identifying with their mothers. This identification process marked the development of narcissistic homosexuality, because, according to Freud, these children now saw themselves *as* the mother and would find a sexual partner representing themselves who desired them in the way that they desired their mother in the early stages of the Oedipus.

Yet, in the same essay, Freud also proposed the shocking concept of "polymorphously perverse disposition." Freud explained that "there is indeed something innate lying behind the perversions but that it is something innate in everyone, though as a disposition it may vary in its intensity and may be increased by the influences of actual life" (2000 [1905], 37). Elaborating on this idea of "polymorphously perverse disposition," Freud suggested that there existed a "latent homosexuality" in everyone, at least in their unconsciousness: "All human beings," wrote Freud, "are capable of making a homosexual object-choice and have in fact made one in their unconscious" (2000 [1905], 11). Although the notions of polymorphous perversity and latent homosexuality may seem like a fairly liberal interpretation of sexual perversion, in his third essay "Transformations of Puberty," however, Freud contended that the most desirable psychosexual developmental path led to heterosexual object choice with coitus as the final aim.

In his section on the "prevention of inversion," Freud stated: "One of the tasks implicit in object-choice is that it should find its way to the opposite sex" (2000 [1905], 95). Thus, Freud ultimately maintained that heterosexual orientation in adulthood represented true sexual maturity and that homosexual orientation was nothing but the result of an arrested childhood psychological development. This layered theory of human sexuality offered 20th-century psychiatrists a language that casts sexual orientation in exclusively psychogenic terms.

Sigmund Freud, ca. 1921. (Library of Congress)

But not all psychiatrists appropriated Freud's theory without hesitation. Following the publication of *Three Essays* and his other works, U.S. psychiatrists and psychoanalysts in particular took on a very conservative interpretation of Freud. They popularized the belief that, because homosexuality was an arrested psychosexual development, it could be "cured" through psychotherapy. In 1940, a year after Freud's death, U.S. analyst Sandor Rado published his influential essay "A Critical Examination of the Concept of Bisexuality," in which he outright refuted Freud's theory of polymorphous perversity and latent homosexuality by arguing that infantile bisexuality was not an universally normal condition. Whereas Freud had stressed in his later years that homosexuality, strictly speaking, was not an illness, Rado rejected the idea of latent homosexuality entirely and insisted that all homosexuality was pathological and thus potentially curable.

Later on in the sociopolitical context of the 1950s and early 1960s, other psychiatrists, such as Edmund Bergler (1956) and Irving Bieber (1962), completely endorsed Rado's psychoanalytic framework. They went on to describe male homosexuality as a form of "psychic masochism," occurring most frequently in boys with detached fathers, or "the absence of strong fatherhood," thereby bolstering the Cold War ideal of nuclear family units. These themes also appeared, for instance, in both *Female Homosexuality* (1954), the first medical monograph devoted to the topic of lesbianism by Dr. Frank Caprio, and *All the Sexes* (1955) by Dr. George Henry, which was written for a lay audience and based on his original 1,000-page tome *Sex Variants*.

After their wartime involvement in screening out mentally "handicapped" military inductees—including those with "homosexual proclivities"—U.S. psychiatrists gained an unprecedented level of social status in the postwar years. In the 1940s, a major generational battle broke out within the psychiatric profession. The American Psychiatric Association (APA) had a long history of representing the interests of public asylum physicians, who predominantly favored the use of somatic methods (such as lobotomy, hydrotherapy, and shock therapy) to treat the mentally ill.

After the war, however, the APA was joined by a younger generation of psychiatrists who had experienced their early careers on the battlefield. They believed that environmental stressors, rather than neurological factors, played the more significant role in causing mental diseases. As such, they contended that local psychotherapy, as opposed to institutionalization, was the more favorable approach to treating psychoneuroses and other more serious psychiatric disorders. This shift in the institutional bases and therapeutic approaches to mental illness, therefore, collided with the overwhelming prevalence of psychoanalytic theory within the psychiatric discourse. The culmination of these historical forces rendered the U.S. mental health profession as one of the most influential cultural authorities to deliver opinions about people's gender and sexual experiences in the 1950s.

Meanwhile, medical doctors had the most difficulty grasping the intertwining relationship between gender and sexuality in dealing with transsexual patients. When transsexuals, individuals who possess a deep-seated desire to become members of the opposite sex, began to seek professional surgical interventions for modifying their own physical sex in the 1940s and the 1950s, physicians debated furiously among themselves over the most appropriate therapeutic response to these requests (Meyerowitz, 2002).

On the one hand, some medical experts, mostly influenced by European perspectives, used the scientific theory of human bisexuality to legitimate the administration of sex reassignment surgery on transsexuals. One of the major proponents of this approach was Harry Benjamin, who received his medical degree in Germany in 1912 and then came to the United States in 1913. Coming from the German tradition of sexology, Benjamin was the key figure to introduce European sexual science to experts and the public of the United States. Having previously collaborated with Magnus Hirschfeld and studied under Eugen Steinach, Benjamin became the main endocrinologist and physician of Christine Jorgensen, who was the first U.S. male-to-female transsexual to undergo sex reassignment surgery abroad in Denmark and who received great notoriety as a result of mass media publicity upon her return to the United States in the 1950s.

Relying on a long tradition of endocrinological research that demonstrated how men and women both had various quantities of male and female hormones, Benjamin and Jorgensen used the scientific theory of

Christine Jorgensen was the first American male-to-female transsexual to undergo sex reassignment surgery. She is shown here in New York City in 1953. (Library of Congress)

universal bisexuality to explain her condition to the public. Furthermore, by emphasizing the biological basis of human bisexuality, they justified her sex change surgery, with the idea that transsexuals were simply extreme versions of an universal bisexual condition.

On the other hand, under the influence of Rado, most U.S. medical professionals, psychiatrists, and psychoanalysts in particular, rejected the view of universal human bisexuality. Instead, they argued that identification and behaviors that did not conform to the rigid opposition of the two sexes were the result of early childhood psychosexual maladjustment and thus mental disorders. In refuting both the Freudian interpretation and the biological model of bisexuality that situated sex on a continuum, this group of experts advocated the necessity of psychotherapeutic intervention for individuals whose behaviors and identifications did not follow the conventional sexual norm. They disapproved of medical intervention in the form of sex change surgery as the ideal method for treating transsexuals.

Implicitly, these psychoanalysts and psychiatrists relied on the rigid notion of two opposite biological sexes to see various forms of atypical sexual identification as a psychological, not a physical, problem. Repudiating the claim of universal bisexuality held up by doctors like Benjamin, the psychogenic model predominated through the 1950s, reflecting the rising authoritative status of psychoanalytically oriented psychiatrists in U.S. society after World War II.

When situated in its proper historical context, however, this medical debate over transsexuality simply reveals the larger cultural dynamic of the Cold War era. Although the two sides of the debate seem to be in strong opposition, in terms of the way medical experts interpreted the phenomenon of transsexuality specifically, both sides nonetheless shared the same normative assumptions about desirable gender orientation and behavior. Anchoring on traditional understandings of the proper alignment between sex and gender—men with masculinity and women with femininity—the opinions of those psychoanalysts and psychiatrists who argued for psychotherapies as the best means to treat transsexuality explicitly endorsed heterosexualized gender norms.

But even physicians like Benjamin, who were outnumbered by the psychoanalysts and psychiatrists, relied on and reinforced traditional gender roles, to some degree, in justifying sex change surgery as the best therapeutic approach to treating transsexuality. This was especially the case, for instance, when Benjamin recommended surgical intervention based on the reasoning that this procedure would balance transsexuals' extreme bisexual condition. The outcome of the surgeries, according to Benjamin, would allow transsexual patients to become normal men and women, conforming to and displaying manners appropriate for their changed sex.

Similarly, Jorgensen's fame and celebrity upon her return to the United States in the winter of 1952 from her sex reassignment in Denmark could also be understood as the result of her careful self-representation and self-embodiment of traditional notions of femininity (Serlin, 1995). Only by presenting herself as a "lady" and adopting the conventional roles and behaviors associated with being a woman could Jorgensen appear in front of the U.S. public as a respectable person, someone even worth celebrating and receiving a great measure of media attention.

Therefore, apart from the psychoanalysts and psychiatrists, voices of others like Benjamin and Jorgenson also adhered to and operated, however implicitly, within the dominant heterosexist and homophobic U.S. cultural imagination of the postwar period. It was a time when interconnected ideas of anti-Communism, civil loyalty, individual morality, gender conformity, normative heterosexuality, private behavior, and public order all took on an unprecedented overlapping role in shaping the American people's anxiety, locally and nationally.

Be it public policies discriminating against people with homosexual tendencies or psychiatric models that consistently psychopathologized sexual deviants, experts in law and medicine each had their own ways of controlling people's gender and sexual expressions. As reflected in the demographic trends of the period, women and men married younger and had more babies in the postwar years than at any other point in the course of the 20th century.

And this was accompanied by the significant decline in divorce rate, generating a historically unique, culturally homogenous, and nationally idealized image of nuclear family units that normalized heterosexuality and traditional gender roles. As historian Elaine Tyler May has put it quite succinctly, "As the cold war began, young postwar Americans were home-ward bound" (1999 [1988], ix). The gender ideology of the postwar era redefined men as breadwinners and women as mothers, because the "self-contained home held out the promise of security in an insecure world" (May, 1999 [1988], ix). This powerful notion of containment—including the containment of acceptable gender and sexual norms—permeated every aspect of U.S. life in the 1950s, serving as the key to national security and the offsetting of Cold War cultural anxiety. Various cultural authorities acted as the human agents of the Cold War surveillance of the gendered and sexualized nature of mid-20th-century U.S. social experience.

* * *

As the Cold War sociopolitical climate intensified, most physicians insisted that the proper alignment between sex and gender represented the most desirable—and perhaps even the most natural—arrangement of sexual development. It was in this context that a group of medical scientists at the Johns Hopkins Hospital proposed a radically different perspective. In hoping to better understand and treat patients born with ambiguous genitalia, a condition also known as intersexuality (although the term used in the 1950s was "hermaphroditism"), John Money, John L. Hampson, and Joan G. Hampson distinguished the concept of gender from the concept of sex, suggesting that these two aspects of an individual's sexual development did not necessarily bear any predetermined (natural) connection.

In an article published in 1955, Money used the phrase "gender role" for "all those things that a person says or does to disclose himself or herself as having the status of boy or man, girl or woman," and the term "gender" to refer to "outlook, demeanor, and orientation" (1955, 254, 258). Both gender role and gender, according to Money's definitions, could be conceptualized irrespective of reproductive anatomy, the main visible marker of one's physical sex.

Based on their study of intersex patients, Joan Hampson and Money posited that "psychosexual maturation is determined by various life experiences encountered and transacted, and is not predetermined as some sort of automatic or instinctive product of the bodily achievement of sexual maturation" (1955, 16). In other words, gender—or the "sex of rearing"— was something culturally manipulable, very different from sex, which was biologically determined. Whether intended or not, in differentiating gender from sex this way, Money's research team had provided Americans with a conception of gender as being socially malleable and not fixed at birth.

This novel language of gender later became a powerful tool for second-wave feminists in the 1960s and 1970s to rework dominant cultural ideas about women's proper role in society as mothers or housewives who maintained the "cult of domesticity." Indeed, the conceptual separation of gender from sex later enabled feminists to claim that women, like men, deserve full public and political involvement, because gender roles do not necessarily correspond to biological sex differences but are simply culturally constructed.

Before the rise of the second-wave feminist movement, however, many women in the 1950s, consciously or not, embraced what Betty Friedan had called "the feminine mystique," an image of sexually passive wives and docile nurturing mothers that had been glorified by journalists, educators, writers, advertisers, and experts alike. This was especially true for white middle-class women who lived in the suburbs.

Other women who did not conform to this Cold War gender ideology, which mirrored and reinforced the heterosexual family ideal of the time, were cast as dangerous, immoral, and deviant. Unwed women, women who sought or performed abortions, prostitutes, and women who desired other women sexually all fell under this category. Scientific researchers, medical professionals, legal authorities, and other disseminators of expert opinions without question played a huge role in mediating the social experiences of these women.

Adding onto their ideas about gender and sexual propriety, male experts worked with one another to define their capacity in intervening women's lives. Physicians, most of them male, for instance, consistently stressed the importance of female sexual health to an enduring marital relationship. Linking vaginal orgasm, as opposed to clitoral orgasm, to marital stability and community security, medical doctors self-proclaimed their authority and competence in ensuring female sexual health through state-mandated premarital consultations (Lewis, 2005). Unmarried women were deemed dangerous to U.S. society because they did not participate in the main building blocks of a secure national community—heterosexual marriage.

Similarly, many women abortionists and their clients faced a tremendous amount of pressure in the 1950s, when male physicians and district attorneys worked together to shut down the clinics run by those licensed female doctors who performed abortions. As such, it became increasingly difficult for women who wanted to end their pregnancy to seek help from female practitioners, at a time when male doctors often refused to perform abortion—especially before *Roe v. Wade,* which legalized abortion in 1973 (Solinger, 1994). Unwed women, female abortionists, and pregnant women who wanted an abortion were all regarded as immoral, because experts saw them as disrupting a secure national community, the main building blocks of which were nuclear family units.

In addition to unwed women and women who sought or performed abortion, prostitutes and lesbians were also viewed as dangerous to the health of the country. Because the idea of containment was so central to national security in the 1950s, female prostitutes and women who desired other women became symbols of female sexual excess and uncontained female sexuality (Penn, 1994). Challenging the Cold War "feminine mystique," female sex workers and lesbians did not embrace the prevalent view of women as sexually passive wives or docile nurturing mothers.

Instead, by the nature of their sexuality, prostitutes and lesbians, much like unmarried women and female abortionists and their clients, disrupted the moral fiber of the country by encouraging sexual mores that undermined and destabilized marital heterosexuality. Before the feminist politicization of the language of gender, many cultural authorities consistently voiced the opinion that the behavior of these hypersexual women resembled domestic subversions and identified them as serious hindrances to establishing a secure cultural environment for the nation.

But John Money's research team was not the first group of experts to unsettle the gender and sexual ideology of Cold War America. Before the distinction between sex and gender emerged in the medical literature during the mid-1950s, Alfred Kinsey and his research associates had already challenged the prevailing cultural assumptions about Americans' sexual practices with the publication of *Sexual Behavior in the Human Male* (1948) and *Sexual Behavior in the Human Female* (1953).

In both volumes, Kinsey's research group provided shocking statistical evidences, documenting the wide prevalence of people's sexual behavior in the nation that did not exactly reflect the conventional moral attitudes of U.S. culture at the time. Presenting empirical findings of various nonreproductive sexual experiences—from homosexual behavior to masturbation to extramarital intercourse to bestiality—the Kinsey reports provoked a wide range of negative criticisms from religious groups and other expert circles, including members of the American Statistical Association and the American Medical Association, especially those psychoanalytically oriented psychiatrists.

Like the work of Money, one of the major contributions of Kinsey's studies was that they provided a new frame of reference for both expert and popular opinions regarding issues of gender and sexuality (Chiang, 2008). Whereas Money provided women and other political activists with a new language of gender and new ways of conceptualizing it, Kinsey's research team promoted a sociological and statistical perspective of normal sexual behavior that drastically departed from the dominant psychoanalytic framework.

Dr. Alfred Kinsey, on the left, standing by sorting machine used to tabulate sexual data collected by scientists. (Wallace Kirkland/Time & Life Pictures/Getty Images)

For instance, reporting a high frequency of homosexual behavior in the nation, Kinsey argued that psychiatrists' pathologizing view of homosexuality was inherently problematic, because their clinical insights were generalized from only a small group of individuals who went to psychotherapy. In contrast, Kinsey insisted that his cross-sectional research method (supposedly) sampled the entire U.S. population, and thus the high statistical rate of homosexual behavior in his findings actually suggested that homosexuality was fairly "normal" (Kinsey et al., 1949).

Many gay men and lesbians welcomed Kinsey's publications, which served as a piece of scientific evidence that they could refer to in challenging the orthodox psychiatric framing of homosexuality as a mental illness.

Alfred C. Kinsey

Best known for his empirical studies on human sexuality, Alfred C. Kinsey (1894–1956) received his ScD in zoology from Harvard University in 1919. His academic training reflected his early career research interest: gall wasps, the topic of his doctoral thesis. Throughout the 1920s, Kinsey not only published scientific papers on gall wasps specifically, but also wrote introductory textbooks in biology for a more general audience. After graduate study, he began research and teaching at Indiana University, where he founded the Institute for Research in Sex, Gender, and Reproduction in 1947.

His interest in human sexuality began in the late 1930s, when he coordinated a new course on marriage at Indiana and was unsatisfied with the quantity and quality of scientific research on human sexuality. This frustration motivated Kinsey to interview his colleagues and students on an informal basis. He then began to sharpen his interview questionnaires that detailed people's sexual history and developed statistical methods that eventually defined his major contribution.

Supported by the Committee for Research in the Problem of Sex, with funds from the Rockefeller Foundation, Kinsey put together a research team, which included two Indiana colleagues: psychologist Wardell B. Pomeroy and statistician Clyde Martin. Together, they published *Sexual Behavior in the Human Male* in 1948 and *Sexual Behavior in the Human Female* in 1953. While working on the second book, they were joined by the anthropologist Paul H. Gebhard.

The findings that they reported in the two "Kinsey Reports," the most famous example being the high incidence of homosexual behavior, shocked the nation. But, although the first volume immediately became a bestseller and acquired an international reputation, the second volume on women invited much harsher criticism. Kinsey and his team ultimately interviewed 5,460 white men and 5,385 white women. This sample has been the subject of long-term criticism for its poor representation of the entire (U.S.) population.

At the time that Kinsey ventured into the study of human sexuality, authoritative inquiries on the subject still largely fell under the realm of the expertise of psychiatrists, gynecologists, and other medically trained doctors. Therefore, one of the most significant contributions that Kinsey's research team made was providing a scientific frame of sexual normalcy that was rooted in sociological thinking that emphasizes the prevalence of sexual behavior. This stood in stark contrast to the earlier clinical frame of sexual normality, advocated by psychiatrists and psychoanalysts, which stressed the development of psychosexual identity.

Although still facing a wide range of hostile persecutions in the public sphere, many gay men and lesbians endorsed Kinsey's framework of sexual normality. They began to think of and portray themselves as healthy individuals and eventually organized around themselves a homosexual emancipation movement—known as the "homophile" movement—in the early 1950s.

This movement consisted of the founding of the Mattachine Society, whose members were mostly men, in 1951 by Harry Hay and a small group of his friends. Soon, its lesbian counterpart organization, the Daughters of Bilitis, was founded in 1955 in San Francisco. Both organizations gradually spawned chapters across the nation, the most prominent ones being in Los Angeles—Mattachine Society's initial headquarters—San Francisco, New

York City, and Washington, D.C., and each organization published its own magazine: the *Mattachine Review* by the Mattachine Society and the *Ladder* by the Daughters of Bilitis. In addition, the homosexual magazine *ONE*, based in Los Angeles, was established in tandem with these efforts. Despite how they seemingly represented separate endeavors, the Mattachine Society, the Daughters of Bilitis, and *ONE* supported and collaborated with one another in a tight underground social network (D'Emilio, 1998 [1983]).

Indeed, what scholars have called the "Lavender Scare"—the Cold War persecutions of gay and lesbian civil servants—posed a real threat to these people's economic status, work routines, means of socialization, and psychological well-being, especially for those federal and private-sector employees working in Washington, D.C. (Johnson, 2004). Thus, these governmental forces of surveillance, in addition to the forces of scientific knowledge in defining sexual normality, also contributed to the formation and consolidation of a gay and lesbian subculture and political consciousness in the 1950s.

Taking the idea that homosexuals were an oppressed minority as their fundamental organizing principle, many homophile leaders in the 1950s emphasized the importance for gay men and lesbians to conform to conventional gender roles in order to gain social respectability (Meeker, 2001). Members of the Mattachine Society and male editors of *ONE* magazine wore suits and ties when presenting themselves to the public, giving the impression that they were intelligent and dignified citizens.

In fact, most of the individuals who participated in the early homophile movement were white, affluent, and had a middle-class background, which made their organizations appear to be even more "normal," "respectable," and "tolerable." For male homophile leaders, embodying a masculine gender orientation reflected both their normalcy and the notion that their identity around which the homophile movement was built was defined around their sexual desire, irrespective of their own gender role preference.

Their retreat to cultural respectability manifested, for example, in their prejudice against other non-gender conformist homosexuals. After World War II, "swish" became the most commonly used term in homophile publications such as *ONE* and *The Mattachine Review* to refer to gay men with obvious effeminate appearance and mannerism. In addition to the homophile leaders and writers for these magazines, many gay male readers from all over the country wrote letters to these homophile publications, expressing their strong disgust toward other swishes and swishness in general (Loftin, 2007).

Much as the reason why Christine Jorgensen self-crafted and maintained a feminine public appearance, gay men's anti-swish sentiment in the 1950s reflected the broader Cold War gender anxieties. Adhering to the dominant masculine and feminine conventionalities that heterosexuals deemed normal (and made heterosexuals normal), the homophile leaders and other gay men rejected swishes and swishness in order to construct their public image as upstanding citizens who were entitled to the rights, protections, and benefits of U.S. citizenship.

Not all sexual minorities, however, believed that their sex at birth determined how they ought to behave. Besides the many swishes who insisted that there was nothing inherently wrong with their effeminate behavior, many individuals with cross-gender identification went directly to medical professionals for altering their physical sex. In fact, prior to the wide publicity of Christine Jorgenson's sex reassignment success story in the 1950s, the U.S. press had already begun to cover sex change cases as early as the 1930s. "From the 1930s to the 1950s," according to historian Joanne Meyerowitz (1998), "certain readers appropriated public stories of sex change and included the quest for surgical and hormonal transformation as a central component of their sense of self" (p. 160).

After Jorgenson returned to the United States and surrendered to her fame and celebrity in the early 1950s, these people with cross-gender identification became more fully aware of who they were and what they could possibly become—with the aid of medical technology in the forms of synthetic hormones and plastic surgery. However ironically, a distinct transsexual identity consolidated in a sociopolitical context that perceived individuals who did not follow traditional gender and sexual norms as dangerous, deviant, and immoral (Stryker, 2008).

* * *

Aware of the broader social anxiety of the Cold War era, most policymakers, state officials, physicians, psychoanalysts, and other cultural authorities maintained that a normative gender and sexual order rooted in the ideal of heterosexual familial lifestyle was crucial to establishing a stable national community. The GI Bill, the McCarran-Walter Act, and psychoanalysts' rejection of the theory of universal bisexuality all stigmatized individuals with gender and sexual expressions that failed to adhere to a heteronormative framework.

At the same time, other scientific and medical experts, such as Harry Benjamin, John Money, and Alfred Kinsey, either directly challenged or provided the conceptual tool for members of the contemporary gender and sexual subcultures to rework the basic tenet of Cold War cultural ideology. Over time, the political effort of these subculture participants began to take shape in the 1950s and culminated in the forceful second-wave feminist and sexual liberation movements by the early 1970s.

Of all the subcultural resistances, the historical significance of the emergence of transsexuality seems the most intriguing. On the one hand, its medical and cultural justification appears to reinforce conventional gender norms: Benjamin and Jorgenson claimed her sex reassignment as favorable only by presenting her to the public as a "feminine," respectable lady after her surgery. And even transvestism and transsexuality hit the sexual liberalism of sex researcher Kinsey, who disapproved of genital surgery as the most desirable medical intervention for those who wanted to become the opposite sex or gender (Meyerowitz, 2001).

On the other hand, after Jorgenson's publicity, people with cross-gender identification began to articulate a distinct transsexual (and later transgender) identity that fundamentally contests unwanted social regulations of one's gender and sexual orientation. Furthermore, initially conceived as part of the gay and lesbian movement, cross-dressers, lesbian butches, drag kings, female impersonators, and intersexed people, among other individuals who transgressed boundaries of sex and gender, eventually organized themselves to support an autonomous transgender movement by the 1990s. In the broader historical shaping of the early Cold War United States, whether as friends or foes, delivering liberating or oppressive expert opinions, cultural authorities defined the social meanings of Americans' gender and sexual experience, which ultimately reflected the hopes and fears that marked their vision of political change in the decades to come.

References and Further Reading

Bergler, Edmund. *Homosexuality: Disease or Way of Live?* New York: Hill and Wang, 1956.

Bieber, Irving, et al. *Homosexuality: A Psychoanalytic Study of Male Homosexuals.* New York: Basic Books, 1962.

Canaday, Margot. "Building a Straight State: Sexuality and Social Citizenship under the 1944 G. I. Bill." *Journal of American History* 90 (2003): 935–957.

Canaday, Margot. "'Who Is a Homosexual?': The Consolidation of Sexual Identities in Mid-Twentieth-Century American Immigration Law." *Law & Social Inquiry* 28 (2003): 351–386.

Caprio, Frank Samuel. *Female Homosexuality: A Psychodynamic Study of Lesbianism.* Foreword by Karl M. Bowman. New York: Citadel Press, 1954.

Chiang, Howard Hsueh-Hao. "Effecting Science, Affecting Medicine: Homosexuality, the Kinsey Reports, and the Contested Boundaries of Psychopathology in the United States, 1948–1965." *Journal of the History of the Behavioral Sciences* 44 (2008): 300–318.

Cory, Donald Webster (pseudonym for Edward Sagarin). *The Homosexual in America: A Subjective Approach.* Introduction by Albert Ellis. New York: Greenberg, 1951.

D'Emilio, John. *Sexual Politics, Sexual Communities: The Making of a Homosexual Minority in the United States, 1940–1970.* 1983. 2nd ed. Chicago: University of Chicago Press, 1998 [1983].

D'Emilio, John. "The Homosexual Menace: The Politics of Sexuality in Cold War America." In *Passion and Power: Sexuality in History.* Edited by Kathy Peiss and Christina Simmons, 226–240. Philadelphia: Temple University Press, 1989.

Freedman, Estelle B. "'Uncontrolled Desires': The Response to the Sexual Psychopath, 1920–1960." *Journal of American History* 74 (1987): 83–106.

Freud, Sigmund. *Three Essays on the Theory of Sexuality*. Translated and edited by James Strachey. New York: Basic Books, 2000 [1905].

Friedan, Betty. *The Feminine Mystique*. New York: Dell, 1963.

Hampson, Joan G., and John Money. "Idiopathic Sexual Precocity in the Female: Report of Three Cases." *Psychosomatic Medicine* 17 (1955): 16–35.

Hansen, Bert. "American Physicians' 'Discovery' of Homosexuals, 1880–1900: A New Diagnosis in a Changing Society." In *Framing Disease: Studies in Cultural History*. Edited by Charles E. Rosenberg and Janet L. Golden, 104–133. New Brunswick, NJ: Rutgers University Press, 1992 [1989].

Henry, George W. *All the Sexes: A Study of Masculinity and Femininity*. Forward by David E. Roberts. Toronto/New York: Rinehart & Company, 1955.

Johnson, David K. *The Lavender Scare: The Cold War Persecution of Gays and Lesbians in the Federal Government*. Chicago: University of Chicago Press, 2004.

Kinsey, Alfred C., Wardell B. Pomeroy, and Clyde E. Martin. *Sexual Behavior in the Human Male*. Philadelphia: W. B. Saunders, 1948.

Kinsey, Alfred C., Wardell B. Pomeroy, Clyde E. Martin, and Paul H. Gebhard. "Concepts of Normality and Abnormality in Sexual Behavior." In *Psychosexual Development in Health and Disease: The Proceedings of the 38th Annual Meeting of the American Psychopathological Association,* held in New York City, June 1948. Edited by Paul Hoch and Joseph Zubin, 11–32. New York: Grune & Stratton, 1949.

Kinsey, Alfred C., Wardell B. Pomeroy, Clyde E. Martin, and Paul H. Gebhard. *Sexual Behavior in the Human Female*. Philadelphia: W. B. Saunders, 1953.

Krafft-Ebing, Richard v. *Psychopathia Sexualis, with Especial Reference to Contrary Sexual Instinct: A Medico-Legal Study*. 7th ed. Translated by Charles Gilbert Chaddock. Philadelphia: F. A. Davis, 1892 [1886].

Lewis, Carolyn Herbst. "Waking Sleeping Beauty: The Premarital Pelvic Exam and the Heterosexuality during the Cold War." *Journal of Women's History* 17 (2005): 86–110.

Loftin, Craig Michael. "Unacceptable Mannerisms: Gender Anxieties, Homosexual Activism, and Swish in the United States, 1945–1965." *Journal of Social History* 40 (2007): 577–596.

May, Elaine Tyler. *Homeward Bound: American Families in the Cold War Era*. Revised and updated ed. New York: Basic Books, 1999 [1988].

Meeker, Martin. "Behind the Mask of Respectability: The Mattachine Society and Male Homophile Practice, 1950s–1960s." *Journal of the History of Sexuality* 10 (2001): 78–116.

Meyerowitz, Joanne. "Sex Change and the Popular Press: Historical Notes on Transsexuality in the United States, 1930–1955." *GLQ: Journal of Lesbian and Gay Studies* 4 (1998): 159–187.

Meyerowitz, Joanne. "Sex Research at the Borders of Gender: Transvestites, Transsexuals, and Alfred C. Kinsey." *Bulletin of the History of Medicine* 75 (2001): 72–90.

Meyerowitz, Joanne. *How Sex Changed: A History of Transsexuality in the United States.* Cambridge, MA: Harvard University Press, 2002.

Money, John. "Hermaphroditism, Gender, and Precocity in Hyperadreno-corticism." *Bulletin of the Johns Hopkins Hospital* 96 (1955): 253–264.

Penn, Donna. "The Sexualized Woman: The Lesbian, the Prostitute, and the Containment of Female Sexuality." In *Not June Cleaver: Women and Gender in Postwar America, 1945–1960.* Edited by Joanne Meyerowitz, 358–381. Philadelphia: Temple University Press, 1994.

Rado, Sandor. "A Critical Examination of the Concept of Bisexuality." *Psychosomatic Medicine* 2 (1940): 459–467.

Serlin, David Harley. "Christine Jorgensen and the Cold War Closet." *Radical History Review* 62 (1995): 136–165.

Solinger, Rickie. "Extreme Danger: Women Abortionists and Their Clients before *Roe* v. *Wade.*" In *Not June Cleaver: Women and Gender in Postwar America, 1945–1960.* Edited by Joanne Meyerowitz, 335–357. Philadelphia: Temple University Press, 1994.

Stryker, Susan. *Transgender History.* Berkeley, CA: Seal Press, 2008.

Mothers, Spy Queens, and Subversives: Women in the McCarthy Era

9

Michella M. Marino

The post-World War II era was both a time of opportunity and discrimination, as many white middle-class families moved in droves to the new suburbs, while families of color and varying ethnic backgrounds were denied the opportunity to pursue this ideal of material happiness because of racial segregation and economic policies. Although not available for all families, the middle-class suburbs represented the idealistic, capitalistic, and democratic American way of life. The government, leading officials, and private sector sought to protect this American way, even if that meant repressing U.S. freedoms and rights to combat the looming evil of the time: Communism and its host country, the Soviet Union.

Toward the end of World War II, U.S. and Soviet relations began to deteriorate. The inherent conflict between U.S. democracy and the Soviet Union's Communism fueled the tension between the former allies as peace plans were negotiated in Europe and the Pacific. While President Harry S Truman articulated a containment policy in order to stop the spread of Communism to Greece and Turkey, Americans naturally became concerned about the spread of Communism abroad and at home. Although the Communist Party (CP) had existed in the United States since 1919, its members, and others associated with it, were labeled as a national threat to the U.S. system and way of life in the postwar era. Fueled by Wisconsin Senator Joseph McCarthy from 1950 to 1954, the campaign to locate, persecute, and punish Communists in the United States during the Cold War became known as McCarthyism.

Although McCarthyism technically sought to eliminate Communism from the U.S. government, most Americans experienced the effects of McCarthyism in some way, shape, or form. Thousands of Americans lost their jobs, and many were unfairly targeted for radical activities not associated with Communism; however, others actually did engage in Communist actions and alliances. In this hunt for the few, many Americans experienced anxiety and fear as a result of the supposed infiltration of Communists in their communities and witnessed the violation of basic U.S. rights in order to squelch the "dangerous" Communist threat. People in all walks of life became targets of McCarthyism: government officials, engineers, lawyers, movie stars, teachers, firemen, janitors, men's room attendants, and housewives. Some employers required their employees to take loyalty oaths to the United States. Even a group of Las Vegas strippers was forced to swear that they had never plotted to overthrow the U.S. government.

Clearly, everyone was a potential Communist threat, but women actually began and ended the mainstream witch hunt associated with McCarthyism, starting with ex-Communist spy Elizabeth Bentley's naming names in 1947 and concluding with the heroic stance of the Women Strike for Peace (WSP) against HUAC activities in 1962.

Active and inactive Communist women existed and potentially posed a national threat, but many women were also unfairly labeled and attacked. Some women served as informers, and some who were unfairly persecuted fought back. But, because of their gender and the traditional ideology that tied women to the home in the late 1940s and 1950s, women proved easy targets for McCarthyism. Women who stepped outside of their traditional boundaries could be targeted as radical and dangerous. Yet women who remained inside their home boundaries could be seen as weak and impressionable to the ever-looming threat of Communism. Because of this contradictory status within the American family and society, McCarthyism targeted women in an often contradictory manner. This unbalanced persecution forced women to react and respond in differing ways, but women were always bound voluntarily or involuntarily within or at odds with the U.S. family.

The contradiction between women's varying roles stems from the social changes that women had experienced during World War II. Because millions of men had voluntarily joined or were drafted into the U.S. armed forces, women were responsible for managing the home front, which included working in the defense industry. Government and industrial propaganda told women that it was their patriotic duty to get out of the kitchen and into the workplace to help win the war. Rosie the Riveter became an icon for wartime women, as a strong, independent worker who supported the boys overseas, while still maintaining her femininity and wholesome American values.

Once the war ended, women were expected to return home and relinquish their jobs to the men, regardless of their particular economic needs for gainful employment. Although many new women war workers had discovered that they enjoyed the independence and economic stability that defense work outside the home provided, they soon found themselves forced out of their wartime jobs, with nowhere to turn but back to their family and home.

With the soldiers returning from overseas and the women returning home, many couples settled down to a life of early marriage and an abundance of children, which resulted in the baby boom generation. The postwar society returned to traditional middle-class gender roles of the male

Esther Brunauer

Colleagues, friends, and even her family doctor hailed Esther Brunauer as a hardworking, loyal, and devoted employee, wife, and mother. They also vouched that she was a staunch anti-Communist. Their testimonies, however, ultimately made no difference, as Brunauer was repeatedly targeted as a Communist or Communist sympathizer in the McCarthy era anti-Red campaigns.

Brunauer worked for the State Department during and after World War II while her husband Stephen, originally a poor Hungarian immigrant, worked for the U.S. government as a renowned chemist and explosives expert. In their younger days, the Brunauers had been involved in some Communist-front organizations, but, by the 1930s, they had fostered a personal, liberal anti-Communist and anti-fascist political belief. Neither ever belonged to the actual Communist Party.

Brunauer was first attacked in 1947 when a congressman misinterpreted one of her speeches as "echoing Soviet propaganda." HUAC investigated her loyalty, but she was declared faithful and left alone, until Joseph McCarthy listed her as a Communist in 1950. His smear campaign against Brunauer was simply inaccurate and misinformed. He accused her of involvement in activities in which she had not participated and confused her participation in non-Communist groups with those of Communist-led organizations. She rebutted McCarthy's flimsy charges and was exonerated yet again.

Brunauer was targeted a third time for simply being married to her husband, whose loyalty was also under review. By 1952, Esther lost her job because the State Department viewed her marriage as a security risk. She remarked, concerning the male panel that presided over her appeal, "Either their opinion of the reliability of women in professional positions was very low, or else they knew of many men who shared State Department secrets with their wives, and thought that a woman . . . must behave the same way."

Defeated, out of work, and with their reputations ruined, the Brunauers moved to Chicago, where necessity forced them to change careers. An unfortunate victim of the Red Scare, Esther Brunauer's entire life was disrupted and destroyed by the careless accusations of Joseph McCarthy and his henchmen.

breadwinner and female homemaker as represented in the family as a way to free themselves from the unstable past and establish a secure future. As the Cold War and anti-Communist hysteria descended upon the United States, U.S. society used the family as a model to, as historian Elaine Tyler May states, "offer a psychological fortress that would protect them against themselves" (May 1999, xxi). Family stability represented a safety net in an insecure world that could help deter the danger of Communism and the Cold War.

As the crusade against Communism emerged in the postwar era, women, their families, and their homes were often paraded as the symbols for which Americans should stand up and fight. This is best represented in what was deemed the "kitchen debate" in 1959 between Vice President Richard Nixon and Soviet Premier Nikita Khrushchev at the American Exhibition in Moscow. Nixon argued with Khrushchev about U.S. superiority—not in terms of weaponry and atomic energy, but instead in terms of U.S. advantages in modern consumer goods such as televisions, washing machines, and stoves. Consumerism represented capitalist success and, ultimately, American freedom.

According to Nixon, distinct gender roles, suburban homes, and a plethora of consumer goods allowed Americans the means for success and happiness. He stated, "To us, diversity, the right to choose, . . . is the most important thing. We don't have one decision made at the top by one government official. . . . We have many different manufacturers and many different kinds of washing machines so that the housewives have a choice" (May 1999, 11). These new appliances provided women with options to make their housework easier so that they could lead happier and more comfortable lives.

Under the Communist system, women were supposedly productive members of society and not tied solely to the home. According to U.S. journalists who witnessed Nixon and Khrushchev's "kitchen debate," Soviet women were productive and hardworking, but they also appeared unfeminine and desexualized. Because of new consumer products and appliances, women in the United States did not have to work as hard as the Soviet women and thus could spend their time on their physical beauty and sexuality, all courtesy of U.S. capitalist ideology.

What both sides failed to grasp was that their country's ideology had failed to live up to its reality. Many women in the United States and the Soviet Union worked outside of the home, but they also were largely responsible for domestic chores. Still, this stereotype of the Soviet woman as an unattractive, desexualized worker led to suspicion of self-supporting, emancipated women in the United States in the postwar era. The United States had decided to combat Communism to protect the American way of life, which included women tucked neatly into the family as the mother, wife, and homemaker, even if this was not the reality that many women lived.

This conflict between the ideology and reality regarding the status of women in the United States was evident in the persecution of women in the McCarthy era and in how women responded to this persecution. The stories of individual women and groups of women who were persecuted represent the dichotomy of types of women involved in U.S. society outside of their homes and how they were differently targeted and harassed by the government and employers.

First, some women legitimately belonged to the CP and worked to promote their belief in Communism in the United States. The American Communist Party often attracted young, educated, liberal women because of its theoretical stance to end discrimination against women. Communist leaders acknowledged women's inequality in society, especially in the workforce and in reference to sexual double standards.

Elizabeth Bentley, a young American woman who joined the Communist ranks and became a top-level Soviet spy, is partially responsible for triggering the paranoia and persecution that became McCarthyism, while also bringing down the Soviet spy ring in the United States. Bentley represents the ability of and reality faced by American women outside of their homes. Although she certainly used her status as a woman in a negative way, she often is not credited for her prominent role in McCarthyism and the Red Scare, partially because of her gender and radical actions as a woman.

In a 1948 radio interview, Elizabeth Bentley discusses her role in Congressional investigations of Communist infiltration of the U.S. government. (Library of Congress)

Bentley was born in New Milford, Connecticut, in 1908 but moved around with her parents until they settled in Rochester, New York, where she graduated from high school. On the surface, it appears that Bentley had a relatively normal childhood, at least in that she took piano lessons, participated in Girl Scouts and church activities, and played basketball. She later claimed, however, that her parents were incredibly strict and old-fashioned. Bentley went on to college at Vassar but was known as a loner. Before she graduated, her mother suddenly died, and, by the time she was 25, her father had passed away as well.

After graduation, Bentley entered into several sexual relationships with different men, a taboo for the time period. She also decided to attend graduate school at Columbia University during a time when 80 percent of doctoral students were men. In 1933, she broke off a marriage engagement to an Arab student with whom she was living, after winning a prized fellowship to attend the University of Florence in Italy.

In Florence, Bentley rebelled against her supposedly strict upbringing by drinking to excess, becoming sexually promiscuous, and cultivating her political extremism. She became actively involved in fascism but recanted when she became sexually involved with her faculty advisor, who convinced her of the evils of fascism and had his assistant write her master's thesis for her.

After returning to New York in 1934, Bentley struggled to find work and leased an apartment near Columbia, where she decided to take some business courses. In her building, Bentley met a woman named Lee Fuhr, and the two became fast friends. Bentley found out that Fuhr was a fervant anti-fascist, so Bentley regaled her with stories of her own active anti-fascism in Italy—but conveniently left out the part of her stay in which she had participated in fascism. As Bentley sought acceptance from Fuhr and her circle of friends, who were Communists, she decided that she too wanted to join the CP.

Bentley found the sense of belonging that she strove for in the CP and threw herself into its activities. Soon after Bentley had joined the CP, its secret underground department realized Bentley's prospect as an agent for Soviet intelligence because of her education and apparent anti-fascist activities. Bentley began an active espionage career for the CP and the Soviets in 1938, and soon began a sexual relationship with her controller, or her spy boss, Jacob Golos.

This relationship pulled her more deeply into the Communist spy ring. Golos essentially taught Bentley the tricks of the job and set her up with a position in a Communist-front business. Within a few years, the FBI had targeted Golos as a foreign agent, and it became clear that he could no longer run the spy network of which he was in charge, so he trained Bentley to slowly take over his duties. Golos's health was also failing, partially because of the stress of his work. His death in late 1943 left Bentley in charge of the U.S. Communist spy ring, which increasingly felt pressure to turn over its authority to Soviet KGB spies in the United States.

Ultimately, the pressure from the KGB, a friend's betrayal of Bentley's sources to the KGB, and a relationship with a so-called spy catcher led her to become an informer for the FBI. Fearful that she would be arrested by the FBI or be killed by the KGB, Bentley went to FBI agents in August 1945 to feel them out. Bentley fed the FBI half-truths and questioned the interrogating agents about her lover, whom she believed was some sort of spy, although they had never heard of him. (It turns out that he was a fake, trying to seduce women.)

It was the defection to the FBI of a former source that frightened Bentley into talking more earnestly with the FBI agents, although she continued to hide information and tell lies about her work and involvement with spying. It was not until November that Bentley felt that her life was in danger, from the CP and KGB, and she told all to the FBI, including the naming of names.

Whittaker Chambers was one of the first defectors to turn in information to the FBI on the Soviet spy ring in 1941, but it was not until Bentley had verified many of his sources four years later that he was taken seriously. Bentley's testimony and list of names led to the discovery of Communist infiltration in the State Department—through Alger Hiss—and, ultimately, to the atomic bomb project—through Abe Brothman to Harry Gold to David Greenglass. This led to the biggest case of them all—Julius Rosenberg, whom Bentley had listed by his first name. In 1947, director of the FBI, J. Edgar Hoover, handed over Bentley's file to certain congressmen to show that national security was indeed in danger and that the U.S. government needed to act.

By 1948, Bentley had launched her career as a professional ex-Communist spy, which entailed testifying at key court cases, appearing on radio talk shows, lecturing around the country about her Communist activities, and writing an autobiography. Using the tropes of American femininity, Bentley posed herself as a naïve schoolgirl or impressionable housewife type who had been easily influenced by the propaganda of those close to her and, thus, could not be held accountable for her own actions and involvement.

Over the next few years, Bentley attempted to manipulate her public image to, as a Bentley biographer calls, "a sort of Communist June Cleaver," particularly when she published part of her autobiography in *McCall's* magazine under the headline, "I Joined the Red Underground with the Man I Loved" (Olmsted 2002, 166). She ultimately was unable to control the media, which demonstrated an inability to mesh her gender and spy status.

Men dominated the postwar journalist profession, and they were not sure what to make of a woman in a traditionally male profession, which explains why many reporters simultaneously praised and denounced Bentley's accounts. The journalists molded Bentley to fit into common 1940s and 1950s stereotypes of Communists and female spies; she became either a devious blond, sexually charged seductress or a sexually starved, bitter, man-hating spinster.

Of course, Bentley was neither, but the culture of the Cold War period revealed the anxiety about independent, emancipated, strong women who were acting as a man would. Bentley manipulated her own image to gain acceptance for her actions and behavior in U.S. society and to deflect her own guilt and responsibility. This, in some ways, exemplifies the complicated status of women in the McCarthy era. They had the capabilities and often the means to seek life outside the traditional gender boundary lines, yet the public was not fully ready to accept these changes, and thus women still had to revert to "proper" gender norms to gain acceptance.

Also problematic, Bentley was an enigmatic figure, seeking attention and acceptance, as she had been for a long time. She was an unreliable witness for the anti-Communists as they attempted to build their cases against Communist spies and agitators, and she often manipulated the FBI while exaggerating or dramatizing her involvement, knowledge (or lack thereof), and influence in the Communist spy rings.

Regardless, Bentley's confession led the government to other supposed Communist spies, including Julius and Ethel Rosenberg, the only two people condemned to death during the McCarthy era. Ethel Rosenberg, like Bentley, had experienced bitter persecution because of her gender, but also because of her status as a mother. The government took the Rosenbergs to trial because of their supposed Communist ties and involvement in a Communist spy ring. The prosecution and, ultimately, the judge of their case accused them of atomic espionage by passing on secrets to the Soviet Union concerning the U.S. development of the atomic bomb, which led to the Soviet achievement of creating and detonating an A-bomb.

Ethel (left) and Julius Rosenberg ride to separate prisons following their espionage convictions on March 29, 1951. (Library of Congress)

Both Rosenbergs denied any involvement with Communism or the Soviet Union, which ultimately led to their execution. The evidence compiled against the couple was not particularly damning, but the political climate aroused by McCarthyism and the threat that Communism posed to the United States probably led to their guilty verdict.

Very little evidence of Ethel's involvement in Communism or a spy ring was ever uncovered. The government used her as leverage to force her husband into admitting his guilt, which he refused to do. One of the Justice Department's attorneys representing the prosecution of the Rosenbergs explained to the Joint Committee on Atomic Energy in a secret session prior to the trial:

> The only thing that will break this man Rosenberg is the prospect of a death penalty or getting the chair, plus that if we convict his wife, too, and give her a stiff sentence of 25 or 30 years, that combination may serve to make this fellow disgorge. (Schrecker, 1998, 178)

The attorney fully admitted that they did not have a strong case against Ethel, because they were unsure whether she was even aware of Julius's activities, but they planned on using her to break her husband's stubbornness to confess by convicting her as well. The convicting trial judge, however, believed that Ethel was every bit as guilty as her husband. He stated,

> The evidence indicated quite clearly that Julius Rosenberg was the prime mover in this conspiracy. However, let no mistake be made about the role which his wife, Ethel Rosenberg, played in this conspiracy. Instead of deterring him from pursuing his ignoble cause, she encouraged and assisted the cause . . . She was a full-fledged partner in this crime. Indeed the defendants . . . placed their

devotion to their cause above their own personal safety and were conscious that they were sacrificing their own children, should their misdeeds be detected—all of which did not deter them from pursuing their course. Love for their cause dominated their lives—it was even greater than their love for their children. (Schrecker 1994, 145)

Ethel Rosenberg's real crime, according to the government and the judge, was to stand by her husband and endanger her children. The government used the Rosenbergs to show how Communism tore apart marriages and families. Many scholars, popular writers, and even some former Communists claimed that the CP forced its members to put it first, even above family and personal relationships. Communist mothers often faced charges that Communism had forced them to neglect their children, much as the government claimed that Ethel had done.

Ethel's behavior while on trial was considered to be cold, aloof, and dispassionate, which led many observers to the belief that she was following Communist doctrine and deserved punishment. Because Ethel was a mother to two young boys, J. Edgar Hoover initially opposed her sentence of execution but reneged his position upon Ethel's rejection of her own mother's plea for her confession to save the Rosenberg children from becoming orphans.

Along with child neglect, Communist women, including Ethel Rosenberg, were purported to have the upper hand in their marriages and were the dominant partners in their marital relationships. Morris Ernst, a close friend of Hoover's and an attorney, wrote a psychological profile of the Rosenbergs that influenced many people in the federal government, including President Eisenhower, who refused to grant the couple clemency.

Morris's report described Ethel as the master of Julius and Julius as her slave. Interestingly though, Morris had never met the Rosenbergs. Yet, his report led Eisenhower to explain to his own son the reason why he was allowing a woman to be executed: ". . . In this instance it is the woman who is the strong and recalcitrant character, the man is the weak one. She has obviously been the leader in everything they did in the spy ring" (Schrecker 1998, 147).

Despite Hoover's and Eisenhower's stereotypical Communist characterizations of Ethel, many people still viewed her as a mere housewife who had not been involved in any serious political dealings. The only espionage item in which federal investigators believed that Ethel had been involved was the stereotypical feminine activity of typing, even though they were also unable to make that case fully. The investigators believed she had been a Communist at some point but did not believe that she had been a true threat.

Anti-Communists and those investigating subversive activities generally ignored women tied to the CP. Politics still fell within the traditional male realm during the McCarthy era, so many investigators dismissed the important role that Communist women played in the CP. The investigators were often more concerned about the activities of the women's husbands, as opposed to the women's involvement themselves in the CP, on the assumption that women were ignorant of political matters and concerned themselves only with their domestic lives. One particularly chauvinistic Ohio investigator questioned an accused Communist woman if she had baked a cake for the Communist cause.

Clearly, Ethel Rosenberg's roles as a woman and potential subversive could not coincide. On the one hand, Ethel was characterized as a mother and housewife who was unaware of the political involvement of her husband. On the other hand, she was a negligent mother and controlling wife who had been duped by the CP to betray her country. We may never know whether either or neither is actually true, but her gender, role as wife and mother, and member of the CP reveal the anxiety of the time concerning women's abilities, influence, and proper roles.

Both men and women involved in liberal politics and labor unions, although they were not necessarily Communist, often found themselves the targets of anti-Communists. Their association with radicalism or left-wing activities led the government to conclude that they were only a few steps away from switching over to Communism because it was believed that Communists began as liberals.

Federal investigators used the well-known, yet clearly unfair, "duck-test" to determine whether someone was a Communist: if the person "walks like a duck and swims like a duck and quacks like a duck, he is a duck" (Schrecker 1998, 276). Radical political or liberal organizations often served as Communist-front groups, in which many Communists were actively involved but not all members belonged to the CP. However, because people with liberal views, according to the government, were highly at risk to become Communists or were just as dangerous as already belonging to the CP, the government viewed the participation of liberal persons in these groups as a sign that they were actual CP members. The policy of the day became "guilt by association" (Schrecker 1998, 276).

Although typical gender roles stated that women belonged in the home, tending to their husbands and children, the reality was that many women had to work to survive or to afford the level of subsistence that their family required. Many women, such as African American women, had never been afforded the opportunity to stay at home, even if they had wanted to, because discrimination in the workplace had forced them to serve as the breadwinners of their families.

With working-class white women and women of other races and ethnicities in the workforce, African American women also joined unions and political groups that supported their rights in general, but also in the workplace. Unions did not always focus on women's issues, but they did encourage involvement and some leadership roles. The CP was not the pinnacle of female equality as it often claimed, but Communists and others involved in labor rights had organized women in labor movements, particularly the underpaid and overworked non-white women employees that the mainstream labor movement had left behind. However, women's involvement in these leftist labor unions often made them the target of the anti-Communist crusades, even if they were not Communists themselves.

Dorothy Bailey serves as a prime example of a non-Communist who was fired from her job because of her supposed liberal politics, union activities, and possibly even her female gender and African American race. Bailey worked at the Department of Labor, where she helped create the educational program's training manuals. She also served as the president of her local United Public Workers union. In 1948, after nine years at the Department of Labor, Bailey was suspended from her job as a result of what the Regional Loyalty Board of the Civil Service Commission claimed was questionable information in her personal file.

Bailey had a loyalty hearing several months later, in which the loyalty board questioned her political views and involvement in the union. The loyalty board inquired about her contacts with supposed Communists in her labor union, but they also asked her opinions on current political matters and international affairs. One question that particularly infuriated the public was, "Did you ever write a letter to the Red Cross about the segregation of blood? . . . What was your personal position about that?" (Schrecker 1998, 282). Communist doctrine objected to the segregation of blood, and, because Bailey was African American, they were testing her stance on racial equality to see if that further aligned her with Communism. Despite the intense questioning and accusations, she was never informed of the specific charges against her or who charged her with any disloyal or subversive acts.

Bailey's union hired prominent lawyers to fight her case, because they realized that it could affect many workers accused of subversion or radical activities by people who were never identified, even to the loyalty review boards themselves. The government disregarded due process rights by not informing the accused of their "crimes" or who had been the informant in the case. The courts justified this illegal behavior in the name of national security.

Bailey's lawyers argued that, because she had not been allowed to confront her accusers, she had been deprived of due process, which was a constitutional right. Her anonymous accusers claimed she had been a member of the CP and that she followed the Communist doctrine and associated with local CP leaders. Bailey openly testified against the accusations and provided character witnesses and affidavits from prominent people attesting to her loyalty, yet the Washington, D.C., Court of Appeals ruled against Bailey, claiming that she did not have a right to a fair hearing because losing her job was not deemed criminal punishment.

Bailey's lawyers were shocked, and they were determined to have the case overturned by the U.S. Supreme Court. By October 1950, it seemed as though five of the judges would overturn the original decision, but the majority slowly shifted, and, in April 1951, the Court was split down the middle, thus upholding the D.C. Court's decision. The Supreme Court provided no public opinions on the case, which meant that the D.C. Court's ruling set the standard for the constitutional use of loyalty review boards and secret government informers. The Supreme Court ultimately permitted the government to punish its workers economically for their political beliefs—by refusing to stand up to the government and its loyalty review policies, which allowed McCarthyism to run rampant. In some ways, as seen in Bailey's case, the government and the courts also allowed race and gender to become potential links to the CP.

The persecution of women involved in labor and liberal politics, such as strikes and civil rights activities, affected the trajectory of the feminist movement itself. McCarthyism did not eradicate women's activism, but it did hinder the burgeoning movement. First, the leftist labor unions and also the CP were the main groups promoting women's rights and equality in the late 1940s and 1950s. With these two groups under constant attack during the McCarthy era, feminism itself came under attack and thus split from its association with the Left, which had placed women's issues alongside concerns of racism and economic injustice.

The United Electrical, Radio, and Machine Workers of America (UE) had grown in strength during World War II and was also spearheaded by Communists and their sympathizers. The UE had attracted more female members than any other major union and led the fight for women's rights during and after World War II. The union aggressively battled for equal pay for equal work and fought against placing women in poorly paid stereotypical women's jobs. Because anti-Communists viewed emancipated, outspoken women and radical labor unionists as threats to the American way of life, their persecution immobilized the UE and its fight for women's rights. Gender issues were ignored and put aside for the time being.

Groups such as the Congress of American Women (CAW) faced a similar demise as the UE women's rights advocates. The organization involved itself in a movement called Popular Front feminism, which entailed combining the leftist struggles for peace, racial equality, and economic justice with women's rights issues. The CAW, founded in 1946, combated the inequality of pay in the workplace, lack of child care, and racism. It attempted to appeal to African American women by integrating CAW's membership and placing black women into leadership roles.

The group's focus on women's issues and opposition of segregation led to its persecution by McCarthyism. The organization was largely destroyed by 1950, after it appeared on the Attorney General's list (AGLOGO) of Communist groups and HUAC featured the group in a special report. The group had been under increasing Communist control, so the Department of Justice demanded that the CAW register as an agent of foreign power. Instead, the group dissolved.

Many gender issues remained unaddressed throughout the rest of the McCarthy era, but they reemerged with Betty Friedan's 1963 publication of *The Feminine Mystique*. But even Friedan and her popular book were not exempt from the legacy of McCarthyism. Daniel Horowitz, a historian and biographer of Friedan, asserts that Friedan left out a large portion of her involvement in the Popular Front—including its feminist aspects, as a writer for the Federated Press and *UE News*—to downplay her radicalism and focus on her status as a suburban housewife.

One of the main critiques of *The Feminine Mystique* is that Friedan ignores the plight of working-class women, particularly African American women, and concentrates only on the problems of educated, white, middle-class women. Friedan, contrary to her own assertions, was involved in improving labor conditions and workers rights for all workers, including

Betty Friedan, author of *The Feminist Mystique* and co-founder of the National Organization of Women.
(Library of Congress)

working-class women and African American women, during her decade-long stint as a journalist for the union and left-wing press.

Horowitz suggests that Friedan shifted her focus to the suburbanites because she had witnessed firsthand the Red-baiting that occurred when fighting for workers' rights and civil rights in the 1940s and 1950s. Friedan closeted her former radical activism to avoid the threat it posed to her book's influence on U.S. middle-class society, as well as to her own credibility and the credibility of the feminist movement.

Thus, the lingering threat of McCarthyism potentially led Friedan to exclude issues of class and race in her book—in order to place it in the realm of acceptable topics, such as those issues surrounding domesticity. Friedan's narrow focus on suburban housewives, although instrumental in sparking the next wave of the feminist movement, alienated many women from relating to larger women's issues surrounding gender inequity and sex discrimination, because they could not relate the problems in their own lives to those of the domesticated housewives that Friedan had spotlighted.

Although the height of the McCarthy era was over by 1960, McCarthyism and its legacy lingered into the new decade. It took a group of dedicated women—fighting for their rights as mothers to protect their children from the unstable nuclear age—to bring McCarthyism to its knees. A women's peace movement's confrontation and symbolic victory against HUAC delivered a knockout punch, by drawing widespread negative criticism of HUAC's tactics and so-called moral superiority (Swerdlow 1982, 504). The women in the peace movement took a stand against the

Red-baiting tactics of HUAC and used the stereotypical gender roles of the era to their advantage by emphasizing their femininity and rights as peace-seeking mothers.

The women's peace movement group had evolved out of a nationwide strike held on November 1, 1961, by approximately 50,000 women across the United States who were worried about the alarming growth in the nuclear arms race. These women took a bold stand by refusing to work inside or outside of their homes during the one-day strike calling for the end of the nuclear arms race.

Within a year after the strike, the women involved had formed a national women's movement that historian Amy Swerdlow describes as "a non-hierarchical participatory network of activists opposed both to rigid ideologies and formal organizational structure" (Swerdlow 1982, 495). The new group, named Women Strike for Peace (WSP), called its structural format "our un-organization" (Swerdlow 1982, 495). WSP largely consisted of white, middle-class, middle-aged women, who established a loose network of communication between their local groups and offices in 60 U.S. cities, although they maintained no paid staff and no official leaders. The women wanted to avoid a hierarchical and bureaucratic structure that would bog down the movement and prevent spontaneous action to an immediate national crisis in their quest for peace and protection of their children against nuclear extinction.

The WSP garnered success in many of its actions, which included lobbying, demonstrations, and petitions, in its first year of existence by influencing public policies and officials, which gained positive press for the group. This attention, however, caught the eye of the FBI and HUAC, who had been targeting peace groups and feminist activities for the past 15 years. In typical fashion, HUAC suspected the WSP of Communist infiltration and influence. One right-wing journalist stated, "There is nothing spontaneous about the way the pro-Reds have moved in on our mothers and are using them for their own purposes" (Swerdlow 1982, 497). In late 1962, HUAC sent out subpoenas to uncover the extent of Communist infiltration into WSP.

WSP made a conscious decision to band together as a family unit, through bonds of sisterhood, and stand up against HUAC and its Red-baiting tactics that had devastated so many other movements since the end of World War II. Months prior to the HUAC hearing, the WSP decided not to question its members on their political affiliations because political beliefs were viewed as personal ones that were subjugated to a national policy that declared, "We are women of all races, creeds and political persuasions who are dedicated to the achievement of general and complete disarmament under effective international control" (Swerdlow 1982, 499).

On top of this, the group refused to bow to the legacy of Cold War ideology. The WSP did not want to purge its own "un-organization" of peace-seeking women, regardless of their political ties. So, in between the three weeks of first receiving HUAC's subpoenas and the actual hearing, the WSP launched a massive campaign that called for the cancellation of the HUAC hearing and for public support of WSP. As for its actual strategy at the hearings, the WSP decided to work against HUAC in the "Good New WSP way" (Swerdlow 1982, 501). This meant that the women would testify because they had nothing to hide or of which to be ashamed, and many women who did not receive an actual subpoena volunteered to talk at the hearing, although their offers were rebuffed.

The witnesses called to testify at the hearing used a variety of strategies, depending on each woman's situation and personal morals. The women combined their testimonies with brave yet articulate homilies toward HUAC concerning their beliefs about atomic weaponry, women's rights, and peace. The women used patriotism, moral guidelines, common sense, and humor to make their case and defend their involvement in their own peace movement. They also used their femininity and status as caring mothers to gain sympathy and support from the U.S. public and mainstream media. Instead of rebuking traditional gender roles, they emphasized these roles, to demonstrate why they felt that their peace movement was important and not at all subversive.

WSP's tactics succeeded, and they won, according to the press. Headlines of major papers included such phrases as "Peace March Gals Make Red Hunters Look Silly" and "Headhunters Decapitated." An article in the *Vancouver (BC) Sun*, similar to what many other papers ran, stated, "The dreaded House Un-American Committee met its Waterloo this week. It tangled with 500 irate women. They laughed at it. Kleig lights glared, television cameras whirred, and 50 reporters scribbled notes while babies cried and cooed during the fantastic inquisition" (Swerdlow 1982, 505). A columnist for the *New York Times* remarked that "If the [HUAC] knew its Greek as well as it knows its Lenin, it would have left the women peace strikers alone . . . Instead with typical male arrogance, it has subpoenaed 15 of the ladies . . . spent several days trying to show them that women's place is not on the peace march route, and has come out of it covered with foolishness" (Swerdlow 1982, 505). The WSP had proved its case using traditional gender roles, even if there were contradictions interlaced within the roles themselves.

Regardless of whether they were actual Communists, Communist sympathizers, or patriotic people who had been mistaken for something they were not, women of all walks of life were targeted in the McCarthy era purges. Women, because of the precarious nature of their gender roles, acted and reacted differently to these targets and attacks. It was the contradictions in women's roles themselves that forced women to bind themselves to their families, to protect the American way of life while also speaking out against social evils, to protect themselves and their families against larger, more powerful forces, often out of their control.

References and Further Reading

Fariello, Griffin. *Red Scare: Memories of the American Inquisition, An Oral History*. New York: W. W. Norton & Company, 1995.

Fried, Richard M. *Nightmare in Red: The McCarthy Era in Perspective*. New York: Oxford University Press, 1990.

Horowitz, Dan. "Rethinking Betty Friedan and *The Feminine Mystique*: Labor Union Radicalism and Feminism in Cold War America." *American Quarterly* 48 (1998): 1–42.

May, Elaine Tyler. *Homeward Bound: American Families in the Cold War Era.* New York: Basic Books, 1999.

Olmstead, Kathryn S. *Red Spy Queen: A Biography of Elizabeth Bentley.* Chapel Hill: The University of North Carolina Press, 2002.

Schrecker, Ellen. *The Age of McCarthyism: A Brief History with Documents.* Boston: Bedford Books, 1994.

Schrecker, Ellen. *Many Are the Crimes: McCarthyism in America.* Boston: Little, Brown and Company, 1998.

Swerdlow, Amy. "Ladies' Day at the Capitol: Women Strike for Peace versus HUAC." *Feminist Studies* 8(3) (Autumn 1982): 493–520.

Duck and Cover: Children's Cold War Experiences in 1950s America

10

Margaret Peacock

On the morning of February 7, 1951, children in Manhattan and the New York boroughs bustled into their classes and began what seemed like an ordinary day. Teachers called the roll and collected lunch money; students sharpened pencils and passed notes in the back of the room. Despite its normal appearance, however, this day was different from any ever experienced by a school child in the United States. At 8:45 a.m., teachers across the New York School District instructed their students to "take cover." Having trained for this event, children crawled under their desks and covered their faces with their hands. Later that day, William Jansen, the superintendent of schools, announced to the press that the drills had been "taken by the children in their stride" and that "sneak attack drills" would be held in the upcoming weeks until the children had developed "automatic reactions" (Sisto, 1951, 35).

For the next 15 years, schools across the United States practiced similar drills, refining the process to accommodate different kinds of nuclear attack. In one town, children scrambled under tables. In another, they hid under sheets. If there was time, they marched to the basements of their schools to assume the "duck and cover" position. Some simply ran home.

For U.S. children in the 1950s, "duck and cover" represented a unique and often contradictory way of living and thinking in the modern age. On the one hand, it held the promise of protection. It stood as an example of U.S. efficiency and of the efforts being made by adults to ensure the safety of their youngest citizens. It ostensibly allowed each child to feel as though he or she could play an active role in fighting the Cold War, and it provided a sense of normalcy and preparedness in the face of nuclear threat.

On the other hand, air raid drills presented an undeniably disturbing view of the world. For many children, "duck and cover" symbolized little more than a placebo meant to calm a population that, in fact, had little control over its own fate. As the writer Doris Kearns Goodwin remembers, although these drills "were not meant to frighten us," in truth, "no amount of preparation . . . could hide the gruesome fact that an atomic bomb would kill tens of thousands of people" (Goodwin, 1997, 60). Children, like their parents, now lived in a world of both unprecedented promise and exceptional danger.

In the years following the World War II, the United States enjoyed unparalleled prosperity. Unlike any previous generation, white middle-class children could look forward to the benefits of a good education, a traditional family (in which the father went to work and the mother stayed home), and a disposable income. Thanks to new legislation, revised textbooks, citizenship training, and civil defense drills, these children were promised a world of domestic security that was protected against Communist infiltration and atomic attack.

Yet in a myriad of ways, the complex realities of the Cold War intruded into the lives of the seemingly insulated youth of the United States. Comic books, movies, the press, and even the parents themselves presented views on the Cold War that often contradicted the idealized image of a defended United States. They expressed fears about atomic annihilation that the promise of "duck and cover" simply could not allay.

As the years passed, these contradictions became increasingly difficult to ignore for the baby boom generation. Many found that they could no longer ignore the Manichaean reality that the Cold War had produced for them. Protest and social upheaval were the result of these deep-seeded dilemmas. This chapter tells the complex story of U.S. children living through the Cold War in the 1950s by looking at how their educations, their homes, and their extracurricular activities created for them a multivalenced understanding of the role of the United States in the world.

Peak Prosperity

The United States in the 1950s seemed to hold great promise, at least for white, middle-class citizens. The same war that demolished Europe had transformed the United States into a superpower of unprecedented strength. In 1946, thousands of factories were running that had not existed before, and the U.S. Treasury was bloated with $140 billion in unspent savings bonds (Bryson, 2006, 5). Large corporations that once made fighter jets and war fatigues switched their focus to the mass production of peacetime consumer goods. This meant that there were jobs to be had and that, each year, middle-class families had more money to spend on newer, previously unavailable items.

An average white middle-class family could generally afford to live on a single income. They could buy one of the new homes, sprouting up seemingly overnight, in suburban developments outside of U.S. urban centers. They could furnish their houses with new appliances, including refrigerators, washing machines, telephones, vacuum cleaners, and electric stoves— all intended to minimize domestic chores and create a happier family life.

And when they wanted to leave the house, mothers, fathers, and their children could go to amusement parks such as Disneyland and Coney Island, conveyed there comfortably in their new cars.

The nation's white middle- and upper-class youth arguably benefited the most from this newfound affluence. By 1955, there were 32 million children in the United States under the age of 12. As one historian has commented, "There were children everywhere, all the time, in densities now unimaginable" (Bryson, 2006, 36). In 1950, these baby boomers, who, in the days of war and rationing, had been forced to play with simple wooden toys and secondhand books, could look forward to playing with Lionel trains, equipped with a rocket launcher car, and pretty dresses with matching gloves and bonnets. Equipped with new war toys, boys could relive in their backyards the U.S. victories that their fathers had achieved in Europe and Japan.

Meanwhile, young girls could rehearse their pending transformations into motherhood with toy kitchens, grocery carts, ironing boards, and the newest Barbie doll. Many children could walk home for lunch everyday and expect their mothers to be waiting, with a warm meal on the table. In the afternoons, there were ample friends with whom to play and baseball games broadcast on the radio. Comic books were available for a dime, and television stations aired imaginative shows such as *Captain Video* and *I Love Lucy*.

For many children, a bright future seemed to lie ahead. Bill Bryson remembers:

> We were going to have underwater cities off every coast, space colonies inside giant spheres of glass, atomic trains and airliners, personal jet packs, a gyrocopter in every driveway, cars that turned into boats or even submarines, moving sidewalks to whisk us effortlessly to schools and offices, dome-roofed automobiles that drove themselves along sleek superhighways allowing Mom, Dad, and the two boys (Chip and Bud or Skip and Scooter) to play a board game or wave to a neighbor in a passing gyrocopter. (Bryson, 2006, 6)

A new age had dawned, spurred by the promise of affluence and science. As Richard Wightman Fox has noted, wealth and consumption became a cultural ideal, "a hegemonic 'way of seeing'" in 20th-century America (Fox, 1983, x).

Even nuclear weapons held certain splendor. On some level, the population could not help but be captivated, "transfixed really, by the broiling majesty and unnatural might of atomic bombs" (Bryson, 2006, 73). In the early 1950s, before the full effects of radiation were understood, families visited Nevada to "watch the tests and enjoy the fallout." They lined up, as scientists in lab coats carrying Geiger counters measured their radiation levels. "What a joy it was to be indestructible," Bill Bryson remembers. Such affluence, such security, helped create an idealized image of a happy America—defined by the microcosm of the family and the child, whose parents could afford the amenities of the "good life" and could ensure the safety and happiness of the next generation.

Communism: The Intangible Threat

Even though the citizens of the United States enjoyed unprecedented comfort, the country also faced threats—inside and outside its borders—that were seemingly impossible to locate and yet potentially disastrous to U.S. national security. The Soviet Union was thought by many to threaten the nation in two important ways: through its ideological messianism and its nuclear capacity. While well-armed Communists marched south in Korea, backed by the Chinese, spies such as Klaus Fuchs and the Rosenbergs, appeared to be infiltrating the nation's most sensitive nuclear projects. Russia, many believed, having swallowed up Eastern Europe, now had its sights set on the conquest of Western capitalism. Because the Marxist theory of historical determinism held that revolution was inevitable, Communism and its apostates appeared single-minded in their commitment to Soviet world domination.

Even more worrisome for most Americans was the awareness that the threat of Communism did not stop at its borders or at the highest levels of government. Indeed, its most menacing aspects lay in its potential to infiltrate and "infect" the daily lives of ordinary citizens, especially its children. This new enemy, in the words of Barbara Holland, "was more dangerous than Hitler because it was invisible, and everywhere, like polio. Your next-door neighbor might be pretending to be an ordinary person, with kids and a lawn mower, when he was really a Communist in disguise, and simply living next door to him might infect you, invisibly" (Holland, 2005, 212). For many adults, the Communist threat appeared to menace children in almost every public and private aspect of their lives. Teachers suspected of Leftist affiliation might propagandize Communist ideology to their students within the privacy of the classroom. Communist filmmakers seemed to have access to the young through television and the big screen. Even parents threatened to influence both their own children and those of others negatively through ideological neglect or through direct Leftist affiliation. As the writer Bob Flournoy remembers, "The Great evil in the world was the Communists, who wanted to take away our baseball card collections, our *Mad* magazines, and our Blessed Virgin" (Flournoy, 2005, 42). As a result of these perceived threats, children became a locus of fear for anti-Communist activists across the United States. While magazines published articles with provocative titles like "Reds Are After Your Child," (*American Magazine*), and "Capture of the Innocent" (*Collier's*), Eugene Lyons and John Roy Carlson hit the bestseller lists with books entitled *The Red Decade: The Stalinist Penetration of America* and *Undercover: My Four Years in the Nazi Underworld of America*, respectively.

Throughout the 1950s and 1960s, men like J. Edgar Hoover and Verne P. Kaub published and spoke prolifically on the topic of Communist infiltration in the nation's schools and homes. Through his popular "Credo for Parents," Hoover warned the nation's adults about dangerous texts, films, and mentors who, for their own political purposes, might take advantage of youth's natural gullibility. As the nation's "number one G-man," Hoover became what Mrs. Francis P. Bolton (wife of the Republican congressman from Ohio) called "one of the few people in the world who has a right to talk to parents although he has no children" (Bolton, 1963). In speeches and articles, Hoover informed the nation that Communists were in the process of making a heated appeal to the youngest citizens of the United States, "not from [an] ennobling regard for the truth, but as a means of furthering the international conspiracy of the party" (Hoover, 1962, 2). *Readers Digest* asked its audience in 1951 "Who Owns Your Child's Mind?" Worried parents and lawmakers began to wonder to what extent their young had become unwitting targets of the global Communist conspiracy (Flynn, 1951, 23).

This widespread fear that Communist subversion was undermining the nation's youth was made all the worse by the threat of nuclear annihilation and by a steady stream of Soviet scientific successes in the 1950s. The Soviet A-bomb, detonated in 1949, represented for Americans not only the tangible, physical threat of Soviet attack, but also their own nation's loss of military superiority, their inability to maintain information security, and the Soviet Union's mastery of the most intricate of sciences over a short period of time.

Over the next decade, the threat of Soviet science made its way into U.S. classrooms, as educators and politicians issued a steady stream of warnings about the dilapidated state of U.S. education and the simultaneous strides being made by students in Soviet schools. Finally, America's worst fears were realized on the fateful morning of October 4, 1957, when the Soviets launched their first satellite, *Sputnik I*. Up to that point, most Americans had been certain that theirs was the best education in the world. *Sputnik* forced the United States to question its assumed position of primacy in the scientific world.

Fred Hechinger, in his 1959 book, *The Big Red Schoolhouse*, summed up the cumulative panic in the United States, a condition that was popularly known as "Sputnikitis":

Because we had more schools, and bigger schools than other nations, and kept our children in them for a longer period of time, we assumed that our system

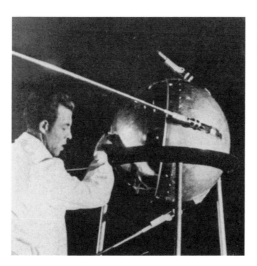

A Soviet scientist makes the final adjustments to the *Sputnik I* satellite before its launch in 1957. (NASA)

:ation must be better than that found in other lands. It was comforting
ve that the Russians substituted propaganda for liberal education, that
.entific and technical schools were inferior to ours, and that they had
been able to develop an atomic bomb only by stealing our secrets. With
Sputnik I, our apathy was replaced by panic. One educator commented that
many people who had never before given much attention to the problems of
education "immediately went into orbit and started beeping." (Hechinger,
1959, 2)

Suddenly, it appeared to scientists and politicians that the Soviets were
doing a better job of educating their children in the "hard" sciences than the
Americans were. The Soviet Communist Party had, over the past 30 years,
transformed its own largely agricultural society into a world power, had
detonated a nuclear weapon, and had put a satellite into space that could
potentially threaten U.S. security in new and terrifying ways. America's
fears about its own children, and concomitant anxieties about Soviet youth,
were no longer simply educational, but geostrategic. An uneducated, ideo-
logically weak child meant danger for the entire nation.

As the 1950s dawned, these fears gave way to new policies and actions
that were meant to shore up the strength and resilience of the next
generation. As a result, U.S. children experienced significant changes in
their educations, their home lives, and in the way that they interacted with
the adult world.

Doing Something: The United States Acts on Its Fears

In the summer of 1949, the National Educational Association published a
report arguing that "East-West tensions will . . . keep the world in a state of
Cold War for years to come . . . Our children will continue to live under an
oppressive shadow of fear." Its recommendations, formulated by a 22-member
panel (one of whom was General Dwight D. Eisenhower, then-president of
Columbia University), were that the nation require a "basic psychological
reorientation" in order to transform education into an "instrument of national
policy" (Educational Policies Commission, 1949, 1). Education, broadly
defined, included the strengthening of the child's intellectual, physical, and
psychological acumen in order to retain the nation's power and security in the
Cold War. If this was going to be a protracted war, as the commission projected,
training children to understand and combat Communism was necessary in
order to create a new generation of future Cold Warriors.

These initiatives in Cold War education sparked a number of changes in
the lives of the nation's children, including the rewriting of their textbooks,
the suspension of their teachers, and the implementation of civil defense
training. Adults across the United States urged their children to practice civil
defense measures calmly. They beseeched the young to work harder in the
sciences, not simply for personal growth, but as an act of patriotism. They
reminded the children that, although their teachers, their friends, and even
their favorite television shows and comic books could be carrying infectious

Soviet propaganda, the young could nonetheless make themselves safe through vigilance and adherence to adult guidance. Adults packaged the Cold War for their children as a serious but manageable threat that required newfound diligence and social conformity in order to ensure survival.

One of the earliest ways that the Cold War affected children was through their learning materials. By 1950, publishers had significantly rewritten most of the nation's history textbooks from only a decade before. Stalin, who was seen by many Americans as a hero during the World War II, had transformed five years later into a dangerous menace. These new perceptions of looming Soviet threat spawned a movement of conservative parents, politicians, and publishers, who sought to ensure that children's literature had made the appropriate adjustments in its portrayals of the Soviet Union. While the American Textbooks Publishers Institute warned parents to be on the watch for "whisperings that your child's textbooks are subversive" (Kahn, 1953, 78), a number of conservative activists, namely Lucille Cardin Crain, who issued the newsletter *The Educational Reviewer,* and Allen Zoll, who was a pro-lific pamphleteer and the head of the National Council for American Education, took it as their mandate to weed out subversive material from public school textbooks. They, along with many other local groups, actively campaigned against texts such as Frank Magruder's *American Government,* which, in their opinion, promoted Communism by supporting the U.N. Charter and by arguing that the U.S. Postal Service was an example of a working socialist system. Such groups were consistently successful in imped-ing the distribution of "subversive" books across the country, including works by Mark Twain, Bertrand Russell, and George Bernard Shaw.

For U.S. children, this control over learning materials meant that their understanding of Communism was formed largely from a normalized, monolithic image of Soviet enmity. In their textbooks, at least, publishers, politicians, and conservative activists carefully managed the child's view of the Soviet Union and the Cold War. They undertook these crusades in order to ensure that the historical narrative presented to children not only complied with the nation's larger views on Communism, but also helped create for the nation's youth an ideological base that could withstand Soviet influence.

The widespread push to shape and monitor public education did not stop with textbooks. Many groups, including the courts, Congress, private organizations, and the schools themselves also assumed the job of watching the country's teachers for Communist infiltration. Teachers, it was argued, had the power to shape the next generation, a power that many believed could prove disastrous if put in the wrong hands. The movement to check the loyalties of civil employees began in 1947, with the Truman Loyalty Oath. It required federal employees to undergo background checks and to affirm that they did not advocate the overthrow of the government. Two years later, New York State passed the Feinberg Law, which, after being upheld by the Supreme Court, not only required that each public school teacher sign a loyalty oath but defined membership in the CP as sufficient evidence for the disqualification of employment. Based on this law, eight teachers in the New York School District were suspended in 1950. The *New York Times* reported on October 12, that, at their trial, the prosecuting attorney argued for four hours in his closing that "teachers who belong to the Communist Party will seek to weaken the government when the time seemed propitious." He declared resoundingly that the classroom provided "ample opportunity" for treasonous behavior. "Academic freedom does not give license to teach evil," he argued to a rapt courtroom.

Private organizations, along with HUAC, made similar efforts to keep a keen eye trained on the country's teachers. While Allen Zoll was busy publishing pamphlets with titles such as "The Commies Are after Your Kids" and "Progressive Education Increases Juvenile Delinquency," HUAC frequently called teachers to testify as a part of their mandate to investigate "Communist penetration" into the public school system.

Throughout the 1950s, HUAC called teachers, such as 54-year-old Eleanor Maki of Detroit, to testify on suspected Communist collusion. As Representative John Wood of Georgia declared during Maki's hearing, "If you are a communist then you have done a grave injustice to every child who has come under your jurisdiction." Mrs. Maki, although never formally indicted, was suspended from her work after 22 years of teaching. As Socrates had learned 2,500 years earlier, even an "extraordinary record in the profession" did not constitute a defense against charges of corrupting the young.

The majority of public school educated children, in turn, received a highly censored version of history—one that avoided many of the nation's continuing domestic and international dilemmas. In addition, the background checks, loyalty oaths, and monitoring of teachers created a sense of uncertainty for some children about the very adults who were supposed to be their mentors.

By the middle of the decade, implementing new programs in the sciences also became a high priority for educators, politicians, and parents. As Bob Myers states in his memoirs, "Knowledge was the key to pushing civilization ahead and beating the Russians" (Myers, 2004, 14). In an effort to mitigate the educational crisis in U.S. schools, academicians such as Arthur Bestor and Harry Fuller called for the reconstruction of the nation's pre-college science education curriculum.

The Committee on Education and Labor passed the National Defense Education Act in 1958, which was intended to "encourage improvement in the quality of education particularly with respect to those aspects which are most important now to national defense." Arguing that the very survival of the country depended in large part "upon the education we provide for our young people now," the Act made specific recommendations that aimed to keep children from dropping out of school and to encourage them (African Americans and girls included) to study physics, math, and chemistry.

Congressional studies committed time and money to the study of how many children with high IQs were failing to finish school; national programs targeted students who showed aptitude in the sciences. In 1958 alone, three important Congressional resolutions granted federal support for school construction and teachers' salaries. Politicians such as Hubert Humphrey, as well as publishers and writers such as Walter T. Ridder, chief of the Ridder Publications Bureau, even looked to Russian education for inspiration. They believed (and argued openly in the press) that the only way to fix the nation's education problem was to adopt the "Russian system," which required that children stay quiet in class, rise when an adult entered the room, and complete assignments immediately.

U.S. children were affected by these many initiatives, which were intended to bring them up to par with their Soviet counterparts. Whereas U.S. education had historically lumped all children together, regardless of their aptitude, the Cold War now dictated that they be segregated into varying levels of aptitude within their grades. For many children, this change had a positive impact upon their lives. High-performing girls, African Americans, and members of the lower class, in particular, found avenues to higher education that had previously been closed to them. For children who had neither wealth nor exceptional academic ability, however, these initiatives often meant further marginalization from the nation's educational infrastructure.

By far the largest and most expensive public effort made to protect U.S. children from the Cold War threat came in the form of civil defense. In its first year, the newly formed Federal Civil Defense Administration (FCDA) staged nearly 2,000 drills in cities across the United States, involving 2,000,000 workers and 42,000,000 private citizens. Civil defense touched U.S. cities and suburbs, schools and homes. It cost millions of dollars and was the preoccupation of many federal employees and regular citizens. It endeavored to generate among the population feelings of security and normalcy about nuclear attack. It attempted to provide a sense of agency to a population that had little personal control over the means of modern warfare. It made possible the idea of nuclear defensibility and, in turn, fostered the public's acceptance of the ongoing conflict with the Soviet Union.

Civil defense had a deep impact on public school education in the 1950s. For officials, the schools represented the possibility of nuclear protection for millions of schoolchildren as they went to class everyday. School air raid drills allowed administrators to inculcate children, first and foremost, into the culture of defense.

The first widely published Civil Defense pamphlet for the schools came out in 1951, entitled "Interim Civil Defense Instructions for Schools and Colleges." In it, the FCDA instructed teachers on how to create "required civil defense behavior patterns" among students and faculty. Among its many suggestions, it proposed that teachers and staff who participated in civil defense drills receive salary bonuses and that children be encouraged to "remain mindful" of civil defense by drawing bomb shelters in art and shop classes. These instructions were accompanied by a large array of publications, directives, and films meant to teach children and their instructors how to go about "doing" civil defense in a manner that would ensure the highest possible survival rate, the most compliance, and the least possible psychological "fallout."

These were the intentions of the 1951 educational film *Duck and Cover* which instructed youths to drop and find shelter at the first sign of an atomic flash. Across the country, children watched the animated character, Bert the Turtle, as he encouraged them to treat nuclear preparedness like

The famous Bert the Turtle appears in a 1952 nuclear propaganda short film designed to help children feel safer during the Cold War. (Photofest)

any other safety precaution and to keep track of their responsibilities, even if alone. When they were in school, the film instructed children to assume a kneeling position on the floor, with their hands clasped behind their necks and their faces covered. Such actions would ostensibly protect children (who were not at ground zero) from the rumbling firestorm.

Civil defense instructions for children actually took many forms. If the explosion was unexpected, taking shelter under desks was the only option. With some warning, children could make their way to the school's basement or hallway, where more shelter could be found. As one set of instructions from the Los Angeles Board of Education read:

A. If inside the school building, the pupil should:
   a. Drop to his knees with back to the window. Knees together.
   b. Fold arms on the floor close to the knees.
   c. Bury face in arms.
B. If outside the school building, the pupil should:
   a. If any protection is within a step or two, crouch or lie down behind building, yard bench, curb or gutter.
   b. If in the open, drop to the ground [and] curl up with back to the blast. (Kahn, 1953, 27)

"Bert the Turtle"

In 1951, Bert the Turtle became the spokesman for the FCDA's civil defense childhood education program. In the widely distributed film *Duck and Cover* Bert instructed children to drop to the ground and find cover in order to ensure their safety from an atomic attack. In the film's opening scenes, Bert protects himself by ducking into his shell to avoid the pop of a fire cracker held over his head by a capricious monkey.

He then demonstrates to his young audience how the very same action can also protect them from the bomb. Replete with destroyed cartoon homes, charred cartoon trees, and a blizzard of flying debris, Bert reminds children that survival is possible as long as they remember to seek cover. In one of the iconic montages of the Cold War, the film demonstrates the possibilities for survival through a series of hypothetical "duck and cover" scenarios: in a school hall, along the side of a building, in a bus, and along the curb of a street. Even when they are alone, the film argues, children should know how to react appropriately in the event of attack.

Duck and Cover received mixed reviews from parents, educators, and experts upon its release in 1951. Although some adults viewed the film as integral to the management of nuclear fear among U.S. children, others saw it as a tool that would generate the very anxieties it was meant to mitigate. For instance, during a preview screening of *Duck and Cover* on January 24, 1951, in New York City, a Board of Education representative applauded the film's "mental hygiene approach" and "its underlying qualities of cheerfulness and optimism."

In contrast, the Committee on War Tensions in Children argued that screening the film to children was "inadvisable" and "more apt to promote anxiety and tension in children . . . than to help them escape injury" (Barclay, 1952, 29).

Today, *Duck and Cover* stands as one of the best-remembered period pieces of the Cold War, reflecting not only the government's response to increasing U.S. fear and anxiety over the age of the atomic bomb, but also a real desire to transform nuclear war into a survivable event, even for the country's children.

As schools constructed and practiced these contingency plans, they integrated civil defense training into their weekly routines. Parents discussed the latest FCDA instructions at their PTA meetings. Superintendents attended conferences and workshops on how to accommodate the new directives. The New York School District spent hundreds of thousands of dollars on dog tags, to enable the identification of children's corpses after attack. Even school architecture experienced marked changes, as officials pushed for stronger buildings with fewer windows in order to minimize the damage inflicted by shattered glass after the explosion.

Children encountered civil defense not only as a shared public event, but as a private exercise held in their homes. Throughout the 1950s and 1960s, the FCDA encouraged families to build bomb shelters that could stand as the nation's first line of defense against nuclear attack. Public service films such as *Operation Scat* (1954) and *Community Shelter Planning* (1966—starring a young Gene Hackman), as well as pamphlets such as *Survival under Atomic Attack* (1950) and *Facts about Fallout Protection* (1958) claimed that habitable bomb shelters could be built "in your backyard for less than two-thousand dollars."

A Pennsylvania family is shown preparing a fallout shelter for use in the event of a nuclear attack. (National Archives)

These materials argued that family security could be realized only so long as the population was willing "to meet the common challenge of national survival." Loaded with canned foods, a washer and dryer, a workbench, and some toys, the U.S. family could ostensibly maintain the belief that survivability was possible and that action could be taken to counter Soviet attack. As the historian Elaine Tyler May has argued, "containment" of the Cold War threat, both physical and ideological, was the key to creating a secure family and nation (May, 1988, 14).

For children, civil defense was intended to prepare the next generation for nuclear attack without unduly traumatizing it. In the 1940s, the psychiatrist Anna Freud published a number of studies on children who had lived through bombings and evacuations during World War II. Not surprisingly, she concluded that warfare caused long-term psychological disorders among the young. Armed with this knowledge, psychologists, teachers, and politicians argued in the 1950s that children needed to be acclimatized to the possibilities of nuclear war in order to prevent such disorders from occurring again. Many viewed civil defense as a "positive mental health program" that would help control atomic apprehension (Brown, 1988, 76). By employing vague language to describe the realities of nuclear holocaust (for instance, by describing nuclear attack as "eventualities that may one day become actualities") and by speaking as little as possible on the long-term effects of fallout, FCDA officials positioned civil defense not as the cause of childhood neurosis but instead as a remedy for anxieties born from the nuclear age (Brown, 1988, 76).

In an effort to mitigate the stresses of the threat, one civil defense memorandum from 1951, for instance, recommended that children take on "constructive tasks" such as handing out civil defense materials to their community, finding buildings that could serve as evacuation centers, and maintaining a list of people who need special attention (Walen, 1951, 93). "Cheeriness" toward the bomb was the target behavior for adults who, in 1952, instructed their students in Detroit's schools to sing songs, tell stories, and play records while in the "refuge area." As a result of these efforts, the bomb in U.S. society was "domesticated." As Joanne Browne has argued, it was transformed from the "unthinkable to the banal." It became little more than an everyday danger, like traffic or fire (Brown, 85).

"And over Us All Lay the Shape of the Mushroom Cloud"

At the Mid-Century White House Conference on Children and Youth, held in Washington, D.C., on December 5, 1950, President Truman, in his opening address, promised the children of the United States that, if they supported his foreign and domestic policies, they would "live in the most peaceful times the world has ever seen." "We cannot insulate our children from the uncertainties of the world in which we live or from the impact of the problems which confront us," he admitted to parents, but with a "good home" and "a better understand[ing of] our democratic institutions," he assured his audience that their children would be safe and happy in the years to come (Porter, 1952, 1).

Yet, under this veneer of promised safety, real anxieties and problems remained. The national myth of a boundless, "fertile, industrious, moral, and always ultimately victorious" Unites States, where the enemy was clear and the battlefields were easily defined, had given way in the past five years to the realities of the nuclear age (Engelhardt, 1995). With the dropping of the first A-bomb in Hiroshima in 1945 and the detonation of the first Soviet bomb in 1949, "victory" became possible only indirectly and under limited conditions.

Moreover, unlike in earlier U.S. wars, when the enemy had been easy to identify and combat, the country's new adversary was difficult to find and even harder to face. Not only could your unsuspecting neighbor be a Communist spy, but your home, town, state, and nation could at any time be the target of a Soviet long-range ballistic missile. From this uncertainty arose, in the words of Tom Engelhardt, the image of a "hydra-headed super enemy," whose many shapes haunted the U.S. psyche.

Adults worked diligently to confront the enemy and protect its citizens (especially its children) from attack. Yet, because the Communist foe was so hard to find and because real success was so impossible to achieve, the long-held U.S. belief in assured victory was replaced in the 1950s by deep uncertainties that were born from the potential horror of ideological infiltration and nuclear holocaust. The comfortable security of the 1950s, with its wealth and promise, now had to coexist with the mocking knowledge that true defense was no longer possible.

Such realizations were not lost on U.S. children. For the first time in human history, an entire generation had to live with the eschatological knowledge that—in one instant—the world that they knew could be destroyed. Ultimately, civil defense, the suspension of teachers, and the monitoring of textbooks could not protect children either from war or from the awareness of war's real impact. In later years, adults remember how, as children, they had lain awake in their beds, "count[ing] slowly to twenty-five," as each potential nuclear plane traveled overhead, "afraid to miss the flash of light that would be [their] only warning" (Brown, 1988, 75).

On the television, in film, and in the press, children encountered uncensored adult perspectives on the Cold War conflict that discussed in realistic terms the nation's inability to protect itself from attack. One of the most complicated visions of the Cold War came from children's television, which enjoyed huge popularity as the T.V. made its way into U.S. households in the early 1950s. In programs such as *Captain Video, Superman, The Incredible Hulk, Mighty Mouse, Buck Rogers*, and *Davy Crockett*, children cultivated an image of the past and future of the United States that was simultaneously hopeful and anxiety-ridden.

On the one hand, these programs provided a reassuring, simplified version of the Cold War conflict for their viewers; producers and directors used heroic protagonists, evil geniuses, and simple narratives to create a universe torn between the forces of good and evil. This was the case for Superman, who, through his dedication to "truth, justice, and the American way," provided a certain level of wish fulfillment for audiences in search of personal and national security. Superman *could* stop a nuclear warhead if called upon. He followed the law, worked with authorities, and stood for all that was ordered, prudent, independent, and strong in U.S. society.

On the other hand, the nation's most popular television heroes regularly faced life-threatening violence, corruption, infiltration, and danger. Despite their superhuman powers, even they, at times, appeared to be overwhelmed by the forces of evil at their doorsteps.

Such "paranoia-producing invader-from-outer-space" shows were then joined by films and comic strips depicting the realistic impact of nuclear attack. Films such as *The Day the World Ended* (1955), *On the Beach* (1959), and *The Day the Earth Caught Fire* (1961) focused on the destruction of nuclear war. Similarly, comic serials such as *Tales from the Crypt, Vault of Horror, Fate*, and *Weird Science* constructed for their readers an unsettling universe that included lynchings, electrocutions, and mob violence—undertaken at the hands of rapists, killers, and thieves.

These varying modalities of apocalyptic media complicated the ideal image of a happy, affluent United States. "Our children are scared," an article in the June 1951 issue of *Today's Woman* began (Fontaine, 1951, 32). Despite their best efforts, adults discovered that they were incapable of maintaining the brinksmanship of the Cold War while protecting their children from all that such brinksmanship implied.

As Seen on TV: Captain Video

The popular television program *Captain Video* ran from 1949 to 1955 on the DuMont Network. The show brought to the U.S. public a handsome, uncomplicated hero (played by Richard Coogan and Al Hidge) who fought an evil genius in the 21st century. With the help of his Atomic Rangers and a multitude of high-tech devices, such as the "Opticon Scillometer" (which allowed him to see through any object) and the "Atomic Rifle" (which shot radioactive rays), this low-budget show provided a fantasy land for its viewers—where the good Captain Video's peering eye was able to see and combat any evil that the world might face.

The show integrated the fight against Communism directly into its screening, as "Video Ranger Messages" warned children that "In the world today, there are those who would destroy our American heritage, tear down our ideals, trample under foot the flag." Yet, as the historian David Weinstein has pointed out, the presence of the evil genius, with his equally destructive weapons and penchant for violence, also reinforced the dominant Cold War discourse of the nuclear–bomb-wielding nemesis who hides away and may or may not be stoppable before he (or sometimes she) destroys the world.

In the 1959 film *On the Beach*, residents of Australia come to terms with the fact that all life will be destroyed in the wake of global nuclear war. (Photofest)

Conclusion: Growing Up in the Cold War

As the baby boomer generation grew up, it retained its awareness of the ultimate indefensibility of the United States in the face of Communist attack. Throughout the 1950s, adults had struggled to create a safe environment for their children by overhauling their ideological and academic educations, by weeding out Communist spies in the schools, and by adopting civil defense measures. Yet through these very efforts, U.S. youth was exposed on a personal level to the disturbing implications of the Cold War.

As the novelist Mary Mackey remembers, "Obediently we would fold our bodies into that attitude of prayer and supplication known only to the children of the fifties: legs folded, head between the knees, hands raised to protect the fragile, invisible nerve that floated somewhere in the blackness behind our eyes" (Brown, 1988, 80). From these exercises, undertaken on a weekly basis for at least a decade, Mackey's generation "never forgot the lesson that their world could someday end in a flash of light, while they were crouched helplessly in gyms and basements among heating ducts and spare blackboards."

Children's awareness of their country's inability to protect itself from nuclear threat played an important role in shaping youth identity in the 1960s. "Is it any wonder that we were the generation who spawned the sixties revolution?" Lucille Maistros asks in her memoirs. "How can you grow up normal in an era that is defined on the one hand by threats of annihilation and on the other by Howdy Doody?" (Maistros, 2004, 32). Great promises had been made, and yet great danger persisted. Where could youth find protection and security in a nation committed to an indefensible arms race? For many youths, this question led them to conclude that, despite the promises of nuclear safety, they were, in fact, on their own.

As the 1960s dawned, such realizations were joined by equally disturbing epiphanies concerning the U.S. promise of social equality and fairness to its own citizens and to the world. Visions of nuclear destruction combined with photographs and descriptions of popular violence against the civil rights movement and, later, slaughtered civilians in Vietnam—to create an image of a nation plagued by deep social contradictions. Ultimately, for a generation of children growing up in the 1950s, the promise of affluence and happiness, spawned by U.S. postwar victory, could not fix the problems of nuclear threat and social inequality that sparked a rebellion a decade later.

References and Further Reading

Association, National Teachers. "A Civil Defense Program for Parent Teacher Associations." *National Parent-Teacher* 45 (1951): 34–45.

Barclay, Dorothy. "Film on Atom War Bad for Children." *New York Times*, November 21, 1952, 29.

Bolton, Francis P. "Francis P. Bolton Speaks on the Floor of Congress." *Congressional Record* (1963): 28743.

Brown, JoAnne. "'A Is for Atom, B Is for Bomb': Civil Defense in American Public Education." *Journal of American History* 75:1 (1988): 68–90.

Bryson, Bill. *The Life and Times of the Thunderbolt Kid: A Memoir*. New York: Broadway Books, 2006.

Educational Policies Commission, *American Education and International Tensions*. Washington, DC: U.S. Gov. Printing Office, 1949, 1.

Engelhardt, Tom. *The End of Victory Culture: Cold War America and the Disillusioning of a Generation*. New York: Basic Books, 1995.

Flournoy, Bob. *Just a Little Rain . . . Baby Boomers and Military Brats Reflect on Childhood, Baseball, and War*. Baltimore: PublishAmerica, 2005.

Flynn, John T. "Who Owns Your Child's Mind?" *The Reader's Digest,* October 1951, 23–28.

Fontaine, Andre. "Our Children Are Scared." *Today's Woman,* June 1951, 32–35.

Fox, Richard Wightman, and T. J. Jackson Lears. *The Culture of Consumption: Critical Essays in American History, 1880–1980*. 1st ed. New York: Pantheon Books, 1983.

Goodwin, Doris Kearns. *Wait till Next Year: A Memoir*. New York: Simon & Schuster, 1997.

Hechinger, Fred M. *The Big Red Schoolhouse*. Garden City, NY: Doubleday and Company, 1959.

Holland, Barbara. *When All the World Was Young: A Memoir*. New York: Bloomsbury, 2005.

Hoover, J. Edgar. "Communist Youth Campaign." *Follow Up Reporter,* August 1962, 2–5.

Kahn, Albert. *The Game of Death: Effects of the Cold War on Our Children*. New York: Cameron & Kahn, 1953.

Maistros, Lucille Maurice. *Growing Up Cold: A Memoir of Growing Up Cold But Longing to Be Cool, in 1950s Vermont*. Baltimore: PublishAmerica, 2004.

May, Elaine Tyler. *Homeward Bound: American Families in the Cold War Era*. New York: Basic Books, 1988.

Myers, Bob. *Bobby and the A-Bomb Factory*. New York: iUniverse, Inc., 2004.

Porter, Russell. "Truman Bids Youth Support His Policy as Means of Peace." *New York Times*, March 16, 1952.

Sisto, Ernest. "Training School Children in the Event of a 'Sneak' Air Attack on the City." *New York Times*, February 8, 1951, 35–37.

Walen, Harry L. "School Programs in Civil Defense." *Educational Leadership* 9 (1951), 92–94.

Primary Documents[*]

J. Edgar Hoover Warns of Communist Infiltration

Editor's Note: J. Edgar Hoover, head of the Federal Bureau of Investigation, was one of the most important Cold Warriors. Given his responsibilities for maintaining domestic security, Hoover worked diligently to ferret out what he saw as widespread evidence of domestic subversion. Hoover's understanding of and tactics in addressing this perceived threat have been widely criticized because he defined virtually any reform movement in mid-century America as representing a potential security risk. The following text comes from his testimony before the House Committee on Un-American Activities on March 26, 1947.

The aims and responsibilities of the House Committee on Un-American Activities and the Federal Bureau of Investigation are the same—the protection of the internal security of this Nation. The methods whereby this goal may be accomplished differ, however. I have always felt that the greatest contribution this committee could make is the public disclosure of the forces that menace America—Communist and Fascist [. . .]

[. . .] They evade the question of force and violence publicly. They hold that when Marxists speak of force and violence they will not be responsible—that force and violence will be the responsibility of their enemies [. . .]

[. . .] The American Communist, like the leopard, cannot change his spots.

The party line: The Communist Party line changes from day to day. The one cardinal rule that can always be applied to what the party line is or will be is found in the fundamental principle of the Communist teachings that the support of Soviet Russia is the duty of Communists of all countries.

One thing is certain. The American progress which all good citizens seek, such as old-age security, houses for veterans, child assistance, and a host of others is being adopted as window dressing by the Communists to conceal their true aims and entrap gullible followers [. . .]

The numerical strength of the party's enrolled membership is insignificant. But it is well known that they are many actual members who because of their positions are not carried on party rolls [. . .]

Identifying undercover Communists, fellow travelers, and sympathizers: The Burden of proof is placed upon those who consistently follow the ever-changing, twisting party line. Fellow travelers and sympathizers can deny party membership, but they can never escape the undeniable fact that they have played into Communist hands thus furthering the Communist cause by playing the role of innocent, gullible or willful allies.

Propaganda activities: The Communists have developed one of the greatest propaganda machines the world has ever known. They have been able to penetrate and infiltrate many respectable and reputable public opinion mediums [. . .]

Infiltration: The Communist tactic of infiltrating labor unions stems from the earliest teachings of Marx, which have been reiterated by party spokesmen down through the years. They resort to all means to gain their point and often succeed in penetrating and literally taking over labor unions before the rank and file of members are aware of what has occurred.

I am convinced that the great masses of union men and women are patriotic American citizens interested chiefly in security for their families and themselves. They have no use for the American Communists but in those instances where Communists have taken control of unions, it has been because too many union men and women have been outwitted, outmaneuvered, and outwaited by Communists.

[. . .] What can we do? And what should be our course of action? The best antidote to Communism is vigorous, intelligent, old-fashioned Americanism with eternal vigilance. I do not favor any course of action which would give the Communists cause to portray and pity themselves as martyrs. I do favor unrelenting prosecution when they are found to be violating our nation's laws.

[. . .] I would have no fears if more Americans possessed the zeal, the fervor, the persistence, and the industry to learn about this menace of Red fascism. I do fear for the liberal and progressive who has been hoodwinked and duped into joining hands with the Communists. I confess to a real apprehension so long as Communists are able to secure ministers of the gospel to promote their evil work and espouse a cause that is alien to the religion of Christ and Judaism. I do fear as long as school boards and parents tolerate conditions whereby Communists and fellow travelers, under the guise of academic freedom, can teach our youth a way of life that eventually will destroy the sanctity of the home, that undermine(s) our faith in God, that causes them to scorn respect for the constituted authority and sabotage our revered Constitution.

I do fear so long as American labor groups are infiltrated, dominated or saturated with the virus of Communism. I do fear the palliation and weasel-worded gestures against Communism indulged in by some of our labor leaders who should know better but who have become pawns in the hands of astute but sinister manipulations for the Communist cause.

I fear for ignorance on the part of all our people who may take the poisonous pills of Communist propaganda.

Source: Investigation of Un-American Propaganda Activities in the United States. Hearings (1947). Washington, DC: U.S. Government Printing Office. Excerpted from http://www.archive.org/stream/investigationofu194702unit/investigationofu194702 unit_djvu.txt

Ronald Reagan Testifies about Alleged Communism in Hollywood

Editor's Note: The following is an excerpt of the transcript from Ronald Reagan's testimony before the House Committee on Un-American Activities on October 23, 1947. Liberals who accused him of "naming names" and betraying colleagues in the industry in which he worked criticized Reagan's testimony. On the other hand, conservatives admired what they saw as Reagan's courage in standing up to left-wing influences in the film industry. The hearings helped ignite Reagan's political career.

CHAIRMAN J. PARNELL THOMAS:	The record will show that Mr. McDowell, Mr. Vail, Mr. Nixon, and Mr. Thomas are present. A subcommittee is sitting. Staff members present: Mr. Robert E. Stripling, chief investigator; Messrs. Louis J. Russell, H. A. Smith, and Robert B. Gaston, investigators; and Mr. Benjamin Mandel, director of research.
STRIPLING:	When and where were you born, Mr. Reagan?
RONALD REAGAN:	Tapioca, Illinois, February 6, 1911.
STRIPLING:	What is your present occupation?
REAGAN:	Motion picture actor.
STRIPLING:	How long have you been engaged in that profession?
REAGAN :	Since June 1937, with a brief interlude of 3 1/2 years— that at the time didn't seem very brief.
STRIPLING:	What period was that?
REAGAN:	That was during the late war.
STRIPLING:	What branch of service were you in?
REAGAN:	Well, sir, I had been for several years in the Reserve as an officer in the United States Cavalry, but I was assigned to the Air Corps.
STRIPLING:	That is kind of typical of the Army, isn't it?
REAGAN:	Yes, sir. The first thing the Air Corps did was loan me to the Signal Corps.
MCDOWELL:	You didn't wear spurs?
REAGAN:	I did for a little while.
CHAIRMAN:	I think this has little to do with the facts we are seeking. Proceed.
STRIPLING:	Mr. Reagan, are you a member of any guild?

REAGAN: Yes, sir, the Screen Actors Guild.

STRIPLING: How long have you been a member?

REAGAN: Since June 1937.

STRIPLING: Are you the president of the guild at the present time?

REAGAN: Yes, sir.

STRIPLING: When were you elected?

REAGAN: That was several months ago. I was elected to replace Mr. (Robert) Montgomery when he resigned.

STRIPLING: When does your term expire?

REAGAN: The elections come up next month.

STRIPLING: Have you ever held any other position in the Screen Actors Guild?

REAGAN: Yes, sir. Just prior to the war I was a member of the board of directors, and just after the war, prior to my being elected president, I was a member of the board of directors.

STRIPLING: As a member of the board of directors, as president of the Screen Actors Guild, and as an active member, have you at any time observed or noted within the organization a clique of either Communists or fascists who were attempting to exert influence or pressure on the guild?

REAGAN: Well, sir, my testimony must be very similar to that of Mr. (George) Murphy and Mr. (Robert) Montgomery. There has been a small group within the Screen Actors Guild which has consistently opposed the policy of the guild board and officers of the guild, as evidenced by the vote on various issues. That small clique referred to has been suspected of more or less following the tactics that we associate with the Communist Party.

STRIPLING: Would you refer to them as a disruptive influence within the guild?

REAGAN: I would say that at times they have attempted to be a disruptive influence.

STRIPLING: You have no knowledge yourself as to whether or not any of them are members of the Communist Party?

REAGAN: No, sir, I have no investigative force, or anything, and I do not know.

STRIPLING: Has it ever been reported to you that certain members of the guild were Communists?

REAGAN: Yes, sir, I have heard different discussions and some of them tagged as communists.

STRIPLING: Would you say that this clique has attempted to dominate the guild?

REAGAN: Well, sir, by attempting to put their own particular views on various issues, I guess you would have to say that our side was attempting to dominate, too, because we were fighting just as hard to put over our views, and I think, we were proven correct by the figures—Mr. Murphy gave the figures—and those figures were always approximately the same, an average of 90 percent or better of the Screen Actors Guild voted in favor of those matters now guild policy.

STRIPLING: Mr. Reagan, there has been testimony to the effect here that numerous Communist-front organizations have been set up in Hollywood. Have you ever been solicited to join any of those organizations or any organization which you considered to be a Communist-front organization?

REAGAN: Well, sir, I have received literature from an organization called the Committee for a Far-Eastern Democratic Policy. I don't know whether it is Communist or not. I only know that I didn't like their views and as a result I didn't want to have anything to do with them.

STRIPLING: Were you ever solicited to sponsor the Joint Anti-Fascist Refugee Committee?

REAGAN: No, sir, I was never solicited to do that, but I found myself misled into being a sponsor on another occasion for a function that was held under the auspices of the Joint Anti-Fascist Refugee Committee.

STRIPLING: Did you knowingly give your name as a sponsor?

REAGAN: Not knowingly. Could I explain what that occasion was?

STRIPLING: Yes sir.

REAGAN: I was called several weeks ago. There happened to be a financial drive on to raise money to build a badly needed hospital called the All Nations Hospital. I think the purpose of the building is so obvious by the title that it has the support of most of the people of Los Angeles. Certainly of most of the doctors. Some time ago I was called to the telephone. A woman introduced herself by name. I didn't make any particular note of her name, and I couldn't give it now. She told me that there would be a recital held at which Paul Robeson would sing, and she said that all the money for the tickets would go to the hospital, and asked if she could use my name as one of the sponsors. I hesitated for a moment, because I don't think that Mr. Robeson's and my political views coincide at all; and then I thought I was being a little stupid because, I thought, here is an occasion where Mr. Robeson is perhaps appearing as an artist, and certainly the object, raising money, is above any political consideration: it is a hospital supported by everyone. I have contributed money myself. So I felt a little bit as if I had been stuffy for a minute, and I said, "Certainly, you can use my name." I left town for a couple of weeks and, when I returned, I was handed a newspaper story that said that this recital was held at the Shrine Auditorium in Los Angeles under the auspices of the Joint Anti-Fascist Refugee Committee. The principal speaker was Emil Lustig, Robert Burman took up a collection, and the remnants of the

Abraham Lincoln Brigade were paraded on the platform. I did not, in the newspaper story, see one word about the hospital. I called the newspaper and said I am not accustomed to writing to editors but would like to explain my position, and he laughed and said, "You needn't bother, you are about the 50th person who had also been listed as sponsors of that affair."

STRIPLING: Would you say from your observation that that is typical of the tactics of the Communists, to solicit and use the names of prominent people to either raise money or gain support?

REAGAN: I think it is in keeping with their tactics, yes sir.

STRIPLING: Do you think there is anything democratic about those tactics?

REAGAN: I do not, sir.

STRIPLING: As president of the Screen Actors Guild, you are familiar with the jurisdictional strike which has been going on in Hollywood for some time?

REAGAN: Yes, sir.

STRIPLING: Have you ever had any conference with any of the labor officials regarding this strike?

REAGAN: Yes, sir.

STRIPLING: Do you know whether the communists have participated in any way with this strike?

REAGAN: Sir, the first time that this word "Communist" was ever injected into any of the meetings concerning the strike was at a meeting in Chicago with Mr. William Hutchinson, president of the carpenters' union, who were on strike at the time. He asked the Screen Actors Guild to submit terms to Mr. (Richard) Walsh, and he told us to tell Mr. Walsh that, if he would give in on these terms, he in turn would [...] run this Sorrell and the other commies out—I am quoting him—and break it up. I might add that Mr. Walsh and Mr. Sorrell were running the strike for Mr. Hutchinson in Hollywood.

STRIPLING: Mr. Reagan, what is your feeling about what steps should be taken to rid the motion picture industry of any Communist influences?

REAGAN: Well, sir, 99 percent of us are pretty well aware of what is going on, and I think, within the bounds of our democratic rights and never once stepping over the rights given us by democracy, we have done a pretty good job in our business of keeping those people's activities curtailed. After all, we must recognize them at present as a political party. On that basis we have exposed their lies when we came across them, we have opposed their propaganda, and I can certainly testify that in the case of the Screen Actors Guild we have been eminently successful in preventing them from, with their usual tactics, trying to run a majority of an organization with a well organized minority. In opposing those people, the best thing to do is make democracy work. In the Screen Actors Guild we make it work by insuring everyone a vote and by keeping everyone informed. I believe that, as Thomas Jefferson put it, if all the American people know all of the facts they will never make a mistake. Whether the party should be outlawed, that is a matter for the government to decide. As a citizen, I would hesitate to see any political party outlawed on the basis of its political ideology. However, if it is proven that an organization is an agent of foreign power, or in any way not a legitimate political party—and I think the government is capable of proving that—then that is another matter. I happen to be very proud of the industry in which I work; I happen to be very proud of the way in which we conducted the fight. I do not believe the Communists have ever at any time been able to use the motion picture screen as a sounding board for their philosophy or ideology.

CHAIRMAN: There is one thing that you said that interested me very much. That was the quotation from Jefferson. That is why this committee was created by the House of Representatives: to acquaint the American people with the facts. Once the American people are acquainted with the facts there is no question but what the American people will do the kind of job that they want done: that is, to make America just as pure as we can possibly make it. We want to thank you very much for coming here today.

REAGAN: Sir, I detest, I abhor their philosophy, but I detest more than that their tactics, which are those of the fifth column, and are dishonest, but at the same time I never as a citizen want to see our country become urged, by either fear or resentment of this group, that we ever compromise with any of our democratic principles through that fear or resentment. I still think that democracy can do it.

Source: U.S. Congress, House Committee on Un-American Activities, Hearings Regarding the Communist Infiltration of the Motion Picture Industry, 80th Congress, 1st Session, October 23–24, 1947 (Washington, DC: U.S. Government Printing Office, 1947).

Hollywood Producers Condemn McCarthyism

Editor's Note: The following statement was released by the Association of Motion Picture Producers to denounce the Hollywood Ten and their allegedly radical political associations. The AMPP was seeking to distance itself from dissident elements within the Hollywood entertainment industry and to discourage the continued interest of the House Committee on Un-American Activities.

Members of the Association of Motion Picture Producers deplore the action of the ten Hollywood men who have been cited for contempt. We do not desire to prejudge their legal rights, but their actions have been a disservice to their employers and have impaired their usefulness to the industry.

We will forthwith discharge or suspend without compensation those in our employ and we will not reemploy any of the ten until such time as he is acquitted or has purged himself of contempt and declares under oath that he is not a Communist.

On the broader issues of alleged subversive and disloyal elements in Hollywood, our members are likewise prepared to take positive action.

We will not knowingly employ a Communist or a member of any party or group which advocates the overthrow of the Government of the United States by force or by illegal or unconstitutional methods. In pursuing this policy, we are not going to be swayed by hysteria or intimidation from any source. We are frank to recognize that such a policy involves dangers and risks. There is the danger of hurting innocent people. There is the risk of creating an atmosphere of fear. We will guard against this danger, this risk, this fear. To the end we will invite the Hollywood talent guilds to work with us to eliminate any subversives, to protect the innocent, and to safeguard free speech and a free screen whenever threatened.

Source: The Producers' Response to the Blacklist: The Waldorf Declaration Statement. http://www.archive.org/stream/reportonblacklis00coglrich/reportonblacklis00coglrich _djvu.txt

Alfred Kinsey Researches Sexuality in American Society

Editor's Note: Alfred Kinsey was a biologist who turned his attention in the mid-1940s to human sexual behavior. He and his team of researchers compiled an enormous database based on interviews asking about more than 500 different issues related to sexual behavior. Although their results have been controversial, the publication of *Sexual Behavior in the Human Male* in 1948 was a groundbreaking book. It sold much better than expected to a general audience, who began discussing sexuality in a far more open manner than had previously been the case. This trend is an interesting juxtaposition to the repressive attitudes toward certain sexual behaviors, especially homosexuality, that some alleged created security risks in a society also focused on Communist infiltration.

For some time now there has been an increasing awareness among many people of the desirability of obtaining data about sex which would represent an accumulation of scientific fact completely divorced from questions of moral value and social custom. Practicing physicians find thousands of their patients in need of such objective data. Psychiatrists and analysts find that a majority of their patients need help in resolving sexual conflicts that have arisen in their lives. An increasing number of persons would like to bring an educated intelligence into the consideration of such matters as sexual adjustments in marriage, the sexual guidance of children, the pre-marital sexual adjustments of youth, sex education, sexual activities which are in conflict with the mores, and problems confronting persons who are interested in the social control of behavior through religion, custom, and the forces of the law. Before it is possible to think scientifically on any of these matters, more needs to be known about the actual behavior of people, and about the inter-relationships of that behavior with the biologic and social aspects of their history.

Source: Kinsey, Alfred C., Wardell B. Pomeroy, and Clyde E. Martin. Sexual Behavior in the Human Male. *Philadelphia: W. B. Saunders Company, 1948, 3.*

Senator Smith Denounces McCarthyism

Editor's Note: Margaret Chase Smith was a Republican Senator from Maine who was one of very few Washington leaders willing to speak out against Joseph McCarthy and the tactics he utilized during his Senate hearings. Smith delivered the following speech, which she titled a "Declaration of Conscience," on the floor of the U.S. Senate on June 1, 1950. Smith was the first woman elected to both the House of Representatives and the U.S. Senate. In 1964, she also became the first woman to have her name formally placed in nomination for the presidency by one of the major political parties. The following speech is sometimes described as marking an early beginning of the end of McCarthy's unchallenged abuse of power.

Mr. President:

I would like to speak briefly and simply about a serious national condition. It is a national feeling of fear and frustration that could result in national suicide and the end of everything that we Americans hold dear. It is a condition that comes from the lack of effective leadership in either the Legislative Branch or the Executive Branch of our Government.

That leadership is so lacking that serious and responsible proposals are being made that national advisory commissions be appointed to provide such critically needed leadership.

I speak as briefly as possible because too much harm has already been done with irresponsible words of bitterness and selfish political opportunism. I speak as briefly as possible because the issue is too great to be obscured by eloquence. I speak simply and briefly in the hope that my words will be taken to heart.

I speak as a Republican. I speak as a woman. I speak as a United States Senator. I speak as an American.

The United States Senate has long enjoyed worldwide respect as the greatest deliberative body in the world. But recently that deliberative character has too often been debased to the level of a forum of hate and character assassination sheltered by the shield of Congressional immunity.

It is ironical that we senators can in debate in the Senate directly or indirectly, by any form of words, impute to any American who is not a senator any conduct or motive unworthy or unbecoming an American—and without that non-senator American having any legal redress against us—yet if we say the same thing in the Senate about our colleagues we can be stopped on the grounds of being out of order.

It is strange that we can verbally attack anyone else without restraint and with full protection and yet we hold ourselves above the same type of criticism here on the Senate floor. Surely the United States Senate is big enough to take self-criticism and self-appraisal. Surely we should be able to take the same kind of character attacks that we "dish out" to outsiders.

I think that it is high time for the United States Senate and its members to do some soul-searching—for us to weigh our consciences—on the manner in which we are performing our duty to the people of America—on the manner in which we are using or abusing our individual powers and privileges.

I think that it is high time that we remembered that we have sworn to uphold and defend the Constitution. I think that it is high time that we remembered that the Constitution, as amended, speaks not only of the freedom of speech but also of trial by jury instead of trial by accusation.

Whether it be a criminal prosecution in court or a character prosecution in the Senate, there is little practical distinction when the life of a person has been ruined.

Those of us who shout the loudest about Americanism in making character assassinations are all too frequently those who, by our own words and acts, ignore some of the basic principles of Americanism:

The right to criticize;
The right to hold unpopular beliefs;
The right to protest;
The right of independent thought.

The exercise of these rights should not cost one single American citizen his reputation or his right to a livelihood nor should he be in danger of losing his reputation or livelihood merely because he happens to know someone who holds unpopular beliefs. Who of us doesn't? Otherwise none of us could call our souls our own. Otherwise thought control would have set in.

The American people are sick and tired of being afraid to speak their minds lest they be politically smeared as "Communists" or "Fascists" by their opponents. Freedom of speech is not what it used to be in America. It has been so abused by some that it is not exercised by others.

The American people are sick and tired of seeing innocent people smeared and guilty people whitewashed. But there have been enough proved cases, such as the Amerasia case, the Hiss case, the Coplon case, the Gold case, to cause the nationwide distrust and strong suspicion that there may be something to the unproved, sensational accusations.

As a Republican, I say to my colleagues on this side of the aisle that the Republican Party faces a challenge today that is not unlike the challenge that it faced back in Lincoln's day. The Republican Party so successfully met that challenge that it emerged from the Civil War as the champion of a united nation—in addition to being a Party that unrelentingly fought loose spending and loose programs.

Today our country is being psychologically divided by the confusion and the suspicions that are bred in the United States Senate to spread like cancerous tentacles of "know nothing, suspect everything" attitudes. Today we have a Democratic Administration that has developed a mania for loose spending and loose programs. History is repeating itself—and the Republican Party again has the opportunity to emerge as the champion of unity and prudence.

The record of the present Democratic Administration has provided us with sufficient campaign issues without the necessity of resorting to political smears. America is rapidly losing its position as leader of the world simply because the Democratic Administration has pitifully failed to provide effective leadership.

The Democratic Administration has completely confused the American people by its daily contradictory grave warnings and optimistic assurances— that show the people that our Democratic Administration has no idea of where it is going.

The Democratic Administration has greatly lost the confidence of the American people by its complacency to the threat of communism here at home and the leak of vital secrets to Russia though key officials of the Democratic Administration. There are enough proved cases to make this point without diluting our criticism with unproved charges.

Surely these are sufficient reasons to make it clear to the American people that it is time for a change and that a Republican victory is necessary to the security of this country. Surely it is clear that this nation will continue to suffer as long as it is governed by the present ineffective Democratic Administration.

Yet to displace it with a Republican regime embracing a philosophy that lacks political integrity or intellectual honesty would prove equally disastrous to this nation. The nation sorely needs a Republican victory. But I don't want to see the Republican Party ride to political victory on the Four Horsemen of Calumny—Fear, Ignorance, Bigotry, and Smear.

I doubt if the Republican Party could—simply because I don't believe the American people will uphold any political party that puts political exploitation above national interest. Surely we Republicans aren't that desperate for victory.

I don't want to see the Republican Party win that way. While it might be a fleeting victory for the Republican Party, it would be a more lasting defeat for the American people. Surely it would ultimately be suicide for the Republican Party and the two-party system that has protected our American liberties from the dictatorship of a one party system.

As members of the minority party, we do not have the primary authority to formulate the policy of our government. But we do have the responsibility of rendering constructive criticism, of clarifying issues, of allaying fears by acting as responsible citizens.

As a woman, I wonder how the mothers, wives, sisters, and daughters feel about the way in which members of their families have been politically mangled in the Senate debate—and I use the word "debate" advisedly.

As a United States senator, I am not proud of the way in which the Senate has been made a publicity platform for irresponsible sensationalism. I am not proud of the reckless abandon in which unproved charges have been hurled from the side of the aisle. I am not proud of the obviously staged, undignified countercharges that have been attempted in retaliation from the other side of the aisle.

I don't like the way the Senate has been made a rendezvous for vilification, for selfish political gain at the sacrifice of individual reputations and national unity. I am not proud of the way we smear outsiders from the floor of the Senate and hide behind the cloak of Congressional immunity and still place ourselves beyond criticism on the floor of the Senate.

As an American, I am shocked at the way Republicans and Democrats alike are playing directly into the Communist design of "confuse, divide, and conquer." As an American, I don't want a Democratic Administration "whitewash" or "cover-up" any more than a want a Republican smear or witch hunt.

As an American, I condemn a Republican "Fascist" just as much I condemn a Democratic "Communist." I condemn a Democrat "Fascist" just as much as I condemn a Republican "Communist." They are equally dangerous to you and me and to our country. As an American, I want to see our nation recapture the strength and unity it once had when we fought the enemy instead of ourselves.

It is with these thoughts that I have drafted what I call a "Declaration of Conscience." I am gratified that Senator Tobey, Senator Aiken, Senator Morse, Senator Ives, Senator Thye, and Senator Hendrickson have concurred in that declaration and have authorized me to announce their concurrence.

Source: Margaret Chase Smith. Declaration of Conscience. June 1, 1950. http://www.senate.gov/artandhistory/history/resources/pdf/SmithDeclaration.pdf

Warnings of Communist Infiltration into the Television Industry

Editor's Note: *Red Channels* was a pamphlet published in 1950 in order to document alleged Communist sympathies or involvement by a wide range of individuals working in the television industry, including directors, producers, writers, and actors. The pamphlet was widely circulated and cited, listing the allegedly subversive organizational and political affiliations of those included. The document led to serious consequences for many of those named, including cancelled contracts, limited employment opportunities, and blacklisting from the industry. The following excerpt is from the pamphlet's introduction.

Testifying before a U.S. Congressional committee on March 26, 1947, J. Edgar Hoover, Director of the Federal Bureau of Investigation, stated: "The (Communist) party has departed from depending upon the printed word as its medium of propaganda and has taken to the air. Its members and sympathizers have not only infiltrated the airways but they are now persistently seeking radio channels."

Director Hoover's concise summary of Communist activities in the radio-TV field will be expanded in the following report to the broadcasting industry and to those who are both its client and judge—the American public.

Basically, the Cominform (previously known as the Comintern) seeks to exploit American radio and TV to gain the following:

1) Channels (known to the Communist Party as "transmission belts") for pro-Soviet, pro-Communist, anti-America, anti-democratic propaganda.
2) Financial support.
3) The great prestige and crowd-gathering power that derives from having glamorous personalities of radio and TV as sponsors of Communist fronts and as performers or speakers at front meeting and rallies (which incidentally adds to the performers' prestige).
4) Increasing domination of American broadcasting and telecasting, preparatory to the day when—the Cominform believes—the Communist Party will assume control of this nation as the result of a final upheaval and civil war.

Source: Red Channels: The Report of Communist Influence in Radio and Television *(1950). http://www.authentichistory.com/1946–1960/redchannels/redchannels.html*

Federal Government Urges Americans to Be Prepared

Editor's Note: The National Civil Defense Administration was established in order to coordinate national and local efforts to prepare for possible military, especially nuclear, attack. The agency published public education pamphlets and materials, made short films, and organized local citizen groups to provide surveillance of potentially vulnerable public facilities (such as hospitals, as described by Dave Mills in his essay in this volume). The following excerpt is from a speech by James J. Wadsworth, deputy administrator for the NCDA, given to local civil defense authorities on January 18, 1952.

At the basis of an adequate civil defense is the self-reliant individual, fortified with every possible training and every possible practice, prepared to do everything he can to protect himself in an emergency with assurance and without panic. In addition he is prepared to extend efficient aid to his family, his neighbors, or the people down the street.

His efforts are duplicated in self-reliance and mutual assistance by family units, neighborhoods, industrial plant populations, communities, states, and even nations. That last word was added to the paper because, as you probably know, we have a civil defense pact with Canada, the basis for which in the preamble appears in language something like this: that in the event of a civil defense emergency Canada and the United States will operate as though there were no border at all.

Every person and every community has a part to play in an effective civil defense program. Remoteness from places considered probable targets or comparatively small size does not exempt any community from playing its part in the over-all program, since evacuee reception and care must be planned and mutual aid and mobile support organized.

This tying together of individuals, homes, industries, blocks, zones, communities, states, and nations is basically the bedrock on which civil defense rests. In the perfected plan, a community takes necessary preattack steps— provision of shelters; dispersal of equipment, manpower and facilities; and the like. If it is attacked, it rides out the storm, using every principle of self-protection to minimize loss and damage. Then its neighbors move in to help. Teams of radiation detectors, fire fighters, and rescue and other workers move to the stricken area. The wounded, dead, and the bombed-out people are moved out. Rehabilitation starts almost before the fires are out.

Even in the event of an attack without warning, civil defense preparations will be of invaluable assistance. Given only a few minutes warning, the casualties can be reduced as much as 50 percent [. . .]

Source: James. J. Wadsworth, January 18, 1952. National Civil Defense Administration. www.ndu.edu/library/ic2/L52–080.pdf

Paul Robeson Defends His Actions and Philosophies

Editor's Note: As discussed in S. Ani Mukherij's essay, Paul Robeson was a prominent African American singer and actor whose support for Communism and the Soviet Union led to ongoing harassment through a variety of mechanisms. He was targeted for surveillance by the FBI, had his passport revoked, and was attacked by a mob at a concert in upstate New York. Robeson insisted that he was a loyal American who had a right to express his political views. His story illustrates the complex interactions between race and radicalism in mid-century America. The following excerpt is from his autobiography.

My views concerning the Soviet Union and my warm feelings for friendship for the peoples of that land, and the friendly sentiments which they have often expressed toward me, have been pictured as something quite sinister by Washington officials and other spokesmen of the dominant white group in our country. It has been alleged that I am part of some kind of "international conspiracy."

The truth is: *I am not and never have been involved in any international conspiracy or any other kind, and do not know anyone who is.* It should be plain to everybody—especially to Negroes—that if the government officials had a shred of evidence to back up that charge, you can bet your last dollar that they would have tried their best to put me *under* their jail! But they have no such evidence, because that charge is a lie. By an arbitrary and, as I am insisting in the courts, *illegal* ruling they have refused me a passport.[. . .] let me say that their denial of my passport is proof of nothing except the State Department's high-handed disregard of civil liberties.

In 1946, at a legislative hearing in California, I testified under oath that I was not a member of the Communist Party, but since then I have refused to give testimony or to sign affidavits as to that fact. There is no mystery involved in this refusal. As the witchhunt developed, it became clear that an important issue of Constitutional rights was involved in the making of such inquiries, and the film writers and directors who became known as the Hollywood Ten challenged the rights of any inquisitors to violate the First Amendment's provisions of free speech and conscience. They lost their fight in the courts and were imprisoned, but since then the Supreme Court has made more liberal rulings in similar cases. The fundamental issue, however, is still not resolved, and I have made it a matter of principle, as many others have done, to refuse to comply with any demands of legislative committees or departmental officials that infringes upon the Constitutional right of all Americans.

Source: Here I Stand by Paul Robeson. *Copyright © 1958, 1988 by Paul Robeson. Reprinted by permission of Beacon Press, Boston, pp. 38–39.*

Labor Organizer Len DeCaux versus HUAC

Editor's Note: Len DeCaux was a labor union leader and journalist who wrote for the Congress of Industrial Organization's newspaper. The CIO had frequently come under attack for tolerating or even encouraging Communist infiltration into the labor movement. DeCaux was purged from the CIO as a Communist but was subsequently able to get a job as a factory laborer. In 1954, he was called to testify before HUAC. The following excerpt comes from his memoir, *Labor Radical.*

When the knock on the door came—after months of the rehabilitation—our family agitation was extreme. It was a subpoena to appear before the House Un-American Activities Committee in Washington, for a hearing on *March of Labor.* I hadn't been connected with the magazine for nearly a year. It has long since moved back from Chicago to New York, where its dying gasps were less and less frequent.

Could I somehow come through without losing my job? I thought there was a fighting chance and began to plot the seemingly impossible—an undiscovered public appearance before HUAC.

Had the hearing been in Chicago, I'd have given up. Exposure, discharge, blacklist, would have been inevitable. If HUAC came to one's city, the only way out was to dodge the subpoena. For years after, I had no telephone in my name, left no forwarding address when I moved. Each place of employment was a closely guarded secret—mentioned not even in family or among friends. At first I thought to dodge the FBI also, then concluded that was asking trouble from an outfit concerned chiefly with knowing my whereabouts. HUAC was the menace to my job, and I figured a local subpoena-server couldn't count on earning his pay by no more than calling the FBI. In this case, however, the HUAC hearing was in Washington [. . .] Could I make the trip to Washington and back without being missed from the job?

[. . .] In Washington, I had breakfast with my lawyer, who discussed my constitutional rights. Besides citing the First Amendment on press freedom, I'd have to claim protection of the Fifth and answer no anti-Communist questions, or I'd be required, under pain of jail and fine, to answer all related questions, inevitably designed to make me an informer against my associates and friends. My chief concern was to protect my job, but the lawyer said they'd certainly ask about it and I'd have to answer.

Sure enough, committee counsel soon asked the questions that could mean discharge and blacklist. I stalled, asking to keep my employer's name from the record—lest he be embarrassed, I said. Congressman Harold Velde [. . .] insisted I give full name, business, address of my employer, spell it out and repeat it [. . .] Unlike the Senate committee, HUAC was arrogant, hectoring, deliberately rude, and inconsiderate. Each time I started to snap back, I felt the cautioning glance of my lawyer, who had advised self-control under provocation, lest I risk extended persecution. When my anger tempted me to disregard him, my fear of publicity bringing job loss stopped me. The sure way to make a news story was to clash with the committee.

[. . .] Once released from the hearing, I sped to Washington airport with but minutes to spare [. . .] [After returning to Chicago], I bought [newspapers] to hunt through them on the way home for further squibs [. . .] I started with the *Chicago Tribune*. I didn't have to hunt; it was no squib. On the second page, with my picture and sprawling over four columns, was a story exclusively about me, my life story and all.

[. . .] The next day was Saturday [. . .] the super called. He sounded genuinely distressed. "Can't tell you how sorry I am," he said, "but I've got to let you go. You can have it any way you like—quit, call it a layoff, a discharge, whatever's best for you. I can't wait till the boss returns. Customers have been calling in all day, and the salesmen are raising hell. They say I've got to fire you at once."

Source: De Caux, Len. Labor Radical: From the Wobblies to the CIO. *Boston: Beacon Press, 1970, 538–545.*

Women Organize against McCarthyism

Editor's Note: Women Strike for Peace was an organization formed as part of the anti-nuclear movement. Their organization coincides with the end of the McCarthy period, but members were nevertheless summoned before HUAC to investigate the allegedly pro-Communist and subversive nature of their program. A group mostly made up of housewives, Women Strike for Peace represents an example of a transitional group from the conformist (and often fearful) liberalism of the 1950s to a more assertive activism in the 1960s. The following excerpt is from the testimony of Mrs. Blanche Hofrichter Posner before the Committee on December 11, 1962.

Mr. Clyde Doyle (Representative from California and Committee Chair): Before we hear the first witness, I have a prepared statement I wish to read, which will give everyone in the hearing room an outline of what the objectives of these hearings today are:

Everyone in the world, every nation in the world—if you can believe their words—wants peace. The cry is universal. It comes from neutralists, from Communists, from anti-Communists. Yet there is no peace because certain persons, groups, and nations in the world—even while they cry peace—foment war and unrest [. . .]

[Doyle continues with a lengthy description of the historical and contemporary threats represented by the Soviet Union and international Communism.]

These very blunt Communist statements make one thing very clear: Present Communist strategy gives No. 1 priority to peace agitation and propaganda in the United States and all other non-Communist nations. It calls for Communist infiltration of, and support for, existing peace organizations, Communist or non-Communist [. . .] The subject of this inquiry is to determine the extent of Communist infiltration in peace organizations, particularly in the Metropolitan New York area and with special reference to Women Strike for Peace. [. . .] The Committee wishes to emphasize these points before the hearings begin: The fact that Communists are active in peace agitation does not mean that everyone who agitates for peace is a Communist or even a fellow traveler [. . .]

MR. ALFRED N. NITTLE (Committee counsel):	Do you hold an official position in an organization known as Women Strike for Peace? [Witness conferred with counsel.]
MRS. POSNER:	I must decline to answer that question and I should be very grateful if you would let me say why.
MR. NITTLE:	We are only interested in whether or not you are presenting a legal reason and basis for your refusal to testify. Therefore, I will ask you simply this, and ask you not to make a statement but to respond to the inquiry: Do you assign as your basis for your next refusal to testify the constitutional privilege of the Fifth Amendment? [Witness conferred with counsel.]
MRS. POSNER:	I should like to decline to answer the question, but I must please plead with you to let me say why. I have—
MR. NITTLE:	Mr. Chairman, I respectfully request that the witness be directed to answer the question addressed to her.
MR. DOYLE:	(Committee Chair): I instruct the witness to answer the question. We believe it is a pertinent question and entirely proper. [Witness conferred with counsel.]
MRS. POSNER:	I don't know, sir, why I am here, but I do know why you are here. I think—
MR. NITTLE:	Mr. Chairman, I must ask for regular order.

MRS. POSNER: —because you don't quite understand the nature of this movement. This movement was inspired and motivated by mothers' love for their children.

MR. NITTLE: Mr. Chairman?

MRS. POSNER: When they were putting their breakfast on the table, they saw not only Wheaties and milk, but they also saw strontium 90 and iodine 131.

MR. DOYLE: Just a moment.

MRS. POSNER: They feared for the health and life of their children. That is the only motivation.

MR. DOYLE: Witness! Now, Witness—

MRS. POSNER: If you gentlemen have children or grandchildren, you should be grateful to the Women Strike for Peace, or whatever peace movement is working to stop nuclear testing. Every nuclear test has resulted in stillbirths, has resulted in leukemia, has resulted in cancer, has resulted in the possibility of nuclear holocaust.

I have given you gentlemen this statement which presents some of the reasons why women are concerned.

MR. DOYLE: Now, Witness, just a minute. I have to declare you out of order. If you insist on interrupting the hearing, we will have to ask that you be removed from the hearing room. I do not want to do that, and you do not want it. So please cooperate. You have made your little speech. Now proceed and either cooperate with the committee or not, just as you choose.

[Witness conferred with counsel.]

MR. DOYLE: I order and direct you to answer that question. We believe it is pertinent legally . . .

[Witness conferred with counsel.]

MRS. POSNER: By virtue of the statement, this will be just the one sentence, Mr. Doyle, by virtue of the statement that you read at this hearing, I must at this point decline to cooperate with the Committee and thank God that the framers of our Constitution and the Bill of Rights included that Fifth Amendment, which I now invoke.

Source: U.S. Congress. House Committee on Un-American Activities. Communist activities in the peace movement (Women Strike for Peace and certain other groups): Hearings before the Committee on Un-American Activities, House of Representatives, 87th Congress, 2nd Session, December 11–13, 1962. Washington, DC: U.S. Government Printing Office, 1963.

Acheson, Dean Acheson was secretary of state from 1949 to 1953 during the Truman Administration. He was secretary during the crucial years when U.S. Cold War policy was put to its first major test. During his term as secretary, the Soviets detonated an atomic bomb, the Chinese Revolution concluded in a Communist victory, and the United States became involved in the Korean War.

Alsop, Joseph Alsop, an outspoken opponent of Communism, was a conservative syndicated columnist. By the early 1950s, Alsop also became a vocal critic of McCarthy and his tactics. He co-wrote "We Accuse!" with his brother Stewart in 1953, in which they argued that the security clearance of J. Robert Oppenheimer ought to be reinstated.

American Federation of Labor The AFL was the largest trade union in the United States, enlisting mostly white male members from skilled trades. Although it had long sought to distance itself from radicalism, during the McCarthy period, the AFL, and most other unions, was accused of harboring Communists. It merged with the Congress of Industrial Organization (CIO) in 1955.

Americans for Democratic Action The ADA was founded in 1947 as a left-leaning but adamantly anti-Communist political organization. Among its members were Eleanor Roosevelt, Hubert Humphrey, and other liberal political and public figures. The ADA supported Harry Truman's Cold War policies, opposed McCarthyism, and was an early advocate for more federal civil rights legislation.

Arbenz Guzman, Jacobo Arbenz was the president of Guatemala who was overthrown in a CIA-sponsored coup in 1954. The United States was concerned about the leftist policies of the Arbenz administration; in addition, John Foster Dulles (secretary of state) and Allen Dulles (head of the CIA) both had financial interests in the United Fruit Company, which was at risk of nationalization by Arbenz.

Army-McCarthy Hearings In 1954, Senator Joseph McCarthy launched accusations at the U.S. Army that it was concealing the identity of known Communists in its ranks. Joseph Welch, Army attorney, was angered by McCarthy's attempts to smear a young lawyer working in Welch's firm, prompting Welch's famous question of McCarthy: "Have you no decency, sir?" The televised Army-McCarthy hearings led to a steep decline in popular support for McCarthy, who, by the end of 1954, had been officially censured by the Senate.

Atlantic Charter The Atlantic Charter was a statement of principles drafted by Winston Churchill, prime minister of Great Britain, and President Franklin D. Roosevelt in August 1941 at a meeting off the Canadian coast. In the Charter, the United States and Britain committed to protecting the sovereignty rights of all nations, in addition to promises of other protections of democracy. Although the Charter was issued in response to the threat of fascism and totalitarianism around the world, in the postwar period, it became a statement of opposition to Communist expansion as well.

Atomic Energy Commission There are actually two atomic energy commissions, one established in the United States and one by the United Nations, both in 1946. The USAEC was charged with monitoring and managing U.S. atomic research, including materials that could be used to manufacture atomic weapons. The U.N. commission was the first international venue in which nuclear disarmament was discussed.

Ball, Lucille Ball was one of the most popular television actresses in the 1950s and 1960s. *I Love Lucy* was one of the highest ranked television series of the era. In 1953, a news report alleged that Ball had been a member of the Communist Party in the 1930s. She testified before HUAC that she had joined the Party at her grandfather's request but had never been an active member. HUAC cleared her of charges, and she was never blacklisted.

Bay of Pigs In April 1961, a group of Cuban expatriates, trained and supplied by the CIA, attempted to invade Cuba and overthrow the revolutionary government of Fidel Castro. Although the plans for the invasion were drawn up by the Eisenhower administration, it was John Kennedy who authorized the operation to go forward. The invasion failed—it was a humiliating defeat for the ex-pats and, by extension, the United States.

Bentley, Elizabeth Bentley was an American woman who, in July 1948, appeared before HUAC to testify to the presence of Communists within the federal government. Bentley herself had served as a Soviet informant in the United States since at least 1945. Although a variety of witnesses challenged Bentley's credibility, her accusations were among the first to stir up a wave of anxieties about Communist infiltration into U.S. society.

Berlin Airlift and Blockade Following World War II, Germany as a whole and Berlin in particular were divided into zones of occupation under the supervision of each major Allied power (British, French, American, and Soviet). By 1948, the British, French, and Americans were seeking to unify the western zones of Germany into a sovereign republic. Josef Stalin, seeing this as a threat to Soviet influence in the East, imposed a blockade of supplies into western Berlin. Truman ordered an airlift of supplies to Berlin in defiance of Stalin's blockade. The airlift lasted for ten months before Stalin backed down, in May 1949.

Berlin Wall In the late 1950s, Soviet Premier Nikita Khrushchev proposed that Berlin become a "free city," belonging to neither East nor West Germany. This reignited an escalation of tensions over the status of the city that remained a potent symbol in the West of anti-Communist resistance. In August 1961, Khrushchev ordered the border between East and West Berlin sealed. This was followed by construction of a wall dividing the city, which remained in place until it was dismantled by anti-Communist protestors in 1989.

Blacklisting Blacklisting is the practice of seeking the denial of employment or other opportunities on the basis of alleged political affiliation. In the Cold War context, it refers to the policy of major television and movie studios, as well as theaters and some major industries, to deny employment to individuals identified as Communists or Communist sympathizers. These charges were not necessarily based on verifiable claims, but the widespread use of blacklists had a chilling effect on mid-20th-century society. The Hollywood Ten were the best-known targets of blacklisting during this era.

Bolshevik The Bolshevik Party was the leading Communist political organization in Russia at the time of the Russian Revolution. Vladimir Lenin, Leon Trotsky, and Josef Stalin were among the important leaders of the Bolshevik Party that had, by 1921, solidified its control over Russia.

Browder, Earl Browder was head of the American Communist Party from 1934 to 1944. He supported the Soviet's Popular Front program during the 1930s and promoted the U.S.-Soviet alliance during World War II. In 1945, Browder was subpoenaed to testify before HUAC, and, in 1946, he was expelled from the Communist Party. In 1950, he was held in contempt for refusing to testify before the Senate and was jailed from 1950 until 1951, when a federal judge ordered him released.

Buckley, William F. Buckley was a prolific author and editorialist who has long been identified with conservative politics in the United States. He gained fame in 1950 when he wrote a book condemning the leftist politics of many academics. He spent time working for the CIA in the early 1950s and then cowrote a book in 1954 defending McCarthy. When this book received little media attention, Buckley decided to establish his own magazine, *National Review*, which became a major conservative voice in U.S. culture.

Castro, Fidel Castro was the leader of the revolutionary forces that toppled the government of Fulgencio Batista in Cuba in 1959. The proximity of Cuba to the U.S. mainland and the anti-American views of Castro led him to become one of the most important opponents of the United States during the Cold War era. Repeated attempts by the United States to assassinate or otherwise remove him from power have failed. In the early 1960s, Castro became an important Latin American ally of the Soviet Union.

Central Intelligence Agency The CIA was created in 1947 as part of the massive National Security Act of 1947, which reorganized the military and security services of the United States. The CIA was initially developed by the Army as the Office of Strategic Services. Although the CIA was originally intended to be an intelligence gathering agency, it increasingly took on a more proactive role during the 1950s in planning and implementing covert operations.

Chambers, Whittaker In 1948, Chambers appeared before HUAC, accusing State Department official Alger Hiss of being a member of the Communist Party. Hiss denied the allegation, leading to one of the best-known dramas of the Cold War era. Eventually, Hiss admitted that he had known Chambers under another name but continued to deny that he was a Communist. He was convicted of perjury and served time in prison. Chambers, a former *Time* magazine editor, spent the rest of his career writing and lecturing on the dangers of leftist ideologies in U.S. life.

Chaplin, Charles Chaplin, one of the most popular and influential movie stars of the early 20th century, was British-born but rose to fame in Hollywood before accusations of Communism led him to return to Europe. In 1948, he supported the presidential candidacy of Henry Wallace and was linked to leftist causes. Although he denied ever being a Communist, he was investigated by McCarthy's Senate subcommittee but never forced to testify.

Chiang Kai-Shek Chiang Kai-Shek was the nationalist leader in China who became an important ally of the United States and led the opposition to the Chinese Communists, led by Mao Zedong. In 1949, Chiang Kai-Shek and his forces were forced to retreat to the island of Taiwan (formerly Formosa), where they established the Republic of China. Despite his anti-Communism, allegations of corruption under his leadership of Taiwan complicated his relationship with the United States.

China Hands This group of Americans working in the State Department were tasked with monitoring the activities and threats represented by Chinese Communist forces in the postwar period. With the defeat of the Nationalists in China, these State Department officials (see John Steward Service) were blamed for the "loss" of China. Several of these men were subsequently questioned by various Congressional committees, and a few had their security clearances revoked or lost their jobs.

Chinese Civil War The Chinese Civil War was one of the first and most important international dramas of the Cold War era. With the defeat of Japan, Communist Chinese, under the leadership of Mao Zedong, sought to overthrow the regime of Chiang Kai-Shek and the pro-Western Nationalists, also called the Kuomintang. In October 1949, Mao and his forces took over Beijing, and Chiang retreated to the island of Taiwan.

Churchill, Winston Churchill was prime minister of Great Britain from 1940 to 1945 and 1951 to 1955. Although perhaps best known for his inspirational leadership during World War II, he was also an important Cold War figure. In 1946, he gave a speech in Fulton, Missouri, in which he coined the phrase "Iron Curtain" in describing Soviet encroachment into Eastern and Central Europe. He also led Britain into the atomic age, when the British detonated a nuclear weapon in 1952. He championed the close alliance between the United States and Britain.

Cohn, Roy Cohn was chief counsel to the Senate Permanent Investigations Subcommittee, when it was chaired by Joseph McCarthy. He was McCarthy's most important investigator and, like McCarthy, engaged in irresponsible and unfounded attacks on a variety of witnesses appearing before the subcommittee. In 1953, Cohn tried to use his influence to secure a desirable assignment for his assistant and friend, David Schine, who had been drafted into the U.S. Army. Cohn's threats against the Army, unless the appointment was made, helped destroy both Cohn's and McCarthy's careers.

Cominform The Communist Information Bureau was created in 1947 for the purpose of disseminating Communist propaganda internationally. It was established in response to the initiation of the Marshall Plan, which Stalin insisted also represented an international propaganda opportunity.

Communist Party of America Before World War I, most Communists in the United States belonged to the Socialist Party, but, in the wake of the Russian Revolution, ideological disagreements led the Socialist Party to split into three parties, one of which was the Communist Party of America. The Communist Labor Party was a second offshoot. These two parties combined had a membership of perhaps 40,000 in 1919 (Brune, 2005, 26). Constant disagreements and splits within the Party's leadership make it difficult to trace the history of any single Communist Party in the United States.

Congress of Industrial Organizations The CIO was formed in 1935 as a union that enlisted membership from among unskilled workers. The CIO was intended to be an alternative to the American Federation of Labor, which traditionally only enlisted skilled workers as members. The CIO included a more leftist, broadly based membership, which led to charges of Communist infiltration.

Containment The containment theory was proposed by George Kennan in 1945. It was at the heart of U.S. Cold War policy and argued, simply, that in order to prevent the global spread of Communism, it must be contained anywhere that it existed. This assessment was turned into official policy through the Truman Doctrine, NSC-68, and other important government statements.

Cuban Missile Crisis In the late summer of 1962, U.S. spy planes detected the construction of missile launch sites on the island of Cuba. These sites appeared to be of Soviet origin and had the potential to launch missiles against the U.S. mainland. President Kennedy insisted on their removal, a demand initially rejected by Soviet leader Khrushchev. After more than a week of very tense negotiations in October 1962, Khrushchev agreed to cease construction if the United States promised to refrain from attacks on Cuba and to withdraw U.S. missiles from Turkey.

The Day the Earth Stood Still This 1951 film, starring Patricia Neal and directed by Robert Wise, portrays the United States confronting an alien invasion. When aliens land in Washington, D.C., the U.S. Army greets them suspiciously, despite the claims of friendship being offered by the alien visitors. The movie ends with the alien warning that either humans must learn to live in peace or face annihilation.

Department of Defense The Department of Defense was created in 1947 as part of the massive National Security Act of 1947. This act unified all branches of the military, under the supervision of the joint chiefs of staff and the secretary of defense (formerly secretary of war). The Pentagon was constructed in order to bring the different branches together, which would increase efficiency and allow for a rapid response to threats.

Dien Bien Phu In May 1954, French forces, fighting to reestablish control over former French colonies in Indochina, were defeated at Dien Bien Phu by Communist forces, led by Vo Nguyen Giap and Ho Chi Minh. Despite the nationalist motivations of the Communists, the United States felt compelled to support the French rather than risk the creation of a Communist state in Southeast Asia.

Disney, Walt Disney was a cartoonist, studio owner, and entertainment mogul who pioneered the idea of the theme park with the opening of Disneyland in 1955. Disney was an outspoken critic of Communism, who testified before HUAC as a friendly witness in 1947; he claimed that Communists were attempting to infiltrate cartoonists' professional organizations in California.

Douglas, Helen Gahagan In 1950, Douglas, a Democratic congresswoman from California, was defeated by Republican congressman Richard Nixon. This race set a new standard for Red-baiting, as Nixon repeatedly attacked Douglas for her allegedly leftist views. Although Nixon won easily, he also picked up a new nickname during the campaign, "Tricky Dick."

Dr. No *Dr. No* is the title of a 1958 novel by Ian Fleming, starring his popular Cold War character, James Bond. Bond is a British agent who works to protect the British and its allies from a variety of threats, in this case the plan of evil Dr. No to blow up a rocket to be launched from Cape Canaveral.

DuBois, W. E. B. DuBois was a African American scholar, educator, and activist who co-founded the NAACP and served as editor of its magazine, *The Crisis*, during its first few decades. As a strong advocate of racial equality, he condemned racism in the United States and was accused by his critics of Communist sympathies. DuBois eventually joined the Communist Party and ultimately exiled himself to Ghana, where he died.

Duck and Cover This 1951 educational film was produced for a school age audience in order to show children what to do in case of atomic attack. Bert the Turtle, a cartoon character, became a Cold War icon by showing children how to drop to the ground and curl up in a ball to protect themselves.

Whether the film increased or alleviated the anxieties of school children living during this age, the film has become a classic of the era.

Dulles, Allen Dulles served as director of the Central Intelligence Agency from 1953 to 1961. As such, he was one of the most powerful Americans of the Cold War era. Because his brother also served as secretary of state during part of this time, Dulles's influence was even greater. Dulles's tenure at the CIA was especially controversial because of his belief that the CIA was justified in engaging in almost any action, including those which appeared to exceed the agency's mandate or were even illegal, in the interests of defending the United States against Communist threats.

Dulles, John Foster Dulles served as secretary of state during the Eisenhower administration. During his tenure, he proved to be both a strong anti-Communist and a pragmatist who was committed to containment. In conjunction with his brother, Allen Dulles, who was director of the CIA at this time, Dulles supported using U.S. resources to bolster forces resisting Communism around the world, notably in Southeast Asia and Latin America.

Dumbarton Oaks Dumbarton Oaks is the location at which agreement was reached among Allied leaders during World War II on the basic format for a new international organization. This organization became known as the United Nations, and its purpose was to create a forum in which diplomacy might be used as a way to avoid future military conflict.

Eisenhower, Dwight D. Eisenhower served two terms as U.S. president from 1953 to 1961. Previously, he had served as commander of U.S. forces in Europe during World War II. Although Eisenhower was a Republican president, he was not particularly ideological and preferred a more pragmatic approach to foreign policy. Although there was a significant arms buildup early in his presidency, by the time he left office, he had come to support arms control talks.

Face the Nation This television program debuted in 1954 and served as an important venue for political figures of all types during the height of the Cold War. The CBS news program scored a particular coup in 1947, when Nikita Khrushchev agreed to appear on a special hour-long edition in which he was questioned by reporters. CBS was criticized for not following up with an anti-Communist commentator.

Federal Bureau of Investigation The FBI was created in 1932 in order to investigate threats to the domestic security of the United States. It is an investigative, not enforcement, agency, but its longtime director, J. Edgar Hoover, focused the agency's efforts on rooting out Communist and other leftist ideologies in U.S. life. During the height of the Cold War, the FBI worked closely with members of Congress and other so-called Cold Warriors in an attempt to identify Communists.

From Russia with Love This novel was published by Ian Fleming in 1957 and again featured the dashing James Bond. In this novel, Bond seeks to break up an international criminal organization seeking to initiate conflict between British and Soviet intelligence agencies. The prize fought over by the various parties is a Soviet deciphering machine.

Fuchs, Klaus Fuchs was a naturalized citizen of Great Britain who worked as a nuclear physicist in the United States as part of the Manhattan Project. As early as 1943, Fuchs began passing classified information about the atomic weapons program to the Soviet Union. In 1949, after an FBI investigation, he confessed to espionage and was sentenced to prison.

Geneva Accords The Geneva Accords were signed in 1954 after the defeat of the French by Vietnamese forces, led by Ho Chi Minh. Under the Accords, which the United States did not sign, France accepted the loss of its Indochinese empire, and Viet Nam was temporarily divided at the 17th parallel—with Communist forces to the North and pro-Western forces to the South. Elections for a unified government were to be held within two years.

Godzilla This 1954 Japanese film reflected anxieties over the impact of nuclear technologies. Godzilla is a sea monster who arises to wreak havoc on the island of Japan. The success of this movie led to several sequels, in which Godzilla evolves into a defender of Japan.

Goldfinger This James Bond novel, published in 1960 and written by Ian Fleming, follows Bond as he tries to prevent a gold-obsessed villain from detonating an atomic bomb inside Ft. Knox. China, seeking to destabilize the United States, had delivered the bomb to Goldfinger.

H-bomb The hydrogen bomb supplanted the atomic bomb as the most destructive weapon of the era. Its development provoked a heated debate by physicists and military experts, many of whom insisted that it had no military value. The first hydrogen bomb was tested by the United States in 1952, followed closely by a Soviet detonation in 1953.

Heston, Charlton Besides Ronald Reagan, Heston was one of the best-known Cold Warriors working in Hollywood. He served several terms as president of the Screen Actors Guild, in addition to making several classic 1950s films focusing on religious and patriotic themes.

Hiss, Alger Hiss was a State Department official, who was accused in 1948 of being a former member of the Communist Party. His accuser, Whittaker Chambers, claimed that both of them had belonged to the party in the 1930s. Hiss insisted that he did not know Chambers and had never been a Communist, but, under extensive questioning and, eventually, two trials, he was found guilty of perjury and served several years in prison.

Ho Chi Minh Ho Chi Minh was a Vietnamese nationalist leader, who was also a founding member of the Vietnamese Communist Party. He fought against the Japanese during World War II, when Japan occupied much of Indochina, and then fought against the French after the war, when France tried to reassert control over its Indochinese empire. By the 1960s, as U.S. involvement in Viet Nam escalated, Ho became one of the most bitter Cold War opponents of the United States.

Hollywood Ten In 1947, ten writers, directors, and producers refused to submit to questioning about their political affiliations when asked to do so by HUAC. Large numbers of Hollywood personalities were called as witnesses, and the Hollywood community split over who testified and who did not. The Ten were subsequently blacklisted in Hollywood and found their careers either over or seriously threatened. Several of the Ten had, at some point, in fact, been members of either the Communist Party or sympathetic organizations.

House Committee on Un-American Activities HUAC, as it is commonly called, was originally set up in 1938 to investigate allegations of Communism and fascism in U.S. society. The Committee focused especially on the entertainment industry. Various well-known figures were called either as defendants or witnesses; whether to appear or not became a major preoccupation for many actors, directors, and writers.

Iron Curtain Speech At a speech in Fulton, Missouri, in 1946, British leader Winston Churchill gave a speech in which he said an "Iron Curtain" was falling across parts of Central and Eastern Europe. His reference to Soviet power in these regions became one of the most familiar descriptions of Soviet domination.

Kennan, George Kennan was perhaps the most important architect of early U.S. Cold War policy. He was a State Department official, with extensive experience in the Soviet Union, who wrote two very influential documents, the "Long Telegram" and the "Mister X" article in *Foreign Affairs*, which promoted the notion of containment as the best way to deal with Soviet Communism. Truman relied heavily on Kennan's arguments in designing his Cold War policies. In 1952, Kennan served briefly as ambassador to the Soviet Union. Later in his career, he urged for a more diplomatic approach to U.S.-Soviet relations.

Khrushchev, Nikita As Soviet leader from 1953 until 1964, Nikita Khrushchev represented a somewhat more moderate leader than Stalin had been. In 1956, Khrushchev denounced Stalin and his brutal rule in the so-called secret speech. In 1959, he became the first Soviet leader to visit the United States. But he was determined to protect Soviet power and did not hesitate to provoke standoffs with the United States, including over Cuba and Berlin.

Korean War The Korean War began in June 1950, when Communist North Korea invaded pro-Western South Korea. The United States asked the U.N. Security Council to authorize a "police action" in order to push North Korea back over the 38th parallel, which divided the country upon the conclusion of World War II. After intense fighting, including the mobilization of large numbers of U.S. and Chinese forces, the war ended in 1953. with no clear resolution but merely a restoration of the prewar status quo.

Kuomintang This was the party of Chiang Kai-Shek and the Chinese Nationalists, who fought against Communist forces led by Mao Zedong. The Party had its origins in the early 20th-century political realignment created by the collapse of the Chinese empire. The Kuomintang was an important U.S. ally and was avowedly anti-Communist, but also frequently charged with corruption.

Lavender Scare This phrase refers to Cold War repression against gays and lesbians in U.S. society. In particular, gays and lesbians working in the federal government were targeted by defenders of McCarthyism, who argued that the sexual preference of these employees made them a security risk because they would be more susceptible to blackmail.

Lenin, Vladimir Lenin was founder and chief ideologue of the Russian Communist party, better known as the Bolshevik Party. He was exiled for many years from Czarist Russia, during which time he revised Marxism into a form that, he argued, was more appropriate for Russian conditions. In particular, he introduced the argument that socialist governments required the leadership of a small, tightly organized ruling party.

MacCarran, Pat MacCarran was a Democratic senator from Nevada and a major architect of U.S. domestic security programs from the 1930s to the 1950s. He was one of the most outspoken Democratic Cold Warriors and pushed for legislation requiring loyalty oaths and other screening mechanisms.

Manhattan Project The Manhattan Project was the World War II-era secret program that eventually succeeded in developing a nuclear weapon. Under the leadership of J. Robert Oppenheimer, the scientists worked at a secret location in New Mexico developing the bomb. In the postwar period, this group of scientists came under scrutiny after classified information was leaked.

Mao Zedong Mao was leader of the Chinese Communist Party. For many years, he fought against the corrupt rule of various postimperial political leaders in China, and then, during World War II, Mao and the Communists fought against Japan's encroachment into China. After the war, civil war in China lasted from 1945 until 1949, when the Nationalist Chinese were defeated and the Communists came to power.

Marshall, George Marshall was a World War II hero, who after the war served as secretary of state during the Truman administration. Despite his military background, Marshall sought to use diplomacy as a way to reduce rising tensions between the United States and the Soviets. He is best known as a supporter of the financial assistance package offered to European nations after World War II that became known as the Marshall Plan.

Marshall Plan The Marshall Plan, introduced by secretary of state George Marshall in 1947 in a speech at Harvard, offered U.S. financial support for postwar reconstruction in Europe; funds were available to any country that had fought against the Axis powers. However, requirements that countries accepting aid provide documentation about national finances deterred the Soviets and their satellite nations from participating.

Mattachine Society This organization, founded in 1951 by Harry Hay and other gay men, sought to challenge 1950s prejudices against homosexuality as a "perversion." The organization had chapters across the nation and published a magazine called *The Mattachine Review*. A sister organization of lesbians was established in 1955 called the Daughters of Bilitis.

McCarthy, Joseph McCarthy was a Republican senator from Wisconsin who was elected in 1946. He had served in the military during World War II, later styling himself "Tail Gunner Joe," although the details of his alleged wartime heroism and subsequent injury could never be documented. McCarthy was at the center of domestic investigations of Communist influence in the United States; his vigorous, even abusive, method of investigation while chairing a Senate subcommittee became a hallmark of the era. McCarthyism refers to the witch hunt that he and his allies launched against alleged subversives.

National Security Act of 1947 The National Security Act of 1947 was passed by Congress in order to create a more efficient and centrally organized military. The Act created the Department of Defense, placing all branches of the military under the supervision of the secretary of defense (eventually housed in the Pentagon). In addition, the Act created the National Security Council and the Central Intelligence Agency, in order to strengthen U.S. intelligence gathering abilities.

National Security Agency The NSA was created in 1952 in order to collect and analyze intelligence information using increasingly sophisticated technologies. These methods relied primarily on remote communications monitoring.

National Security Council The NSC was created as an advisory group to the president. Its director, the National Security Advisor, is based in the White House and is positioned to offer the president the most current intelligence findings. This position was created and quickly assumed increasing prominence and significance during the Cold War period.

Nixon, Richard Nixon was elected to the U.S. House in 1946 and the U.S. Senate in 1950. He then served as vice president during the Eisenhower administration, ran unsuccessfully for president in 1960, and eventually was elected president in 1968 and 1972. In 1974, he became the first president to resign from office, in the wake of the Watergate scandal. Nixon first made his name as a Cold War Warrior while serving on HUAC; he played an important role in the Hollywood Ten hearings.

North Atlantic Treaty Organization NATO was formed in 1949, in the wake of the Berlin Blockade crisis. The members of NATO promise to treat an attack on any member as though it were an attack on all. Membership in NATO originally included most of Western Europe; several years later, the Soviet Union formed an analogue to NATO with the Warsaw Pact. NATO now has a membership extending into the former Soviet satellite nations.

NSC-68 NSC-68 was a policy paper authored by the National Security Council in 1949. It argued that the Soviet Union was determined to seek world domination, that it could not be trusted as a negotiating partner, and that, given these realities, the United States ought to escalate its defense spending massively. Only the threat of overwhelming force could deter the Soviets from military action.

Nuclear Weapons The first nuclear weapon was detonated in a test held at Alamogordo, New Mexico, in July 1945. The successful detonation of the bomb gave President Harry Truman a new weapon to use in the war against the Japanese. The subsequent use of the bomb in an attack on Hiroshima, Japan, on August 6, 1945, and on Nagasaki, Japan, on August 9, 1945, led to the end of World War II. In 1949, the Soviet Union tested its own bomb, launching an arms race between the two nations and the intensification of the Cold War.

Oppenheimer, J. Robert Oppenheimer was the nuclear physicist placed in charge of the development and testing of a nuclear bomb by the United States. He joined the Manhattan Project in 1942 and set up the research facility at Los Alamos, New Mexico, that successfully developed a bomb. After the end of World War II, Oppenheimer and other scientists opposed the development of a "super" or hydrogen bomb as militarily unnecessary. Based on these views, Oppenheimer fell under suspicion and had his security clearance revoked in 1953.

Reagan, Ronald Reagan served as governor of California from 1967 to 1975 and as president of the United States from 1981 to 1989. His early career was as an actor in Hollywood, and, in 1947, he testified before HUAC in qualified support of the Hollywood Ten. However, he later said that he was "naïve" about the presence of Communism in Hollywood, and, by the end of the 1950s, he was an outspoken critic of leftist politics in his former profession. As a political leader, Reagan strongly identified with anti-Communist programs and political initiatives.

Robeson, Paul Robeson was one of the best-known African American entertainers in mid-century America, renowned as an actor and singer. He also became well-known as a target of Red-baiting after he expressed support for the Soviet Union in the late 1940s. Robeson's career was effectively ended by the controversy following these remarks.

Rosenberg, Julius and Ethel Julius Rosenberg was a longtime Communist, who was accused in 1950 of being involved in a spy ring seeking to sell nuclear secrets to the Soviet Union. Evidence suggests that Julius was almost certainly involved in illegal activities, but no such evidence was ever produced in reference to his wife, Ethel. She was arrested in an attempt to put pressure on Julius to confess and provide information. The two were both convicted of espionage and were executed in June 1953.

Service, John Stewart Service was a leading China expert in the State Department, who was born and lived much of his early life in China. As a member of the U.S. Foreign Service, he was assigned to China in 1944. Service became convinced that the Chinese Communists would eventually prevail over the Nationalists. After being charged with Communist sympathies by Joseph McCarthy, Service was fired by the State Department in 1951. In

1957, after the United States Supreme Court upheld his challenge to his firing, Service was reinstated.

Spillane, Mickey Spillane was a very popular mystery writer and novelist who published during the McCarthy era. Spillane's best-known fictional character is Detective Mike Hammer, who engaged in a variety of crime-fighting activities, including tracking down Communist spies.

Stalin, Josef Stalin was one of the most important figures in the Russian Revolution. After the death of Lenin in 1924, Stalin ruthlessly sought to suppress any challengers to his power. By 1929, Stalin had secured power as the dominant figure in the Soviet Communist Party. Stalin was a brutal tyrant, who authorized the execution of thousands of his opponents. He led the Soviet Union during World War II and through the early years of the Cold War, until his death in 1953.

Stevenson, Adlai Stevenson was governor of Illinois in 1952 when he became the Democratic nominee for the presidency. He lost that race to Eisenhower and lost again in 1956 when he was again the Democratic nominee. Stevenson was best known for his wit and effectiveness as a speaker. However, his inability to articulate a strong Cold War policy proved a weak link in his candidacy. His defeat was seen by many as a defeat of liberalism in U.S. society.

Symington, William Stuart (Stu) Symington was a Democratic senator from Missouri who served on the Senate subcommittee that Joseph McCarthy chaired. Symington expressed opposition to McCarthy's tactics and claims but was unable to seriously challenge his use of the subcommittee to threaten and harass people. Nevertheless, his was one of the few voices raised to challenge McCarthy during the hearings.

Truman, Harry Truman was serving as U.S. senator from Missouri when he was tapped by Franklin Roosevelt to become his running mate in 1944. Only a few months after becoming vice president, Truman became president when Roosevelt died in April 1945. Truman served as president during the crucial early years of the Cold War, from 1945 to 1951, and the hard-line approach that he developed remained a key aspect of the Cold War for the next 40 years.

Truman Doctrine In 1947, the political situation in Greece and Turkey was very unstable, and the United States feared that pro-Communist forces might gain control of the governments in those nations. In response to this situation, but also intended as a broader statement of U.S. policy, Truman announced what became known as the "Truman Doctrine" in a speech to Congress. This doctrine said that the United States would "support free peoples who are resisting subjugation by armed minorities or outside pressures."

Union of Soviet Socialist Republics (USSR) The USSR was the formal name for the federation of states led by Russia but including 14 other republics established in 1922. The USSR was primarily made up of the lands that had previously comprised Czarist Russia.

United Nations The United Nations was created in 1945, in the wake of World War II. The purpose of the organization was to create an international organization in which conflicts and other international problems could be resolved through diplomacy and cooperation. The United Nations also encompassed the U.N. Security Council, with a permanent membership that included the "Big Five" (the United States, the Soviet Union, China, Britain, and France), the countries that could veto any Council decision. The Security Council controlled the U.N. military forces and was a stage for many Cold War debates.

Venona Venona was a code word for an operation conducted by the United States and Great Britain to decode Soviet intelligence transmissions; it now refers to a collection of decrypted Cold War-era files that document the extent of a Soviet spy network within the United States and Western nations. These documents confirm the accuracy of charges made against some high-profile targets of McCarthyism but cast doubt on the accusations made against others.

Wallace, Henry Wallace was a leading proponent of liberalism in the postwar period. He was an Iowan who served as vice president during Roosevelt's third term, from 1941 to 1945. In the election of 1944, Roosevelt replaced him with Harry Truman because of Wallace's outspoken support for civil rights. After the war, Wallace served as Truman's secretary of commerce, until he was asked to resign after making public statements in which he criticized Truman's hard-line policies toward the Soviet Union. In 1948, Wallace ran as a third-party candidate for the Progressive Citizens of America Party.

Warsaw Pact The Warsaw Pact was a mutual security treaty, signed in 1955 by the Soviets and its satellite countries. It was intended as an analogue to NATO and, in particular, was a response to the rearmament of West Germany. The only military action that the Warsaw Pact engaged in was the Soviet suppression of dissent activities in Czechoslovakia in 1968.

White, Harry Dexter White was a treasury department official in the 1940s who played an important role in creating the International Monetary Fund and World Bank. He was also accused in the late 1940s of being a Soviet spy. The Venona documents appear to confirm that White may indeed have been working for Soviet intelligence. White testified in front of HUAC in 1948 and died of a heart attack days later.

Yalta Conference The Yalta Conference was held beginning in February 1945 between the "Big Three" Allied leaders: Churchill, Stalin, and Roosevelt. At the Yalta meeting, discussions about the postwar organization of a demilitarized and denazified Germany were held. Critics of Roosevelt later charged that he had given Stalin too many concessions in allowing Soviet influence to spread into Eastern and Central Europe.

Zwicker, Ralph Zwicker was a World War II veteran and U.S. Army General, who commanded Fort Kilmer in 1953, when one of the soldiers stationed there, Major Irving Peress, was accused by Joseph McCarthy of being disloyal. Although Peress was honorably discharged, McCarthy wanted him court-martialed and, in the course of questioning Zwicker, became outraged over the fact that Zwicker refused to provide details about the case. McCarthy's attacks on Zwicker angered Army leadership and ultimately led to the Army-McCarthy hearings, which ended in the collapse of McCarthy's popular support and credibility.

Bibliography

Aaron, Daniel. (1961) *Writers on the Left: Episodes in American Literary Communism*. New York: Harcourt, Brace and World.

Abt, John, with Michael Myerson. (1993) *Advocate and Activist: Memoirs of an American Communist Lawyer*. Urbana: University of Illinois Press.

Acheson, Dean. *Present at the Creation*. (1974) New York: Holt, Rinehart and Winston.

Ainsfield, Nancy, ed. (1991) *The Nightmare Considered: Critical Essays on Nuclear War Literature*. Bowling Green, OH: The Popular Press.

Altschuler, Glenn C. (2003) *All Shook Up: How Rock 'n' Roll Changed America*. New York: Oxford University Press.

Alves, Teresa. (2001) "'Some Enchanted Evening': Tuning in the Amazing Fifties, Switching off the Elusive Decade." *American Studies International*, 39:25–40.

Ambrose, Stephen, and Douglas Brinkley. (1981) *Ike's Spies: Eisenhower and the Espionage Establishment*. Garden City, NY: Doubleday and Co.

Ambrose, Stephen, and Douglas Brinkley. (1997) *Rise to Globalism: American Foreign Policy Since 1938*. New York: Penguin.

The American Dream: The 50s. (1998) By Editors of Time Life Books. Alexandria, VA: TimeLife, Inc.

Anderson, Jack, and Ronald May. (1952) *McCarthy*. Boston, MA: Beacon Press.

Andrews, Bart. (1976) *Lucy & Ricky & Fred & Ethel: The Story of "I Love Lucy."* New York: Dutton.

Aptheker, Herbert, ed. (1990) *A Documentary History of the Negro People in the United States*. Vols. 5 & 6. New York: Carol Publishers.

Applebaum, Irwyn. (1984) *The World According to Beaver*. New York: Bantam.

Appy, Christian, ed. (2000) *Cold War Constructions: The Political Culture of United States Imperialism, 1945–1966*. Amherst: University of Massachusetts Press.

Arms, Thomas S. (1992) *Encyclopedia of the Cold War*. New York: Facts on File.

Aronson, James. (1970) *The Press and the Cold War*. Boston, MA: Beacon Press.

Balio, Tino, ed. (2005) *The American Film Industry*. Madison: University of Wisconsin Press, 1985. August 18, 2005. http://www.thirdworldtraveller.com/McCarthyism/HUAC_Rise_AntiCommun.html.

Barrettt, Edward. (1951) *The Tenney Committee: Legislative Investigation of Subversive Activities in California*. Ithaca, NY: Cornell University Press.

Barrett, James R. (1999) *William Z. Foster and the Tragedy of American Radicalism*. Urbana: University of Illinois Press.

Barth, Alan. (1952) *The Loyalty of Free Men*. New York: Viking.

Bayley, Edwin. (1981) *Joe McCarthy and the Press*. Madison: University of Wisconsin Press.

Belfrage, Cedric. (1989) *The American Inquisition, 1945–1960: A Profile of the "McCarthy Era."* New York: Thunder's Mouth Press.

Belfrage, Sally. (1994) *Un-American Activities: A Memoir of the Fifties*. New York: Harper Collins.

Belknap, Michael. (1977) *Cold War Political Justice: The Smith Act, the Communist Party, and American Civil Liberties*. Westport, CT: Greenwood.

Benson, Robert Louis, and Michael Warner, eds. (1996) *VENONA: Soviet Espionage and the American Response*. Washington, DC: National Security Agency, Central Intelligence Agency.

Bentley, Elizabeth. (1951) *Out of Bondage: The Story of Elizabeth Bentley*. New York: Devin-Adair.

Bentley, Eric. (1971) *Thirty Years of Treason: Excerpts from Hearings before the House Committee on Un-American Activities, 1938–1968*. New York: Viking.

Berger, Roger A. (1989) "'Ask What You Can Do for Your Country': The Film Version of H. G. Wells's The Time Machine and the Cold War." *Literature/Film Quarterly*, 17 (3):177–187.

Bernstein, Carl. (1989) *Loyalties: A Son's Memoir*. New York: Simon and Schuster.

Bird, Kai. (2006) *American Prometheus: The Triumph and Tragedy of J. Robert Oppenheimer*. New York: Knopf.

Biskind, Peter. (1983) *Seeing Is Believing: How Hollywood Taught Us to Stop Worrying and Love the Fifties*. New York: Pantheon Books.

Biskind, Peter. (1985) "Pods, Blobs, and Ideology in American Films of the Fifties." In Georg Slusser and Eric S. Rabkin, eds. *Shadows of the Magic Lamp: Fantasy and Science Fiction in Film*. Carbondale: Southern Illinois University Press, 58–72.

Bondi, Victor. (1995) *American Decades, 1940–1949*. Detroit, MI: Gale Research, Inc.

Bontecou, Eleanor. (1953) *The Federal-Loyalty Security Program*. Ithaca, NY: Cornell University.

Boyer, Paul. (1985) *By the Bomb's Early Light: American Thought and Culture at the Dawn of the Atomic Age*. New York: Pantheon Books.

Brands, H. W. (1993) *The Devil We Knew: Americans and the Cold War*. New York: Oxford University Press.

Brians, Paul. (1987) *Nuclear Holocausts: Atomic War in Fiction, 1895–1984*. Kent, OH: Kent State University Press.

Briley, Ron. (1990) "Reel History: U.S. History, 1932–1972, as Viewed through the Lens of Hollywood." *The History Teacher*, 23 (May 1990): 228–229.

Breines, Winni. (1992) *Young, White, and Miserable: Growing Up Female in the Fifties*. Boston, MA: Beacon.

Broadwater, Jeff. (1992) *Eisenhower and the Anti-Communist Crusade*. Chapel Hill: University of North Carolina.

Broderick, Mick. (1991) *Nuclear Movies: A Critical Analysis and Filmography of International Feature Length Films Dealing with Experimentation, Aliens, Terrorism, Holocaust and Other Disaster Scenarios, 1914–1990*. Jefferson, NC: McFarland & Co.

Brown, Ralph. (1958) *Loyalty and Security: Employment Tests in the United States*. New Haven, CT: Yale University Press.

Brune, Lester, and Richard Dean Burns. (2006) *Chronology of the Cold War*. New York: Routledge.

Bryson, Bill. (2006) *The Life and Times of the Thunderbolt Kid: A Memoir*. New York: Broadway Books.

Buckley, William F., and L. Brent Bozell. (1954) *McCarthy and His Enemies: The Record and its Meaning*. Chicago: Henry Regnery.

Buckley, William F., Jr. (1962) *The Committee and Its Critics*. New York: Putnam.

Budd, John W. (2005) *Labor Relations: Striking a Balance*. New York: McGraw-Hill/Irwin.

Budenz, Louis. (1947) *This Is My Story*. New York: McGraw-Hill.

Burnham, James. (1954) *The Web of Subversion*. New York: John Day and Co.

Calder, Nigel. (1980) *Nuclear Nightmares*. New York: Viking Press.

Carini, Susan M. (2003) "Love's Labors Almost Lost: Managing Crisis during the Reign of 'I Love Lucy'" *Cinema Journal*, 43:1, 44–62.

Carleton, Don E. (1985) *Red Scare! Right Wing Hysteria, Fifties Fanaticism, and Their Legacy in Texas*. Austin: Texas Monthly Press.

Carr, Robert K. (1952) *The House Committee on Un-American Activities*. Ithaca, NY: Cornell University Press.

Caute, David. (1978) *The Great Fear: The Anti-Communist Purge under Truman and Eisenhower*. New York: Simon and Schuster.

Ceplair, Larry, and Steven Englund. (1980) *The Inquisition in Hollywood: Politics in the Film Community, 1930–1960*. Garden City, NY: Anchor Books.

Chambers, Whittaker. (1952) *Witness*. New York: Random House.

Chase, Harold W. (1955) *Security and Liberty: The Problem of Native Communists, 1947–1955*. Garden City, NY: Doubleday.

Cherny, Robert, William Issel, and Kieran Walsh Taylor, eds. (2004) *American Labor and the Cold War*. New Brunswick, NJ: Rutgers University Press.

Clifford, Clark. (1991) *Counsel to the President: A Memoir*. New York: Random House.

Clute, John, and Peter Nicholls, eds. (1992) *The Encyclopedia of Science Fiction*. New York: St. Martin's Press.

Cochran, Bert. (1977) *Labor and Communism: The Conflict That Shaped American Unions*. Princeton, NJ: Princeton University Press.

Cogley, John. (1954) *Report on Blacklisting*. New York: Fund for the Republic.

Cohn, Carol. (1987) "Slick 'Ems, Glick 'Ems, Christmas Trees and Cookie Cutters: Nuclear Language and How We Learned to Pat the Bomb." *Bulletin of the Atomic Scientists* 43:5 (June 1987), 17–24.

Coontz, Stephanie. (1992) *The Way We Never Were: Families and the Nostalgia Trap*. New York: Basic Books.

Corber, Robert J. (1997) *Homosexuality in Cold War America: Resistance and the Crisis of Masculinity*. Durham, NC: Duke University Press.

Corker, Charles, ed. (1955) *Digest of the Public Record of Communism in the United States*. New York: Fund for the Republic.

Crosby, Donald F. (1978) *God, Church, and Flag: Senator Joseph R. McCarthy and the Catholic Church, 1950–1957*. Chapel Hill: University of North Carolina Press.

Cunningham, Jesse G., and Laura K. Egendorf. (2003) *The McCarthy Hearings*. San Diego, CA: Greenhaven.

Darby, William. (1987) *Necessary American Fictions: Popular Literature of the 1950s*. Bowling Green, OH: Bowling Green University Popular Press.

Davies, Carol Boyce. (2001) "Deportable Subjects: US Immigration Laws and Criminalizing of Communism," *South Atlantic Quarterly* (Fall 2001) 100:4, 949–966.

Davis, Benjamin. (1969) *Communist Councilman from Harlem.* New York: International Publishers.

Davis, Kenneth C. (1984) *Two-Bit Culture: The Paperbacking of America.* Boston, MA: Houghton Mifflin.

Davis, Ronald L. (1997) *Celluloid Mirrors: Hollywood and American Society since 1945.* Fort Worth, TX: Harcourt Brace College Publishers.

Daynes, John Gary. (1996) "Making History: Joseph R. McCarthy, Martin Luther King, Jr. and the Place of the Past in American Public Life." PhD Dissertation: University of Delaware.

D'Emilio, John. (1993) *Sexual Politics, Sexual Communities: The Making of a Homosexual Minority in the United States, 1940–1970.* Chicago: University of Chicago Press.

Dennis, Peggy. (1977) *The Autobiography of an American Communist.* Westport, CT, and Berkley, CA: Lawrence Hill and Co., Creative Arts Books Co.

Diamond, Sigmund. (1992) *Compromised Campus: The Collaboration of Universities with the Intelligence Community, 1945–1955.* New York: Oxford University Press.

Diggins, John P. (1975) *Up from Communism: Conservative Odysseys in American Intellectual History.* New York: Harper and Row.

Diggins, John P. (1988) *The Proud Decades: America in War and in Peace, 1941–1960.* New York: Norton.

Dillard, Annie. (1987) *An American Childhood.* New York: Harper and Row.

Dodds, John W. (1965) *Everyday Life in Twentieth Century America.* New York: Putnam.

Doherty, Thomas. (1993) *Cold War, Cool Medium: Television, McCarthyism and American Culture.* New York: Columbia University Press.

Donovan, Robert J. (1977) *Conflict and Crisis: The Presidency of Harry S Truman, 1945–1948.* New York: Norton.

Douglas, William O. (1980) *The Court Years, 1939–1975.* New York: Random House.

Draper, Theodore. (1957) *The Roots of American Communism.* New York: Viking.

Duberman, Martin Bauml. (1988) *Paul Robeson.* New York: Knopf.

Duden, Jane. (1989) *1950s.* New York: Crestwood House.

Dudziak, Mary. (2000) *Cold War Civil Rights: Race and the Image of American Democracy*. Princeton, NJ: Princeton University Press.

Dyson, Lowell K. (1982) *Red Harvest: The Communist Party and the American Farmer*. Lincoln: University of Nebraska Press.

Einstein, Daniel. (1987) *Special Edition: A Guide to Network Television Documentary Series and Special News Reports, 1955–1979*. Metuchen, NJ: Scarecrow Press.

Eisler, Benita. (1986) *Private Lives: Men and Women of the Fifties*. New York: Franklin Watts.

Engelhardt, Tom. (1995) *The End of Victory Culture: Cold War America and the Disillusioning of a Generation*. New York: Basic Books.

Fariello, Griffin. (1995) *Red Scare: Memories of the American Inquisition, An Oral History*. New York: Norton.

Faulk, John Henry. (1983) *Fear on Trial*. Austin: University of Texas Press.

Field, Bruce E. (1998) *Harvest of Dissent: The National Farmers Union and the Early Cold War*. Lawrence: University Press of Kansas.

Field, Hermann, and Kate Field. (1999) *Trapped in the Cold War: The Ordeal of an American Family*. Stanford, CA: Stanford University Press.

Filene, Peter. (1974) *Him/Her/Self: Sex Roles in Modern America*. New York: Harcourt Brace Jovanovich.

Filippelli, Ronald L., and Mark McColloch. (1995) *Cold War in the Working Class: The Rise and Decline of the United Electrical Workers*. Albany: State University of New York Press.

Fitzgerald, Brian. (2007) *McCarthyism: The Red Scare*. Minneapolis, MN: Compass Point Books.

Fleming, Ian. (1953; 1964) *Casino Royale*. New York: Signet.

Flournoy, Bob. (2005) *Just a Little Rain . . . Baby Boomers and Military Brats Reflect on Childhood, Baseball, and War*. Baltimore, MD: PublishAmerica.

Fones-Wolf, Elizabeth A. (1994) *Selling Free Enterprise: The Business Assault on Labor and Liberalism, 1945–1960*. Urbana: University of Illinois Press.

Foreman, Joel, ed. (1997) *The Other Fifties: Interrogating Midcentury American Icons*. Urbana: University of Illinois Press.

Foster, Edward H. (1992) *Understanding the Beats*. Columbia: University of South Carolina Press.

Fox, Richard Wightman, and T. J. Jackson Lears. (1983) *The Culture of Consumption: Critical Essays in American History, 1880–1980*. 1st ed. New York: Pantheon Books.

Frankel, Benjamin. (1992) *The Cold War, 1945–1991*. Vols. 1–3. Detroit, MI: Gale Research, Inc.

Freedman, Estelle B., and John D'Emilio. (1988) *Intimate Matters: A History of Sexuality in America*. New York: Harper and Row.

Freeland, Richard. (1974) *The Truman Doctrine and the Origins of McCarthyism: Foreign Policy, Domestic Politics, and Internal Security, 1946–1948*. New York: Schocken.

Freeman, Joshua B., and Steve Russwurm. (1992) "The Education of an Anti-Communist: Father John Cronin and the Baltimore Labor Movement" *Labor History* 33:2 (Spring 1992), 217–247.

Fried, Richard. (1976). *Men against McCarthy*. New York: Columbia University Press.

Fried, Albert, ed. (1990) *Nightmare in Red: The McCarthy Era in Perspective*. New York: Oxford University Press.

Fried, Albert, ed. (1997) *McCarthyism: the Great American Red Scare: A Documentary History*. New York: Oxford University.

Friedman, Andrea. (2005) "The Smearing of Joe McCarthy: The Lavender Scare, Gossip, and Cold War Politics," *American Quarterly* 57:4 (December 2005), 1105–1129.

Friedman, Andrea. (2007) "The Strange Career of Annie Lee Moss: Rethinking Race, Gender, and McCarthyism" *Journal of American History* 94:2 (September 2007), 445–468.

Fuller, Linda K. (1990) "The Ideology of the 'Red Scare' Movement: McCarthyism in the Movies." In Paul Loukides and Linda K. Fuller, eds. *Beyond the Stars*. Bowling Green, OH: Bowling Green University Popular Press, 229–248.

Gaddis, John. (1972) *The United States and the Origins of the Cold War, 1941–1947*. New York: Columbia University Press.

Gaddis, John. (1987) *The Long Peace: Inquiries into the History of the Cold War*. New York: Oxford University Press.

Gaddis, John. (2006) *The Cold War: A New History*. New York: Penguin.

Gardner, David P. (1967) *The California Oath Controversy*. Berkeley: University of California Press.

Gates, John. (1958) *The Story of an American Communist*. New York: Nelson.

Gilbert, James B. (1976) "Wars of the Worlds." *Journal of Popular Culture*, X(2), 326–336.

Gillon, Steven M. (1992) *Politics and Vision: The ADA and American Liberalism*. New York: Oxford University Press.

Goldman, Eric. (1960) *The Crucial Decade and After: America, 1945–60*. New York: Vintage Books.

Goldstein, Alvin H. (1975) *The Unquiet Death of Julius and Ethel Rosenberg*. New York: Hill.

Goldstein, Robert J. (2006) "Prelude to McCarthyism: The Making of a Blacklist," *Prologue* 38:3 (Fall 2006), 22–33.

Goldston, Robert C. (1973) *The American Nightmare: Senator Joseph R. McCarthy and the Politics of Hate*. Indianapolis, IN: Bobbs-Merrill.

Goodman, Walter. (1968) *The Committee: The Extraordinary Career of the House Committee on Un-American Activities*. New York: Farrar, Straus and Giroux.

Goodwin, Doris Kearns. (1997) *Wait till Next Year: A Memoir*. New York: Simon & Schuster.

Griffith, Robert. (1987) *The Politics of Fear: Joseph R. McCarthy and the Senate*. 2nd ed. Amherst: University of Massachusetts.

Griffith, Robert, and Athan Theoharis, eds. (1974) *The Specter: Original Essays on the Cold War and the Origins of McCarthyism*. New York: New Viewpoints.

Halberstam, David. (1993) *The Fifties*. New York: Random House.

Hamby, Alonzo. (1973) *Beyond the New Deal: Harry S Truman and American Liberalism*. New York: Columbia University Press.

Hardin, Michael. (1997) "Mapping Post-War Anxieties onto Space: Invasion of the Body Snatchers and Invaders from Mars." *Enculturation: A Journal for Rhetoric, Writing, and Culture* 1(1) (Spring 1997).

Harper, Alan. (1969) *The Politics of Loyalty: The White House and the Communist Issue, 1946–1952*. Westport, CT: Greenwood.

Harrison, Gordon A. (1954) *The Road to the Right: The Tradition and Hope of American Conservatism*. New York: Morrow.

Hart, Hornell. (1952) *McCarthy versus the State Department; Toward Consensus on Certain Charges against the State Department by Senator Joseph McCarthy and Others*. Rev. ed. Durham, NC.

Hart, Jeffrey Peter. (1982) *When the Going Was Good: American Life in the Fifties*. New York: Crown.

Harvey, Brett. (1993) *The Fifties: A Women's Oral History*. New York: Harper Collins.

Haynes, John Earl. (1996) *Red Scare or Red Menace? American Communism and Anticommunism in the Cold War*. Chicago: Ivan R. Dee.

Heale, Michael J. (1990) *American Anticommunism: Controlling the Enemy Within, 1830–1970*. Baltimore, MD: Johns Hopkins University Press.

Heale, Michael J. (1998) *McCarthy's Americans: Red Scare Politics in State and Nation, 1935–1965*. Athens: University of Georgia Press.

Healey, Dorothy, and Maurice Isserman. (1990) *A Life in the American Communist Party*. New York: Oxford University Press.

Heinlein, Robert A. (1951; 1979) *The Puppet Masters*. New York: Signet Books.

Hendershot, Cyndy. (1999) *Paranoia, the Bomb, and 1950s Science Fiction Films.* Bowling Green, OH: Bowling Green State University Popular Press.

Hendershot, Cyndy. (2003) *Anti-Communism and Popular Culture in Mid-Century America.* Jefferson, NC: McFarland.

Henriksen, Margot. (1997) *Dr. Strangelove's America: Society and Culture in the Atomic Age.* Berkeley: University of California Press.

Hiss, Alger. (1957) *In the Court of Public Opinion.* New York: Knopf.

Hiss, Alger. (1988) *Recollections of a Life.* New York: Holt.

Hixson, Walter L. (1998) *Parting the Curtain: Propaganda, Culture and the Cold War, 1945–1961.* New York: St. Martin's Press.

Hofstadter, Richard. (1970) *Anti-Intellectualism in American Life.* New York: Knopf.

Holland, Barbara. (2005) *When All the World Was Young: A Memoir.* New York: Bloomsbury.

Holmes, David. (1989) *Stalking the Academic Communist.* Hanover, NH: University Press of New England.

Horne, Gerald. (1986) *Black and Red: W. E. B. DuBois and the Afro-American Response to the Cold War, 1944–1963.* Albany: State University of New York Press.

Horne, Gerald. (1988) *Communist Front? The Civil Rights Congress, 1946–1956.* Rutherford, NJ: Farleigh Dickinson University Press.

Honey, Michael K. (2004) "Operation Dixie, the Red Scare, and the Defeat of Southern Labor Organizing." In R. Alton Lee, ed. *Truman and Taft-Hartley.* Lexington: University of Kentucky Press.

Horowitz, Daniel. (1998) *Betty Friedan and the Making of The Feminine Mystique: The American Left, the Cold War and Modern Feminism.* Amherst: University of Massachusetts Press.

Invasion of the Body Snatchers. (1956) Dir. Don Siegel. Allied Artists.

Isserman, Maurice. (1982) *Which Side Were You On? The American Communist Party during the Second World War.* Middletown, CT: Wesleyan University Press.

Isserman, Maurice. (1987) *If I Had a Hammer . . . The Death of the Old Left and the Birth of the New Left.* New York: Basic Books.

Jackson, Kenneth. (1985) *Crabgrass Frontier: The Suburbanization of the United States.* New York: Oxford University Press.

Jenkins, Philip. (1999) *The Cold War at Home: The Red Scare in Pennsylvania.* Chapel Hill: University of North Carolina Press.

Johnson, David K. (2004) *The Lavender Scare: The Cold War Persecution of Gays and Lesbians in the Federal Government.* Chicago: University of Chicago.

Johnson, Haynes. (2005) *The Age of Anxiety: McCarthyism to Terrorism.* Orlando, FL: Harcourt.

Kahn, Albert. (1953) *The Game of Death: Effects of the Cold War on Our Children.* New York: Cameron & Kahn.

Keeran, Roger. (1980) *The Communist Party and the Auto Workers Unions.* Bloomington: Indiana University Press.

Keller, William W. (1989) *The Liberals and J. Edgar Hoover: Rise and Fall of a Domestic Intelligence State.* Princeton, NJ: Princeton University Press.

Kimeldorf, Howard. (1988) *Reds or Rackets? The Making of Radical and Conservative Unions on the Waterfront.* Berkeley: University of California Press.

King, David. (1981) *How Can I Keep from Singing? Pete Seeger.* New York: McGraw Hill.

Kirshner, Jonathan. (2001) "Subverting the Cold War in the 1960s: Dr. Strangelove, The Manchurian Candidate, and The Planet of the Apes." *Film & History,* 31(2), 40–44.

Kovel, Joel. (1994) *Red Hunting in the Promised Land: Anticommunism in the Making of America.* New York: Basic Books.

Kretzmann, Edwin M. J. (1967) "McCarthy and the Voice of America," *Foreign Service Journal,* 44 (February 1967), 26–27, 44–45.

Kutler, Stanley I. (1982) *The American Inquisition.* New York: Wang and Hill.

Kuznick, Peter J., and James Gilbert, ed. (2001) *Rethinking Cold War Culture.* Washington, DC: Smithsonian Institution Press.

Latham, Earl. (1966) *The Communist Controversy in Washington from the New Deal to McCarthy.* Cambridge, MA: Harvard University.

Layman, Richard, ed. (1994) *American Decades, 1959–1959.* Detroit, MI: Gale Research Group.

Leab, Daniel J. (1984) "How Red Was My Valley: Hollywood, the Cold War Film, and I Married a Communist." *Journal of Contemporary History,* 19:1 (January 1984), 59–88.

Leab, Daniel J. (1993) "Hollywood and the Cold War, 1945–1961." In Robert Brent Toplin, ed. *Hollywood as Mirror: Changing Views of "Outsiders" and "Enemies" in American Movies.* Westport, CT: Greenwood Press.

Lebow, Richard Ned. (1993) *We All Lost the Cold War.* Princeton, NJ: Princeton University Press.

Leffler, Melvyn. (1992) *A Preponderance of Power: National Security, the Truman Administration, and the Cold War.* Stanford, CA: Stanford University Press.

Leffler, Melvyn. (1994) *The Specter of Communism: The United States and the Origins of the Cold War, 1917–1953.* New York: Hill and Wang.

Leuchtenberg, William F. (1973) *A Troubled Feast: American Society since 1945.* Boston, MA: Little, Brown.

Levenstein, Harvey A. (1981) *Communism. Anticommunism, and the CIO.* Westport, CT: Greenwood.

Lewis, Jon (2000). "'We Do Not Ask You to Condone This.' How the Blacklist Saved Hollywood." *Cinema Journal*, 39:2, 3–30.

Lewis, Peter. (1978) *The Fifties.* New York: Lippincott.

Lichtenstein, Nelson, Susan Strasser, and Roy Rosenzweig. (2000) *Who Built America? Working People and the Nation's Economy, Politics, Culture, and Society.* Vol. 2. New York: Worth Publishers.

Lieberman, Robbie. (1989) *"My Song Is My Weapon": People's Songs, American Communism and the Politics of Culture, 1930–1950.* Urbana: University of Illinois Press.

Lieberman, Robbie. (2000) *The Strangest Dream: Communism, Anticommunism, and the U.S. Peace Movement, 1945–1963.* Syracuse, NY: Syracuse University Press.

Lindey, Christine. (1990) *Art in the Cold War: From Vladivostok to Kalamazoo, 1945–1962.* London: The Herbert Press.

Lipschutz, Ronnie D. (2001) *Cold War Fantasies: Film, Fiction and Foreign Policy.* Lanham, MD: Rowman and Littlefield.

Lipsitz, George. (1994) *Rainbow at Midnight: Labor and Culture in the 1940s.* Urbana: University of Illinois Press.

Loeb, P. (1986) *Nuclear Culture: Living and Working in the World's Largest Atomic Complex.* Philadelphia, PA: New Society Publishers.

Long, Edward L. (1950) *The Christian Response to the Atomic Crisis.* Philadelphia, PA: Westminster.

Low, David. (1960) *The Fearful Fifties: A History of a Decade.* New York: Simon & Schuster.

Lucanio, Patrick. (1987) *Them or Us: Archetypal Interpretations of Fifties Alien Invasion Films.* Bloomington: Indiana University Press.

Lyons, Paul. (1982) *Philadelphia Communists, 1936–1956.* Philadelphia, PA: Temple University Press.

MacDonald, J. Fred. (1988) *Television and the Red Menace.* New York: Praeger.

Maistros, Lucille Maurice. (2004) *Growing Up Cold: A Memoir of Growing Up Cold but Longing to Be Cool, in 1950s Vermont.* Baltimore, MD: PublishAmerica.

Marable, Manning. (2007) *Race, Reform and Rebellion: The Second Reconstruction and Beyond in Black America, 1945–2006*. Jackson: University of Mississippi Press.

Marling, Karal Ann. (1994) *As Seen on TV: The Visual Culture of Everyday Life in the 1950s*. Cambridge, MA: Harvard University Press.

Matthews, Christopher. (1996) *Kennedy and Nixon: The Rivalry That Shaped Postwar America*. New York: Simon and Schuster

Matusow, Allen J. (1970) *Joseph R. McCarthy*. Englewood Cliffs, NJ: Prentice-Hall.

Matusow, Harvey. (1955) *False Witness*. New York: Cameron and Kahn.

May, Elaine Tyler. (1999) *Homeward Bound: American Families in the Cold War Era*. New York: Basic Books.

May, Larry. (1989) *Recasting America: Culture and Politics in the Age of the Cold War*. Chicago: University of Chicago Press.

McAuliffe, Mary Sperling. (1978) *Crisis on the Left*. Amherst: University of Massachusetts Press.

McCormick, Charles H. (1989) *This Nest of Vipers*. Urbana: University of Illinois Press.

McEnaney, Laura. (2000) *Civil Defense Begins at Home: Militarization Meets Everyday Life in the Fifties*. Princeton, NJ: Princeton University Press.

McGilligan, Patrick, and Paul Buhle. (1997) *Tender Comrades: A Backstory of the Hollywood Blacklist*. New York: St. Martin's.

Meeropol, Michael, and Robert Meeropol. (1986) *We Are Your Sons*. Chicago: University of Illinois Press.

Merritt, Jeffrey. (1979) *Day by Day: The Fifties*. New York: Facts on File.

Meyerowitz, Joanne, ed. (1994) *Not June Cleaver: Women and Gender in Postwar America, 1945–1960*. Philadelphia, PA: Temple University Press.

Miller, Douglas T., and Marion Nowak. (1977) *The Fifties: The Way We Really Were*. Garden City, NY: Doubleday.

Mintz, Stephen, and Susan Kellogg. (1988) *Domestic Revolutions: A Social History of American Family Life*. New York: Free Press.

Mischler, Paul. (1999) *Raising Reds: The Young Pioneers, Radical Summer Camps, and Communist Political Culture in the United States*. New York: Columbia University Press.

Modell, John. (1989) *Into One's Own: From Youth to Adulthood in the United States, 1920–1975*. Berkeley: University of California Press.

Montgomery, John. (1966) *The Fifties*. London: George Allen & Unwin.

Murphy, Brian. (1982) "Monster Movies: They Came from beneath the Fifties." In Michael T. Marsden, John G. Nachbar, and Sam L. Grogg, Jr., eds. *Movies as Artifacts : Cultural Criticism of Popular Film.* Chicago: Nelson-Hall.

Murray, Robert. (1955) *Red Scare.* Minneapolis: University of Minnesota Press.

Myers, Bob. (2004) *Bobby and the A-Bomb Factory.* New York: iUniverse, Inc.

Nash, George. (1976) *The Conservative Intellectual Movement in America since 1945.* New York: Basic Books.

Navasky, Victor S. (2003) *Naming Names.* 3rd ed. New York: Hill and Wang.

Nelkin, Dorothy. (1972) *The University and Military Research: Moral Politics at M.I.T.* Ithaca, NY: Cornell University Press.

Neve, Brian. (1992) *Film and Politics in America: A Social Tradition.* London and New York: Routledge.

Oakley, J. Ronald. (1986) *God's Country: America in the Fifties.* New York: Dembner Books.

O'Brien, F. S. (1968) "The 'Communist-Dominated' Unions in the United States since 1950," *Labor History,* 9, 184–205.

O'Donnell, Victoria. (2003) "Science Fiction Films and Cold War Anxiety." In Peter Lev, ed. *Transforming the Screen, 1950–1959.* New York: Charles Scribner's Sons.

Okun, Rob A. (1988) *The Rosenbergs: Collected Visions of Artists and Writers.* New York: Universe Press.

Olmstead, Kathryn S. (2002) *Red Spy Queen: A Biography of Elizabeth Bentley.* Chapel Hill: The University of North Carolina Press.

O'Reilly, Kenneth. (1983) *Hoover and the UnAmericans: The FBI, HUAC, and the Red Menace.* Philadelphia, PA: Temple University Press.

O'Reilly, Kenneth. (1994) *Black Americans: The FBI Files.* New York: Carroll and Graf.

Oshinsky, David M. (1976) *Senator Joseph McCarthy and the American Labor Movement.* Columbia: University of Missouri Press.

Oshinsky, David M. (1983) *A Conspiracy So Immense: The World of Joe McCarthy.* New York: Free Press.

Packer, Herbert L. (1962) *Ex-Communist Witnesses.* Palo Alto, CA: Stanford University Press.

Painter, Nell Irvin. (1979) *The Narrative of Hosea Hudson: His Life as a Negro Communist in the South.* Cambridge, MA: Harvard University Press.

Parrett, Geoffrey. (1979) *A Dream of Greatness: The American People, 1945–1963.* New York: Coward, McCann, and Geoghegan.

Parrish, Thomas. (1996) *The Cold War Encyclopedia*. New York: Henry Holt.

Paterson, Thomas. (1992) *On Every Front: The Making and Unmaking of the Cold War*. New York: Norton.

Pells, Richard H. (1985) *The Liberal Mind in a Conservative Age: American Intellectuals in the 1940s and 1950s*. New York: Harper and Row.

Pessen, Edward. (1993) *Losing Our Souls: The American Experiences in the Cold War*. Chicago: I. R. Dee.

Philbrick, Herbert. (1952) *I Led Three Lives: Citizen, "Communist," and Counterspy*. New York: McGraw-Hill.

Powers, Richard Gid. (1983) *G-Men: Hoover's FBI in American Popular Culture*. Carbondale: Southern Illinois University Press.

Powers, Richard Gid. (1995) *Not without Honor: The History of American Anticommunism*. New York: Free Press.

Pritchett, C. Herman. (1954) *Civil Liberties in the Vincent Court*. Chicago: University of Chicago Press.

Quart, Leonard, and Albert Auster. (1984) *American Film and Society since 1945*. London: Macmillan.

Radosh, Ronald, and Joyce Milton. (1983) *The Rosenberg File: A Search for Truth*. New York: Holt, Rinehart & Winston.

Reeves, Thomas. (1982) *The Life and Times of Joe McCarthy*. New York: Stein and Day.

Reeves, Thomas C, ed. (1989) *McCarthyism*. 3rd ed. Malabar, FL: R. E. Krieger.

Rogin, Michael. (1967) *The Intellectuals and McCarthy: The Radical Specter*. Cambridge, MA: M.I.T. Press.

Rogin, Michael. (1984) "Kiss Me Deadly: Communism, Motherhood, and Cold War Movies." *Representations* 6 (Spring 1984), 1–36.

Rogin, Michael. (1987) *Ronald Reagan, the Movie: And Other Episodes in Political Demonology*. Berkeley: University of California Press.

Rose, Lisle. (1999) *The Cold War Comes to MainStreet: America in 1950*. Lawrence: University of Kansas Press.

Rosteck, Thomas. (1994) *See It Now Confronts McCarthyism: Television Documentary and the Politics of Representation*. Tuscaloosa: University of Alabama Press.

Rovere, Richard H. (1995) *Senator Joe McCarthy*. Berkeley: University of California.

Record, Wilson. (1964) *Race and Radicalism: The NAACP and the Communist Party in Conflict*. Ithaca, NY: Cornell University Press.

Reynolds, Lloyd G, Stanley H. Masters, and Colletta H. Moser. (1998) *Labor Economics and Labor Relations*. Upper Saddle River, NJ: Prentice Hall.

Rosenberg, Rosalind. (1992) *Divided Lives: American Women in the Twentieth Century*. New York: Hill and Wang.

Rudolph, John L. (2002) *Scientists in the Classroom: The Cold War Reconstruction of American Science Education*. New York: Palgrave.

Ryan, James G. (1997) *Earl Browder: The Public Life of an American Communist*. Tuscaloosa: University of Alabama Press.

Sanders, Jane. (1979) *Cold War on the Campus: Academic Freedom at the University of Washington*. Seattle: University of Washington Press.

Sayre, Nora. (1982) *Running Time: Films of the Cold War*. New York: Dial Press.

Scales, Junius Irving, and Richard Nickson. (1987) *Cause at Heart: A Former Communist Remembers*. Athens: University of Georgia Press.

Schneir, Walter, and Miriam Schneir. (1965) *Invitation to an Inquest*. New York: Doubleday.

Schrecker, Ellen. (1986) *No Ivory Tower: McCarthyism and Universities*. New York: Oxford University Press.

Schrecker, Ellen. (1994) *The Age of McCarthyism: A Brief History with Documents*. Boston, MA: Bedford Books.

Schrecker, Ellen. (1998) *Many Are the Crimes: McCarthyism in America*. Boston, MA: Little, Brown and Company.

Schwartz, Richard Alan. (1998) *Cold War Culture: Media and the Arts, 1945–1990*. New York: Facts on File.

Schwoch, James. (1993) "Cold War, Hegemony, Postmodernism: American Television and the World System." *Quarterly Review of Film and Video* 14 (1993), 9–24.

Seed, David. (1999) *American Science Fiction and the Cold War: Literature and Film*. Chicago: Fitzroy Dearborn.

Selcraig, James T. (1982) *The Red Scare in the Midwest, 1945–55: A State and Local Study*. Ann Arbor, MI: UMI Research.

Shils, Edward A. (1956) *The Torment of Secrecy: The Background and Consequences of American Security Policies*. New York: Free Press.

Smith, Geoffrey S. (1992) "National Security and Personal Isolation: Sex, Gender, and Disease in Cold War United States." *International History Review* 14 (1992), 307–337.

Smith, M. (1989) "Advertising the Atom." In M. J. Lacey, ed. *Government and Environmental Politics: Essays on Historical Developments since World War Two*. Washington, DC: Woodrow Wilson Center Press.

Solberg, Carl. (1973) *Riding High: America in the Cold War*. New York: Mason and Lipscomb.

Southern, David W. (1987) *Gunnar Myrdal and Black-White Relations: The Use and Abuse of an American Dilemma, 1944–1969*. Baton Rouge: Louisiana State University Press.

Steinberg, Peter. (1984) *The Great "Red Menace": United States Prosecution of American Communists, 1947–1952*. Westport, CT: Greenwood.

Steins, Richard. (1997) *Postwar Years: The Cold War and Atomic Age, 1950–1959*. Brookfield, CT: Millbrook Press.

Storrs, Landon R. (2006) "Left-Feminism, The Consumer Movement, and Red Scare Politics in the United States, 1935–1960." *Journal of Women's History* 18:3, 40–67.

Super, John C. (2005) *The Fifties in America*. Vols. 1–3. Pasadena, CA: Salem Press, Inc.

Swerdlow, Amy. (1990) "Ladies' Day at the Capitol: Women Strike for Peace versus HUAC." In Ellen Carol DuBois and Vicki L. Ruiz, eds. *Unequal Sisters: A Multi-Cultural Reader in U.S. Women's History*. New York: Routledge, 400–417.

Tanenhaus, Sam. (1997) *Whittaker Chambers: A Biography*. New York: Random House.

Theoharis, Athan G. (1971) *Seeds of Repression: Harry S Truman and the Origin of McCarthyism*. Chicago: Quadrangle.

Theoharis, Athan G., and Robert Griffith, eds. (1974) *The Specter*. New York: Franklin Watts.

Theoharis, Athan G, ed. (1982) *Beyond the Hiss Case*. Philadelphia, PA: Temple University Press.

Theoharis, Athan, ed. (1991) *From the Secret Files of J. Edgar Hoover*. Chicago: Ivan Dee.

Thompson, Francis. (1979) *The Frustration of Politics: Truman, Congress, and the Loyalty Issue, 1945–1953*. Rutherford, NJ: Farleigh Dickinson University.

Toropov, Brandon. (2000) *Encyclopedia of Cold War Politics*. New York: Facts on File.

U.S. Department of Labor. (1946) "Work Stoppages Caused by Labor-Management Disputes in 1945," 62, 716–735.

Von Hoffman, Nicholas. (1988) *Citizen Cohn: The Life and Times of Roy Cohn*. New York: Doubleday.

Walton, Richard J. (1974) *Henry Wallace, Harry Truman and the Cold War*. New York: Viking.

Wang, Jessica. (1999) *American Science in the Age of Anxiety: Scientists, Anticommunism, and the Cold War*. Chapel Hill: University of North Carolina Press.

Watson, Steven. (1995) *The Birth of the Beat Generation: Visionaries, Rebels and Hipsters, 1944–1960*. New York: Pantheon Books.

Weart, Spencer R. (1998) *Nuclear Fear: A History of Images*. Cambridge, MA: Harvard University Press.

Weigand, Kate. (2001) *Red Feminism: American Communism and the Making of Women's Liberation*. Baltimore, MD: Johns Hopkins University Press.

Weinstein, Allen. (1978) *Perjury: The Hiss-Chambers Case*. New York: Knopf.

Weinstein, Allen, and Alexander Vassiliev. (1999) *The Haunted Wood: Soviet Espionage—The Stalin Era*. New York: Random House.

Weisberg, Jacob. (1999) "Cold War without End." *New York Times Magazine* (November 28, 1999), 116–123, 155–158.

Whitfield, Stephen. (1991) *The Culture of the Cold War*. Baltimore, MD: Johns Hopkins University Press.

Wicker, Tom. (2006) *Shooting Star: The Brief Arc of Joe McCarthy*. New York: Harcourt.

Williams, Selma. (1993) *Red-Listed: Haunted by the Washington Witch Hunt*. Reading, MA: Addison-Wesley.

Winkler, Allan M. (1993) *Life under a Cloud: American Anxiety about the Atom*. New York: Oxford University Press.

Wyndham, John. (1957; 1976) *The Midwich Cuckoos*. New York: Ballantine Books.

Yarmolinsky, Adam. (1955) *Case Studies in Personnel Security*. Washington, DC: Bureau of National Affairs.

Yergin, Daniel. (1977) *Shattered Peace: The Origins of the Cold War and the National Security State*. Boston, MA: Houghton Mifflin.

Yoder, Edwin M., Jr. (1995) *Joe Alsop's Cold War: A Study of Journalistic Influence and Intrigue*. Chapel Hill: University of North Carolina Press.

Zinn, Howard. (1971) *Postwar America, 1945–1971*. Indianapolis, IN: Bobbs-Merrill.

Zion, Sidney. (1988) *The Autobiography of Roy Cohn*. Secausus, NJ: Lyle Stuart.

Index

1960 Presidential campaign, 10–11

Abortion, 120–121
Acheson, Dean, 34, 181
Adler, Larry, 57
African Americans
  and anti-Communism, 108
  Bailey, Dorothy, 138–139
  Communist Party and, xvii
  deportations of, 105
  entry into World War II and, 97–98
  Lee, Canada, 56–57
  McCarthyism and violence against, 95
  public humiliation of major figures, 101
  Robeson, Paul, blacklisting and, 56
  service during World War II, 97
  transformation of lives (1910–1940), 96–97
  and United Nations, 98
  See also individual African Americans
Air Defense Command, Ground Observer Corps
    and, 64
Air raid drills, 145–146
Alien Registration Act of 1940 (Smith Act),
    100
Alsop, Joseph, 181
Amalgamated Clothing Workers Union, 86
American Civil Liberties Union (ACLU), and
    Dies, Martin, 52
American Communist Party
  history of opposition to racism and support
    for workers, 53–54
  See also Communist Party (CP)
American Federation of Labor (AFL), 181
  versus Committee for Industrial
    Organization (CIO), 87

founding of, 80–81
Taft-Hartley Act and, 87
American Psychiatric Association (APA), 116
Americans for Democratic Action, 181
Anti-Communism
  children became locus of fear for, 148
  and civil rights, 107
  elasticity of, 13–14
  federal government and, 83–84
  groups supporting, 84
  hysteria, 34
  individual behavior and, 119
  investigations of liberals, 100–101
  irrationality of, 13
  and organized labor, 92
  partisan politics and, 84
  political use of, 8
  pressuring Kennedy, John, 11
  roots of U.S., 81
  Senate attitudes toward, 7
  and South Vietnam, 13
  Soviet response to, 11
  stereotypical view of Communist women,
    137–138
  and union membership, 81
  and World War II, 2
Arbenz Guzman, Jacobo, 13, 181
Army, United States. *See* United States Army
Army-McCarthy hearings (1954), 25–26,
    182
Arnaz, Desi, 58. *See also* Ball, Lucille
Atkinson, General Joseph H., on Ground
    Observer Corps, 76
Atlantic Charter, 182
Atomic Energy Commission, 90, 182

Attorney General's List of Totalitarian, Fascist, Communist, Subversive, and Other Organizations (AGLOSO), xix, 16
  adoption of, 17–18
  legal basis for, 15

Baby boom, 146–147
Bailey, Dorothy, 138–139
Ball, Lucille, xxi, 34, 182
  beats the blacklist, 58
Bankhead, Tallulah, 52
Bay of Pigs, 182
Bazer, Julia Older, 54
Beck, Dave, 87
Belfrage, Cedric, 106
Benjamin, Dr. Harry, 117–118
Bentley, Elizabeth, xxiii, 130, 132–135, 182
Bergler, Edmund, 116
Berlin Airlift and blockade, 182–183
Berlin Wall, 183
Bessie, Alvah, 55
Bestor, Arthur, 152
Biddle, Francis, 15
Bieber, Irving, 116
Big Red Schoolhouse, The (Hechinger), 149–150
Bilyeu, Florence (Ground Observer Corps volunteer), 67–68
Bisexuality, varying views on, 118. *See also* Gay movement; Homosexuals and homosexuality; Kameny, Franklin E.; Lesbianism; Transsexuals and transsexuality
Blacklisting, 56–58, 183
  Ball, Lucille, beats, 58
  Hollywood Ten and, 56
  music industry and, 56
Body Snatchers, The (Finney), 36–38
Bolsheviks, 183
Bond, James (fictional character), 42–43
Borden, William, 24
Braude, Beatrice, 28
Braudel, Fernand, xi, xiii
Bridges, Harry, 91
Briggs, Cyril, 107
Brotherhood of Sleeping Car Porters, 97
Brothman, Abe, 134
Browder, Earl, 50, 52, 183
Brown v. Board of Education, xxiv, 98
Brunauer, Esther, 131
Brunauer, Stephen, 131
Bryson, Bill, 147
Buckley, William F., 183

Burr, Pamela (Ground Observer Corps volunteer), 65
Business interests versus worker interests, 81

Caprio, Dr. Frank, 116
Captain Video (TV program), 159
Castro, Fidel, 183
  observations on U.S. (1959), 12–13
Caute, David, on McCarthy, Joseph, 34
Central Intelligence Agency (CIA), 184
Chambers, Whittaker, xix, 4
  as defector, 134
  versus Hiss, Alger, 19
Chaplin, Charlie, 34
Chiang Kai-Shek, 184
Children
  awareness of their country's inability to protect itself, 160
  and changes in science education, 152
  and civil defense, 153
  and Cold War, 145–146, 158
  "duck and cover," 145–146, 153–154, 155
  nuclear weapons and, 147
  received highly censored version of history, 152
  vision of bright future for, 147
  White House Conference on Children and Youth (1950), 157
China, Communists take control of, xix, 34
China Hands, 184
Chinese Civil War, 184
Christoffel, Harold, 90
Churchill, Winston, 184–185
  Iron Curtain speech, 189
CIA. *See* Central Intelligence Agency (CIA)
CIO. *See* Committee for Industrial Organization (CIO)
Civil defense, 153–155
  as "positive mental health program" for youth, 156–157
Civil rights
  anti-Communism and, 108
  national security upheld over, 90
  and violent persecution of perceived racial subversion, 104
Civil Rights Congress (CRC), 95, 105
Civil rights movement
  anti-Communism and, 108
  attacks on, xxiv
  silent on questions of U.S. foreign policy, 108
Civil Service Commission, 17
Clark, Tom, on Communists in federal government, 16

Clubb, O. Edmund, 20

Cogley, John, HUAC testimony, 59

Cohn, Roy, 7, 22, 107, 185

Cold War

 access to economic benefits during, 112

 air raid drills, 145–146

 anxieties among U.S. public (1949), xix–xx

 anxiety about independent women, 135

 atmosphere of fear and distrust, xxi–xxii

 and attitudes toward sexuality and gender roles, xxii–xxiii

 axioms during, 9

 battles against organized labor during, 90–92

 broad coalitions during, 11

 business use of, 88–89, 89–90

 children and, 145–146

 chronology, xxix–xliv

 CIA-sponsored coups in Iran (1953) and Guatemala (1954), 13

 civil defense, 153–155

 dates for, xv

 "duck and cover," 145

 and explosion of social protest (1960s), xxiv–xxv

 fear of Communism and, 111

 fear of Communist subversion, 149

 fear of leftist political radicalism, xxiv

 first varying of levels of aptitude within school grades, 153

 gender and sexuality issues during, 111–112

 gender ideology, 111–112, 118–121

 Ground Observer Corps (GOC) (*see* Ground Observer Corps (GOC))

 homosexual persecutions during, 111

 homosexuals during, xxi, 26–27

 Immigration and Naturalization Service (INS) and, 91

 impact on U.S. life, xvi

 initiatives in education during, 150–151

 "Lavender Scare," 26-27, 124

 left wing during, 4

 media coverage and, xx

 notion of containment, 119

 partisan politics and, 84

 popular culture and (*see* Popular (Pop) Culture (U.S.))

 and postwar prosperity, 146–147

 preparing for attack without trauma, 156–157

 push to shape and monitor public education, 151–152

 satire and, xxv

 stereotypical views of Communist women, 137–138

 targeting members of gender and sexual subcultures, 112

 and television, xx-xxi

 tensions and loyalty oath program, 16

 textbooks and, 151

 threat of Soviet science, 149

 and U.S. education, 149–153

 U.S. family during, 131–132

 views on gender during, 118–119

Cole, Lester, 55

Comics

 scrutiny of, 39

 strips, 39–40

 women in, 39

Cominform, 185

Committee for Industrial Organization (CIO)

 versus American Federation of Labor (AFL), 87

 Communists and, 86–87

 federal impact on, 104

 founding, 82

 Taft-Hartley Act and, 87

 unions expelled from, 89

Committee on Civil Rights, and Truman, Harry S, 98

Committee to Defend Negro Leadership, 105–106

Communism

 and children, 148

 deep uncertainities about winning against, 157–158

 threat of, 148

Communist Control Act (1954), 89

Communist Party

 African Americans and, xvii, 107 (*see also* African Americans)

 and Bentley, Elizabeth, 132–135

 claims about party control of women, 137

 deep uncertainties about winning against, 157–158

 disenfranchised workers and, 86

 equality for women and, 138

 fear of infiltration in the nation's schools and homes, 148

 fomented discord between Mafia and, 10

 foreign-born members, 105

 and Great Depression, 82

 immunity to *lanting*, 105

 Jones, Claudia, and, 106

 and labor union organization, 86

 prosecutions of members, 105

Communist Party *(continued)*
 racial equality and, 86
 reduced role in African American groups by
 mid-1950s, 106–107
 Soviet, and threats to United States, 83
 U.S. membership (1936–1939), xvii
 and women, 130, 132
 women living under, 132
 and women's role in family, 137
 See also American Communist Party;
 Communist Party of America
Communist Party of America, 185
Congress (U.S.), and organized labor, 91–92
Congress of American Women (CAW), and
 McCarthyism, 140
Congress of Industrial Organizations (CIO), 3, 185
 excerpt from memoir of DeCaux, Len,
 177–178
Conservatives (U.S.), and popular culture
 (1950s), 33-34
Containment, 185
Cooper, Gary, xviii
Coughlin, Father Charles, 50–51
Counter-Attack (weekly publication), 55
Crane, Lucille Cardin, 151
Cuban Missile Crisis, 9, 185

Daughters of Bilitis, 123–124
Daughters of the American Revolution, 39
Davies, John Paton, 20
Davis, Ben, 107
Day the Earth Stood Still, The (film), 186
DeCaux, Len, excerpt from memoir, 177–178
Department of Defense (U.S.), 186
Department of State. *See* State Department
 (U.S.)
Deportation, 105
Dickinson, Edwin, 15
Dickinson Committee, 15
Dien Bien Phu, 186
Dies, Martin (Dem., Texas)
 and African Americans, 99–100
 and American Civil Liberties Union
 (ACLU), 52
 claims of lists of Communists, 52
 and HUAC, 51–53, 99–100
Disney, Walt, 186
Documents, primary source
 Association of Motion Picture Producers,
 statement against "Hollywood Ten,"
 169–170
 DeCaux, Len, excerpt from his memoirs,
 177–178

Hoover, J. Edgar, warns of Communist infiltration, HUAC, March 26, 1947,
 163–165
Kinsey, Alfred, excerpt from book on human
 sexuality in American society,
 170–171
National Civil Defense Administration,
 excerpt from speech by Wadsworth,
 James J., 175–176
Posner, Blanche Hofrichter, excerpt from
 HUAC testimony of (December 11,
 1962), 178–180
Reagan, Ronald, on alleged Communism in
 Hollywood, HUAC, October 23, 1947,
 165–169
Red Channels pamphlet, excerpt from,
 174–175
Robeson, Paul, defending his actions and
 philosophies, 176–177
Smith, Margaret Chase, "Declaration of Con-
 science" speech, June 1, 1950,
 171–174
Douglas, Helen Gahagan, 186
 campaign against Nixon, Richard (1950), 5
Dr. No (Fleming), 186
Dubois, W. E. B., xxii, 186
 campaign against, 102–103
 and NAACP, 102
Duck and Cover (educational film, 1951),
 153–154, 155, 186–187
"Duck and cover" education program, 145
"Duck-test," 138
Dulles, Allen, 187
Dulles, John Foster, 187
Dumbarton Oaks, 187

EC Comics, 39
Education, U.S.
 civil defense and, 153–155
 during Cold War, 149–153
 first varying of levels of aptitude within
 grades, 153
Eisenhower, Dwight D., xxiv, 187
 and McCarthy, Joseph, 24–25
 and Nixon, Richard, 5
 plea for Ground Observer Corps
 volunteers, 66
 refusal to grant clemency to Rosenbergs,
 137
 view of McCarthy, Joseph (1954), 8
Ernst, Morris, 137
Espionage
 Bentley, Elizabeth, 132–135

Chambers, Whittaker, 134
Soviet, 134–135
women and, 132
See also individual espionage agents
Executive Orders
8802 (Committee on Fair Employment Practices), 97
9835 (loyalty-security order), xix, 17

Face the Nation (TV program), 187
Family units, idealized image of, 119
Fast, Howard, 22
Faulk, John Henry, 57
FBI. *See* Federal Bureau of Investigation (FBI)
Federal Bureau of Investigation (FBI), 187. *See also* Hoover, J. Edgar
Federal Civil Defense Administration (FCDA), 153–155
"Bert the Turtle," 155
Federal employees, loyalty oath program and, 15–21
Federal Loyalty Oath Program
alleged Communist infiltration of the federal government and, 16
Braude, Beatrice, case of, 28
Cold War tensions and, 16
effects of, 28
federal employees and, 15–21
follow-up investigations by Congress, 19
House Committee on Un-American Activities and, 18
McCarthy's Senate subcommittee and, 18
no federal agency free from, 24
and Oppenheimer, J. Robert, 23–24
ostensible purpose of, 18
Feinberg Law, 151–152
Feminine Mystique, The (Friedan), 140–141
Feminist movement, 140
Film industry
blacklisting in, 56
HUAC investigation of, 54–56
Finney, Jack, 36–38
First Red Scare. *See* Red scare, first (1919–1920)
Flanders, Ralph (Rep., Vermont), 7
Fleming, Ian, 42–43
Flournoy, Bob, 148
Food, Tobacco, Agricultural and Allied Workers (FTA) union, Local 22
activities and membership (1941), 79
and refusals to sign non-Communist affidavits, 88
Fox, Richard Wightman, 147
France, social history in, xi

Freud, Anna, 156
Freud, Sigmund, on male homosexuality, 114–116
Friedan, Betty, 120
Feminine Mystique, The, 140–141
From Russia with Love (Fleming), 187–188
Fuchs, Klaus, xx, 188
Fuller, Harry, 152
Fund for the Republic, 59

Gaines, William, 39
Garner, John Nance, 69
Garvey, Marcus, 97
Gaston, Herbert, 16
Gaston Committee, 16
Gay movement, and Kameny, Franklin E., 27. *See also* Bisexuality, varying views on; Homosexuals and homosexuality; Kameny, Franklin E.; Lesbianism; Transsexuals and transexuality
Gender and sexuality
Cold War views on, 118–119
"gender role" term, 119–120
issues remain unaddressed during McCarthy era, 140
Kinsey's research on, 121–123
"Lavender Scare," 124
nuclear family units, idealized image of, 119
postwar culture and, 111–112
traditional outlooks and foundations for future changes of views, 125
See also Bisexuality varying views on; Gay movement; Homosexuals and homosexuality; Kameny, Franklin E.; Lesbianism; Transsexuals and transsexuality
Geneva Accords, 188
GI Bill (1944)
restricting access to benefits under, 112–113
women's benefits, 113
Godzilla (Japanese film), 188
Gold, Harry, 134
Goldfinger (Fleming), 188
Gompers, Samuel, 81
Government Operations Committee, 6
Great Britain, alliance with U.S.S.R. during World War II, xvii
Great Depression (1929–1939), xvi–xvii
Americans during, xviii–xix
and questioning of capitalism, 82
unemployment during,
Greenglass, David, 134
Ground Observer Corps (GOC)
and Alaska, 73–74

Ground Observer Corps (GOC) *(continued)*
    Bilyeu, Florence (volunteer), 67–68
    Burr, Pamela (volunteer), 65
    citizen pride and, 75
    criminals as volunteers, 71
    disbanding of, 64, 76
    donations to, 64–65
    emergencies and, 74–75
    ethnic groups and, 72
    evaluation of, 76
    Filter Center (FC), 64
    fire watch towers and, 72
    handicapped volunteers, 68–69
    Hollywood personalities and, 67
    immigrants and, 68
    Lehr, Janina (volunteer), 68
    McCauley, General James W., on, 64
    Native Americans and, 72–73
    origins of, 63–64
    post locations, 72
    Prohosky, Jane (volunteer), 63
    recruiting for, 66
    Scouting and, 70–71
    Swayze, William (volunteer), 68
    telemarketing campaigns and, 66
    veterans and older Americans as volunteers, 69
    volunteers, 64–67
    women volunteers, 67–68
    youth as volunteers, 70
Guatemala, coup in (1954), 13

H-bomb, 188
Hampson, Joan G., 119
Hampson, John L., 119
Harris, Reed, 28
Hartnett, Vincent, 55, 57
Hatch Act (1939), 15, 16
Hay, Harry, 123–124
Hechinger, Fred, 149
Heinlein, Robert A., 35–36
Hellman, Lillian, 52
Henry, Dr. George, 116
Heston, Charlton, 188
Hillman, Sidney, 86
Hines, Frank, 112
Hiss, Alger, xix, 34, 134, 188
    versus Chambers, Whittaker, 19
    HUAC testimony, 19–21
    and Nixon, Richard, 3–5
histoire totale, defined, xiii
Historiograph, defined, xv
History
    social (*see* Social history)

    study of xv-xvi
Ho Chi Minh, xvii, 188
Hoey, Clyde (Dem., North Carolina), 26
Holland, Barbara, 148
Hollywood Ten, xvii, 189
    Association of Motion Picture Producers
        statement against, 169–170
    HUAC hearings and, 55–56
Homosexuals and homosexuality
    as a clinical pathology, 114
    "curing," 116
    equation with Communists, 113
    as form of mental illness, 114
    and Immigration and Nationality Act
        (McCarran-Walter Act; 1952), 113
    "Lavender Scare," 26–27, 124, 190
    and "psychopaths," 114
    retreat to respectability, 124
    "swishes," 125
    treatment during Cold War, xxi, 26–27, 111
    See also Bisexuality, varying views on; Gay
        movement, and Kameny, Franklin E.;
        Lesbianism; Transsexuals and transex-
        uality
Hoover, J. Edgar, xx, xxiv
    anti-Communism and, 9–10
    and Bentley, Elizabeth, 134–135
    charges against Oppenheimer, J. Robert, 24
    first Red Scare, 10
    fomenting discord between Communist
        Party and Mafia, 10
    illegal wiretaps, 10
    monitoring of political activity and, 100
    and Tolson, Clyde, 10
    use of disinformation, 10
    warnings against Communist infiltration in
        schools and homes, 148–149
Horowitz, Daniel, 140, 141
House Committee on Un-American Activities
    (HUAC), 189
    Chambers, Whittaker, and, 19
    Cogley, John, testimony of, 59
    creation of, xviii
    DeCaux, Len, and his testimony before,
        177–178
    and Dies, Martin (Dem., Texas), 51–53,
        99–100
    early years of, 52
    focus on entertainment industry, 53–56
    focus on film industry, 54–56
    founding of, 51
    Hiss, Alger, testimony before (1948),
        19–21

Hollywood Ten, xviii
"Hollywood Ten," 55–56
Hoover, J. Edgar, testimony, March 26, 1947,
     163–165
  investigation of FTA Local 22, 79
  and labor unions, 79
  as model for inquiries by others, 104
  oversight of teachers, 152
  Posner, Blanche Hofrichter, excerpt from tes-
     timony of (December 11, 1962),
     178–180
  purges of left-led unions, 79
  quality of evidence, 54
  Women Strike for Peace (WSP) and,
     141–143
HUAC. *See* House Committee on Un-American
     Activities (HUAC)
Hughes, Langston, campaign against, 103–104
Humphrey, Hubert, 152

I, the Jury (Spillane), 41–42
Immigration and Nationality Act (McCarran-
     Walter Act; 1952), anti-homosexual
     provisions, 113
Immigration and Naturalization Service (INS),
     and Cold War on U.S. labor, 91
Institute for Propaganda Analysis (IPA), 51
Internal Security Act (1950), 105
International Brotherhood of Teamsters, 87
Invasion of the Body Snatchers (film), 36–38
Iran, coup in (1953), 13
Iron Curtain speech (Churchill, Winston), 189

Jackson, Esther C., 106
Jackson, Henry (Dem., Washington), 6, 7, 9
Jackson, James E., 105
Jansen, William, 145
Jews, charged with disloyalty, 53
Jones, Claudia, 106
Jorgensen, Christine, 117–118, 118–119,
     124–125
Justice Department (U.S.), and hunt for possible
     threats, 104–105
Juvenile delinquency, Senate subcommittee
     investigation of, 39

Kameny, Franklin E., 27
Kaub, Verne P., warnings against Communist
     infiltration in schools and homes,
     148–149
Kelly, Walt, 40
Kennan, George, 189
Kennedy, John F. (President), 9, 10

anti-Communist pressure on, 11
Kennedy, Robert (Dem., Massachusetts), 7
Khrushchev, Nikita, 189
  "kitchen debate" with Nixon, Richard,
     131–132
King, Rev. Martin Luther, Jr., 10
Kinsey, Alfred, xxii, 121–123
  excerpt from book about human sexuality,
     170–171
Kirkpatrick, Theodore (Ted), 55
"Kitchen debate," 131–132
Knox, Colonel Frank, 51
Kohlberg, Alfred, 20–22
Korean War, 189
  outbreak of, 6
Khrushchev, Nikita, 131–132, 189
Krafft-Ebing, Richard v., 114
Kuomintang, 189

Labor movement, Cold War and, xxii. *See also*
     Organized labor
Labor unions, Cold War and, xxii. *See also* Orga-
     nized labor
Ladd, Dr. Milton, 16
Lanting, 104–105
Lardner, Ring, Jr., 55
"Lavender Scare," 26–27, 124, 190. *See also*
     Bisexuality, varying views on; Gay
     movement; Homosexuals and homo-
     sexuality; and Kameny, Franklin E.;
     Lesbianism; Transsexuals and
     transsexuality
Lehr, Janina (Ground Observer Corps
     volunteer), 68
Lenin, Vladimir, 190
Lesbianism
  early scientific literature on, 116
  See also Bisexuality, varying views on;
     Gay movement; Homosexuals and
     homosexuality; and Kameny,
     Franklin E.; Transsexuals and
     transsexuality
Lewis, Fulton, Jr., 53
Lewis, John L., 86
Loeb, Philip, 57
Longshoreman's and Warehousemen's Union,
     91
Loyalty oaths, 53
  federal employees and, 15–21
  teachers and, 151–152
  See also Federal Loyalty Oath Program
Loyalty Review Board, 17
Loyalty Security Program, effects of, 28

Mackey, Mary, 160

Maistros, Lucille, 160

Maki, Eleanor, 152

Manhattan Project, 190

Mao Zedong (Mao Tse-tung), 190
  takeover of China, xix, 34, 111

Marshall, General George C., 25, 190

Marshall Plan, 190

Martin, Manning, effects of Cold War on federal
      government, xix

Marx, Karl, 81

Mattachine Society, 27, 123–124, 190–191

May, Elaine Tyler, on U.S. family during Cold
      War, 131

McCarran, Patrick, 20, 190

McCarran-Walter Act (Immigration and Nation-
      ality; 1952), anti-homosexual provi-
      sions, 113

McCarthy, Joseph R. (Rep. Wisconsin), 191
  Army-McCarthy hearings, 25–26
  burning his bridges, 7–8
  Caute, David, comments on, 34
  censure vote, 7
  charges against Service, John S., 21
  charges against State Department, 18–19
  death, 8
  election of, 84
  fall of, xxiii–xxiv, 8, 25–26, 58–60
  Government Operations Committee and, 6
  and loss of China to Communists, 20
  modern views of, 60
  Moss, Annie Lee, and, 107
  and overseas State Department libraries,
      21–22
  painted as a racial bully, 107
  and Pearson, Drew, 7
  reprimanded, 26
  smear campaign against Brunauer, Esther,
      131
  speech, Wheeling, West Virginia (Feb. 9,
      1950), xx, 6, 18, 49
  State Department firings and, 21
  targeting of NAACP, xxii
  targeting U.S. Army, 7, 24–26
  and testimony of Hughes, Langston,
      103–104
  unethical practices, 25

McCarthy era, chronology, xxix–xliv

McCarthy Select Committee, resignations
      and, 6

McCarthyism
  accusation same as guilty, 57
  attacks on, in comics, 40
  backlash against, xxv
  Belfrage, Cedric, on goal of, 106
  business use of, 88–89, 89–90
  children and, xxiii
  chronology, xxix–xliv
  and civil rights, 80
  civil rights movement and, xxii
  Congress of American Women (CAW) and,
      140
  defamation and intimidation and, 105
  defined, 49, 79–80
  denounced by Smith, Senator Margaret
      Chase, 171–174
  feminist movement and, xxiii, 140
  following McCarthy's fall from power, xxiv
  human cost of, 109
  impact on individuals, 129–130
  and labor unions, 79
  "Lavender Scare," 26–27, 124, 190
  legacies, xxv
  legacy lingered into 1960s, 141–142
  and models for inquiries by others, 104
  partisan politics and, 84
  period of political power, 1–2
  Posner, Blanche Hofrichter, excerpt from
      HUAC testimony of (December 11,
      1962), 178–180
  protection of status quo, xxii
  purges of left-led unions, 79
  segregationists and, 84
  targeting of NAACP, xxii
  ultraconservative versions of, 84
  use of, 105
  variety of groups supporting, 84
  violent aspects of, 95–96
  women as easy targets, 130
  women targeted, 143

McCauley, General James W., on Ground
      Observer Corps, 64

McClellan, John (Dem., Arkansas), 6

Media, the
  and Cold War anxiety about independent
      women, 135
  Red Scare and, 49
  and the rise and fall of McCarthy, Joseph, 59
  See also Radio; Television

Mental diseases, changes in views of causes, 116

Midwich Cuckoos, The (Wyndham), 38

Money, John, 119

"Monsters Are Due on Maple Street, The" (TV
      program; *Twilight Zone* episode), 44–45

Morgan v. Virginia (1946), 98

Moss, Annie Lee, appearance before McCarthy's Senate Subcommittee, 107, 108

Mossadeagh, Mohammed, 13

Muir, Jean, 57

Murray, Philip, 86, 88

Murrow, Edward T., xxi
  and downfall of McCarthy, Joseph, 58–59
  and Radulovich, Milo, 24

Music industry, blacklisting in, 56–57

Myers, Bob, 152

NAACP. *See* National Association for the Advancement of Colored People (NAACP)

National Association for the Advancement of Colored People (NAACP)
  anti-Communist stance, 99
  and DuBois, W. E. B., 102
  growing membership in, 97, 99
  McCarthyism and, xxii
  and societal norms, xxii–xxiii
  Southern legislators and challenges to, xxii
  Truman, Harry S, cooperation with, 99
  union encouragement of membership in, 79

National Civil Defense Administration, excerpt from speech by Wadsworth, James J., 175–176

National Council for American Education, 151

National Defense Education Act (1958), 152

National Educational Association, 150

National Labor Management Relations Act of 1947. *See* Taft-Hartley Act (National Labor Management Relations Act of 1947)

National Labor Relations Act (Wagner Act), 82–83

National Labor Relations Board (NLRB), decertifying unions, 89

National security
  perceived threats and civil liberties, xxi
  upheld over civil rights, 90

National Security Act (1947), 191

National Security Agency, 191

Nationality Act (1952), 105

NATO. *See* North Atlantic Treaty Organization (NATO)

New Deal, 82

Nixon, Richard, xx, xxiv, 191
  and Douglas, Helen (1950 campaign), 5
  and Eisenhower, Dwight, 5
  harnessing anti-Communist zeal, 3-4
  and Hiss, Alger, 3–5, 20

HUAC hearings and, 53
  "kitchen debate" with Khrushchev, Nikita (1959), 131–132
  presidential campaign (1960), 10
  and Voorhis, Jerry (1946 campaign), 3, 4

North Atlantic Treaty Organization (NATO), 191

NSC-68 (National Security Council paper, 1949), 191–192

Nuclear family units, idealized image of, 119

Nuclear weapons, 192
  children and, 147

On the Beach (film), 159

One Lonely Night (Spillane), 41–42

Oppenheimer, J. Robert, 23–24, 192

Organized labor
  attacks on, 84–85, 92
  campaign against opportunistic, 92
  common practices against, 91
  Communists in, 87
  and Congress, 91–92
  defined, 80
  disenfranchised workers, 86
  distrust of, 89
  and doubts about capitalism (1933–1939), 82
  federal impact on, 104
  first union leader jailed during Cold War Red Scare, 90
  founding of American Federation of Labor (AFL), 80–81
  government-related Cold War battles against, 90–92
  history and goals, 80
  industrialized mass production and, 82
  loss of support for, 89
  membership levels, 81
  and National Labor Management Relations Act of 1947 (Taft-Hartley Act), 85, 87–88
  non-Communist affidavit, 85, 87–88
  purges of left-led unions, 79
  strikes (1945–1946), 84
  union-organized work stoppages, 84
  and unions led by Communists or their allies, 86
  U.S. law generally unfavorable to, 82
  and women workers, 86
  worker interests versus business interests, 81
  during World War II, 83
  See also individual labor organizations

Pahlavi, Reza, 13

Palmer, A. Mitchell, xvi

and Hoover, J. Edgar, 10

Patterson, William L., 105

Peace Information Center (PIC), 103

Pearson, Drew, 7

Pepper, Claude (Dem., Florida), 8

Peress, Major Irving, 25

Permanent Subcommittee on Investigations, 6

Perry, Pettis, 105

Peurifoy, John, 26

Plessy v. Ferguson (1896), 98

Poland, Warsaw Uprising, 2

Political activity, monitoring of, 100

Popular (Pop) Culture (U.S.)
    anti-Communist hysteria, 34
    attitudes toward women (1950s), 36, 38
    Cold War politics and, 33–34
    comic books, 39–40
    film industry and, 34–35
    focus on subversion and paranoia, 35
    the nuclear family and, 43
    paradigm shift in, 44–45
    patriarchal order and, 39
    pulp fiction, 40–44
    science fiction and, 35–38
    slow rejection of political conservatism, 43–45
    spy stories featuring James Bond, 42–43
    theme of societal threat, 38
    and threats from within, 44–45
    traditional family values and, 35–36

Popular Front (in U.S.), U.S.S.R. sponsorship of, xvii

Popular Front feminism, 140

Posner, Blanche Hofrichter, excerpt from HUAC testimony of (December 11, 1962), 178–180

Postwar society, women and, 130–131

Potsdam Conference, xvii–xviii
    Truman, Harry S, and, 2

President's Temporary Commission on Employee Loyalty, 2–3, 16–17

Prohosky, Jane, 63

Psychopathia Sexualis (Krafft-Ebing), 114

Psychopaths, and homosexuality, 113–114

Pulp fiction
    depiction of women in, 40–41
    and social and political conservatism, 40–41
    Spillane, Mickey, and, 41–42

Puppet Masters, The (Heinlein), 35–36

Quakers (Society of Friends), denunciation of, 100

R. J. Reynolds Tobacco Company, unions and, 79

Racial equality
    Communist Party and, 86
    contradictions in fighting Nazism abroad while supporting segregation at home, 98
    growing electoral power, 98
    McCarthyism and, 84

Racism
    Alien Registration Act (Smith Act) and, 100
    and anti-Communism, 107–108
    and civil rights, 108
    and delimiting forms of black loyalty, 104
    and fears of Communism, 100
    and McCarthyism, 84, 95–96
    postwar political repression and, 99
    prewar stifling of black radicalism and, 99–100
    Robeson, Paul, stand against, 95
    violent persecution of perceived racial subversion, 104

Radio
    conservative assessments of, 51
    and Coughlin, Father Charles, 50–51
    critics of, 50
    denying leftist leaders access to air time, 50
    freedom of speech and, 51
    HUAC hearings and, 53
    impact of *Red Channels* pamphlet on, 49
    Lewis, Fulton, Jr., and, 53
    political coverage, 50
    power of, 50
    role in society (U.S. and European), 50–51
    "War of the Worlds" broadcast, 51

Rado, Sandor, 116

Radulovich, Milo, 24

Randolph, A. Philip, 97

Rankin, John (Dem., Mississippi), 53

Reagan, Ronald, xviii, xxiv, 34, 192
    HUAC testimony (October 23, 1947), 55, 165–169

Reconversion, defined, 84

Red Channels pamphlet, xx–xxi
    excerpt from, 174–175
    impact on media personnel, 49
    refutation of, 59

"Red Fascism," 2

Red scare
    and attitudes toward pre-World War II Russian contacts, 54
    Brunauer, Esther, as victim of, 131
    first (1919–1920), xvi, 10

Republican Party, anti-Communism issue and, 53

Ridder. Walter T., 152

Riot, Peekskill (New York), 95–96

Robeson, Eslanda, 106

Robeson, Paul, xxii, 192
    appearance in Peekskill, New York, 95
    blacklisting and, 56
    campaign against, 101–102
    defense of his actions and philosophies,
        176–177

Robinson, Jackie, 101

Rogin, Michael, 36

Roosevelt, Eleanor, 52

Roosevelt, Franklin D. (President), xvi, xvii, 52, 82

Rosenberg, David, xx

Rosenberg, Julius and Ethel, xx, 134, 135–136,
    192
    depictions of Ethel, 138
    little evidence of Ethel's involvement, 136
    real crime of, 137
    trial judge on, 136–137

Rosie the Riveter, 130

Rothschild, Edward, 24

Russell, Richard (Dem., Georgia), and Cuban
    Missile Crisis, 9

Russia. *See* Union of Soviet Socialist Republics
    (USSR)

Russian Revolution (1917), xvi

Schine, David, 22, 25

Schlesinger, Arthur, Jr., 102

Schrecker, Ellen, xviii

Seduction of the Innocent (Wertham), 39

Seeger, Pete, 56

Senate Subcommittee Investigation of Juvenile
    Delinquency, 39

Senate Subcommittee on Internal Security, 15

Sentner, William, 87

Service, John Stewart, 20, 21, 192

Sexual Behavior in the Human Female (Kinsey;
    1953), 121–123

Sexual Behavior in the Human Male (Kinsey;
    1948), 121

Shelley v. Kramer (1948), 98

Shepard, John, III, 50

Smathers, George (Dem., Florida), anti-
    Communism and, 8–9

Smith, Margaret Chase, Senate speech, June 1,
    1950, 171–174

Smith Act (Alien Registration Act; 1940), xviii,
    100

Social history
    defined, xi
    emphasis in, xvi
    in France, xi
    in United States, xi–xii

Society of Friends (Quakers), denunciation of,
    100

South Vietnam, 13

Southern Negro Youth Congress, 105

Soviet Communism, and threats to United
    States, 83

Spillane, Mickey, 41–42, 193

Spying. *See* Espionage

Stalin, Joseph, and Warsaw Uprising, 2

State Department (U.S.)
    Brunauer, Esther, 131
    Brunauer, Stephen, 131
    McCarthy blaming traitors in, for
        Communist takeover in China, 20
    McCarthy's charges against, 18–19
    overseas libraries and Voice of America, 6,
        21–22
    purging of Far East Bureau, 20
    targeting of information centers and
        libraries, 21–22
    Voice of America, 22–23

Steele, Walter S., 100

Stennis, John (Dem, Mississippi), 7–8, 9

Stevens, Robert T., 25

Stevenson, Adlai, 193

Subversive Activities Control Board, and left-led
    unions, 89

Supreme Court (U.S.)
    and Bailey, Dorothy, 139
    Brown v. Board of Education (1954), xxiv, 98
    Morgan v. Virginia (1946), 98
    Plessy v. Ferguson (1896), 98
    Shelley v. Kramer (1948), 98
    upholding national security over civil
        rights, 90

Swayze, William (Ground Observer Corps vol-
    unteer), 68

Symington, William Stuart (Dem., Missouri),
    6–7, 193

Taft-Hartley Act (National Labor Management
    Relations Act of 1947)
    employer's use of, 88
    failure to overturn in courts, 89
    non-Communist affidavit (Section 9(h)), 85,
        87–88

Taft-Hartley Act (National Labor Management
        Relations Act of 1947) *(continued)*
    refusals to sign Section 9(h) affidavits, 88
    union power struggles and, 88
Teachers
    HUAC oversight of, 152
    loyalty oaths and, 151–152
Television
    broadcasting of HUAC hearings, 59
    Cold War coverage, xx–xxi
    and downfall of McCarthy, Joseph, 59
    excerpt from *Red Channels* pamphlet,
        174–175
    impact of McCarthy and blacklisting, 57–58
    public response to HUAC hearing
        broadcasts, 59
    Red Channels pamphlet, xx–xxi
    See also Media, the; Radio
Thomas, J. Parnell (Rep., New Jersey), 53
Thomas, Norman, 50
Three Essays on the Theory of Sexuality (Freud),
    114–116
Tolson, Clyde, 10
Transport Worker's Union (TWU), New York, 86
Transsexuals and transsexuality, 116–119
    Jorgensen, Christine, 117–118, 118–119,
        124–125
    See also Bisexuality, varying views on; Gay
        movement; Homosexuals and
        homosexuality; Kameny, Franklin
        E.; Lesbianism
Truman, Harry S (President), xvii–xviii, 193
    allegations he had not been tough enough
        on Communism, xviii–xix
    and Committee on Civil Rights, 98
    cooperation with NAACP, 99
    Executive Order No. 9835 (1947), 17
    insecurity of, 3
    limiting of social activism, 11
    loyalty-security program, xix, 17
    plea for Ground Observer Corps
        volunteers, 66
    Potsdam Conference (1945), 2
    and the President's Temporary Commission
        on Employee Loyalty, 2–3, 16–17
    and public opinion, 1
    stability versus democracy under, 3
    White House Conference on Children and
        Youth (1950), 157
Truman Doctrine, 193
Trumbo, Dalton, 55

Union of Soviet Socialist Republics (U.S.S.R.), 194
    acquisition of atomic bomb, xix–xx
    alliance with U.S. during World War II, xvii
    collapse of alliance with U.S. after World
        War II, xviii
    distrust of Allies, 2
    espionage within U.S. borders, 11–12
    German invasion of (1941), xvii
    loyalty program, 2–3
    and Popular Front, xvii
    President's Temporary Commission on
        Employee Loyalty, 2–3
    reports of targeting U.S. homosexuals by, 26
    U.S. recognition of, xvi
United Auto Workers Union, Local 248 strike
    (1946), 90
United Electrical, Radio, and Machine Workers
    of America (UE), and fight for
    women's rights, 140
United Kingdom. *See* Great Britain, alliance with
    U.S.S.R. during World War II
United Mine Workers, 86
United Nations, 193–194
    and African Americans following World
        War II, 98
United Office and Professional Workers of
    America, 90
United States (U.S.)
    apocalyptic media coverage of Cold War and,
        158–159
    and attitudes toward sexuality and gender
        roles, xxii–xxiii
    attitudes toward treason, 54
    attitudes toward U.S.S.R. (1939–1945), xvii
    baby boom, 146–147
    Castro, Fidel, observations on (1959), 12–13
    collapse of alliance with U.S.S.R. after World
        War II, xviii
    conservatism in (early 1950s), 33
    executive branch and anti-Communism, 84
    and explosion of social protest (1960s),
        xxiv–xxv
    fears of political radicalism, xxiv
    impact of Cold War on life in, xvi
    law generally unfriendly to labor unions, 82
    postwar prosperity, 146–147
    priority for anti-Communism, 83–84
    roots of anti-Communism in, 81
    social history in, xi-xii
    Soviet espionage within, 11–12
    and Soviet science and education, 149–153

union membership and anti-Communism
in, 81
women and their roles, xxiii
See also State Department (U.S.)
United States Army
McCarthy's investigation of, 24–26
targeting of, by McCarthy, 7
United Steelworkers of America, 86
Universal Negro Improvement Association
(UNIA), 97
U.S. *See* United States (U.S.)
U.S.S.R. *See* Union of Soviet Socialist Republics
(U.S.S.R.)

Vanech, A. Devitt, 16
Venona, 194
Vietnam War, 9. *See also* South Vietnam
Village of the Damned, The (film), 38
Vincent, John Carter, 20
Voice of America, investigation of, 22–23

Wagner Act (National Labor Relations Act),
82–83
Wallace, Henry, 194
War, conventional definitions of, xv. *See also*
Cold War
"War of the Worlds" broadcast, 51
Warsaw Pact, 194
Warsaw Uprising, 2
Weavers, The, 56
Welch, Judge Joseph, hearing statement, 25–26
Welles, Orson, 51
Wertham, Frederick, 39
White, Harry Dexter, 34, 194
White, Walter, 99
White House Conference on Children and
Youth (1950), 157
Whitehead, General Ennis C., 64
Wilson, Woodrow, xvi
World War II
overview, 129
U.S. cooperation with Chinese Communists
during, xvii
U.S.–Soviet relationship during, xvii
and women's roles, 130
Women
abortion and, 120–121
in books by Fleming, Ian, 42–43
changing roles for, 130

Cold War anxiety about independent, 135
Cold War attitudes toward, xxiii, 36, 38
in comic books, 39
Communist, 130
Communist and left-led unions and, 86
conflict between the ideology and reality
faced by, 132
and espionage, 132–135
"the feminine mystique," 120
GI Bill benefits restricted, 113
Ground Observer Corps volunteers, 67–68
immoral and dangerous, 120–121
living under Communism, 132
Posner, Blanche Hofrichter, excerpt from
HUAC testimony of (December 11,
1962), 178–180
in pulp fiction, 40–10
reality versus stereotypes, 138
Sexual Behavior in the Human Female (Kinsey;
1953), 121–123
stereotypical views of Communist,
137–138
suspicion of self-supporting, emancipated,
132
unfairly labeled and attacked, 130
United Electrical, Radio, and Machine Workers of America (UE), and women's
rights, 140
unmarried, 120
Women Strike for Peace, 130, 178–180
working, 79, 138
Women Strike for Peace (WSP), 130, 141-142,
178–180
HUAC testimony, 142–143
public and media reaction to HUAC
testimony, 143
Wood, John (Rep., Georgia), 152
Wyndham, John, 38

Yalta Conference, 194
Youth
fear of Communist subversion of, 149
and Ground Observer Corps, 70
Soviet education and its impact on U.S.
schools, 149–153
See also Children

Zoll, Allen, 151
Zwicker, General Ralph, 7, 25, 194–195